EDUCATION 14–19: CRITICAL PERSPECTIVES

RA⁻   ⁻ning hours:

WITHDRAWN

Education 14–19
Critical Perspectives

Edited by

Sally Tomlinson

THE ATHLONE PRESS
London and Atlantic Highlands, NJ

First published 1997 by
THE ATHLONE PRESS
1 Park Drive, London NW11 7SG
and 165 First Avenue,
Atlantic Highlands, NJ 07716

British Library Cataloguing in Publication Data
*A catalogue record for this book is available
from the British Library*

ISBN 0 485 11512 3 hb
0 485 12131 X pb

Library of Congress Cataloguing in Publication Data

Perspectives on education, 14–19: critical perspectives/edited by
Sally Tomlinson
    p.   cm.
Includes bibliographical references
ISBN 0-485-11512-3 (hardcover).—ISBN 0-485-12131-X (pbk.)
1. Education, Secondary—Great Britain. 2. Postsecondary
education—Great Britain. 3. Vocational education—Great Britain.
4. Educational change—Great Britain. 5. Education and state—Great
Britain. I. Tomlinson, Sally.
LA635.P45   1997
373.41—dc21   97–13528
                                                          CIP

Typeset by
RefineCatch Limited, Bungay, Suffolk

Printed and bound in Great Britain by
Cambridge University Press

Contents

Notes on the Contributors

Stephen Ball is Professor of Education at King's College, London, and has been involved in research into educational policy developments for a considerable period, publishing widely. He is the editor of the *Journal of Education Policy*.

Jenny Corbett is a Senior Lecturer in Special Education at the University of London Institute of Education. Her research in the post-school sector began with a PhD case study of integration in further education presented in 1987. Since then she has carried out research projects for the Further Education Unit (FEU) and for Skill: the National Bureau for Students with Disabilities, and has written extensively on learning support provision and practice in further and higher education. Her most recent book in this area is *Opening Doors: Learning Support in Higher Education*, co-edited with Sheila Wolfendale (Cassell 1996).

Roger Crombie-White has been a teacher since graduating from York University in 1970, most recently employed at the University of West of England's Faculty of Education, where his main responsibilities are for international activities and 14–19 curriculum issues. With Richard Pring and David Brockington he wrote the Royal Society of Arts document *14–19 Education and Training: Implementing a Unified System of Learning*.

David Gillborn is Reader in the Sociology of Education and Associate Director of the Health and Education Research Unit (HERU) at the Institute of Education, University of London. He has researched and written extensively in the field of race and racism in schools. His most recent publications include *Racism and Antiracism in Real Schools* (Open University Press 1995) and *Recent Research on the Achievements of Ethnic Minority Pupils* (HMSO 1996, with Caroline Gipps). He is editor of a new international journal, *Race, Ethnicity and Education*, and a member of the editorial board of the *International Journal of Inclusive Education*.

Tamsyn Imison has been Headteacher of Hampstead School in Cricklewood, North London, since 1984, where 55 percent of the roll has English as a second language, over 81 home language are spoken and there are 150 refugees. She is currently Chair of the Secondary Heads Association Equal Opportunities Committee, Educational Adviser to the Women's Playhouse Trust, and initiator and co-ordinator of the National Schools Playwright Commissioning Group. She is also a member of Councils of the University of London, and a number of other trusts and associations, and was a member of the Secondary Examination Council 1986–88.

Sheila Macrae has a background in secondary school teaching and has taught in both Scotland and England. She now works as a Research Fellow in the School of Education, King's College, London.

Meg Maguire taught for many years in London including a spell as a headteacher. She is the course leader of the MA in Urban Education as well as the part-time Postgraduate Certificate in Education in the School of Education, King's College, London. She has published on teacher education and issues of equity.

Richard Pring is Professor of Educational Studies, University of Oxford; He was previously Professor of Education at University of Exeter, a lecturer in curriculum studies at University of London, and a teacher in two London comprehensive schools. He is joint editor of *British Journal of Educational Studies.*

Roger Slee is Professor and Head of the Department of Educational Studies at Goldsmiths College, University of London. Roger was a school teacher and lecturer in Australia prior to this appointment. He is the foundation editor of the *International Journal of Inclusive Education* and has written a number of books including: *Is There A Desk With My Name On It? The Politics of Integration* (Falmer 1993) and *Changing Theories and Practices of Discipline* (Falmer 1995).

Alan Smithers is Director of the Centre for Education and Employment Research which has recently moved from Manchester to Brunel University. He has written influentially on vocational education and many other topics including teacher supply, technology in schools, education 16–19, higher education, science education, and single-sex schooling. He trained as a scientist, and was a Professor of Education at Manchester for twenty years before taking up his present appointment. He has served on a number of national committees including the National Curriculum Council and the Beaumont Committee on Vocational Qualifications.

Geoff Stanton is a Senior Research Fellow at the University of Greenwich School of Post Compulsory Education and Training. For eight years he was director of the Further Education Unit (FEU), before which he was vice-principal at a tertiary college and head of department in an FE college. He has served on working groups of NCVQ and the National Curriculum Council, and is on the FE policy committees of the RSA Examinations Board, City and Guilds, and the Church of England Board of Education.

Sally Tomlinson is Professor of Educational Policy and Management at Goldsmiths College, University of London. She has written and researched extensively in the areas of educational policy, school effectiveness, the education of ethnic minorities and special education. Her most recent books are *Educational Reform and its Consequences* (Rivers-Oram Press for IPPR 1994) and *Ethnic Relations and Schooling Policy and Practice in the 1990s* (edited with Maurice Craft) (Athlone 1995). She carried out a pilot project for the NUT in 1994–95 on 'Teachers' views of the 14–19 curriculum'.

Geoffrey Walford is Reader in Educational Policy (Sociology) in the Department of Educational Studies, University of Oxford, and is a Fellow of Green College, Oxford. He was previously senior lecturer in Sociology and Education Policy at Aston Business School, Aston University, Birmingham. He is author or editor of 15 books which include: *Life in Public Schools* (Methuen 1986), *Restructuring Universities: Politics and Power in the Management of Change* (Croom Helm 1987), *Privatization and Privilege in Education* (Routledge 1990), *City Technology College* (with Henry Miller) (Open University Press 1991), *Choice and Equity in Education* (Cassell 1994), *Educational Politics* (Avebury 1995) and *Researching the Powerful in Education* (editor) (UCL Press 1994).

Foreword

Tony Edwards

Learning to Compete (December 1996) was celebrated by the Secretary of State responsible for it as being the first White Paper to avoid treating 16+ as a 'natural' transition point. The innovation of treating 14–19 as a critical educational stage has an obvious explanation. The end of compulsory education is no longer the end of full-time education for most young people, a fact evident in what the White Paper records as 'dramatic improvements' in participation and achievement since 1985. Yet although the contributors to this book agree on the stage they have wished to explore, they question whether its various transformations may be perpetuating rather than solving old problems. Like another recently completed book (Edwards *et al.*, 1997), they begin with the separation of leaders from followers which has traditionally marked English secondary and post-secondary education. If the 'education of the ablest is what the English system does best', as the Crowther Committee observed nearly forty years ago, it has continued to draw sharp lines between the 'liberal education' of the 'thinking classes', the utilitarian training of some of the rest, and those who could be left to pick up whatever knowledge and skills they needed in the course of being employed. Within what has certainly been a remarkable expansion, at least when viewed from a national rather than an international perspective, a deeply divided system remains.

It would be nice to attribute the expansion to a vision of what an educated democracy should be. But, as Richard Pring argues, it has been driven largely by portrayals of the kind of workforce required to sustain a modern competitive economy. Even within that dominant frame of reference, as other contributors also note, there are practical objections to defining the 'needs' of employment too narrowly when 'serial redundancy' and frequent changes of occupation will be facts of working life for much of the population. The priority given to extended general education both by teachers and by many employers would seem to be more practical as well as more humane.

I am less certain than Sally Tomlinson is, however, that the three-track system of academic, vocational and occupational (with all its connotations of the gold, the silver and the iron) is becoming even more firmly embedded. The tracking is taking different forms, but the problem seems to be more that old failings have survived what should have been a conclusive indictment of their educational and social costs. This was both recognised and trivialised by Sir Ron Dearing when, having noted the 'unequal worth' traditionally attached to achievement on the 'academic and vocational pathways', he refers to students' 'stereotypes of the ways forward' as though those supposedly self-defeating stereotypes were their fault rather than being grounded in realistic perceptions of very unequal opportunities. His brief required him to keep the pathways distinct, thereby retaining that essential choice between the 'academic' and the 'vocational' which most of the book's contributors wish to remove and which has ensured that so much innovation has brought so little fundamental change. Alan Smithers' is a dissenting voice. But while he defends a differentiated system and renews his onslaught on the National Vocational Qualifications (NVQ) model of learning, he too deplores the continuing lack of coherent, well thought-out alternatives to what Dearing called the 'innate quality' of A-level.

Even the pace of innovation has reflected the wide gap in prestige between the venerable and the arriviste. It is certainly possible to exaggerate the capacity of A-level to remain intact while all around it changes, and it too has been undergoing a process of 'creeping modernisation' (Higham *et al.* 1996). But even if the Higginson proposals for broader and leaner academic studies had been accepted, the consequent syllabus changes would not have taken effect for at least four years. Geoff Stanton contrasts that leisurely pace with the rush from GNVQ proposals in October 1991 to the piloting of a new qualification from September 1992 and its formal introduction a year later. Paul Black (1993, p. 46) has described the National Curriculum as a huge experiment without prior trialling. If it had been a new drug, he remarked, 'its application even for those in dire need would not be allowed with this degree of untried novelty'. Yet GNVQs were developed from an NVQ 'drug' already regarded by critics as an ineffective remedy for an under-skilled workforce and as having very damaging side-effects. Hasty innovation might be explained by an eagerness to get the right things done if only there had been broad agreement on what the right things were. Instead, Stanton's analogy is justifiably provocative. Very different educational models have been designed by separate units of the same company (UK plc) with no co-ordination, no clear assessment of their complementary positioning in the qualifications 'market', and without even a common vocabulary with which to compare the designs. If innovation has been uncoordinated, it has also been very much a matter of imposition. The book is therefore to be welcomed for including a rare survey of how teachers assess the progress and limitations of reform, a glimpse of how students themselves perceive the apparent superiority of those following 'the more intellectual side' of the alternative 'pathways', and some searching accounts of how a preoccupation with improving qualifications has diverted attention from larger questions about educational purposes which extend beyond a hard-edged emphasis on skills. Educational credentials may no longer provide a 'solid bulwark' against the uncertainties of the labour market, but some are much less frail than others and different categories of student are still very unequally placed to obtain them. As several of these chapters indicate in well-documented detail, educational expansion and more equal opportunities may not go side by side.

When so much has been happening, at the same time if not 'together', the range of perspectives and concerns reported here is especially valuable. If there is another main theme discernible than the perpetuation of old divisions in new guises, it is the damage done by reforms made piece-meal and without any comprehensive view of what their accumulating effects are and what their accumulated effects should be. Less haste, more thought, less prejudice, more evidence, and above all some vision – these would seem to constitute a better prescription for progress than the fumbling around which this book constructively deplores.

REFERENCES

Black, P. (1993) 'The shifting scenery of the National Curriculum', in C. Chitty and B. Simon (eds), *Education Answers Back: Critical Responses to Government Policy*. London: Lawrence and Wishart.

Edwards, T., Fitz-Gibbon, C., Hardman, F., Haywood, R. and Meagher, N. (1997), *Separate but Equal? A-levels and Advanced GNVQs*. London: Routledge.

Higham, J., Sharp, P. and Yeomans, D. (1996), *The Emerging 16–19 Curriculum: Policy and Provision*. London: David Fulton.

Professor Tony Edwards
University of Newcastle upon Tyne
January 1997

Acronyms

ADHD	attention deficit hyperactivity disorder
ASDAN	Award Scheme for Development and Accreditation Network
BTEC	Business and Technology Education Council
CGLI	City and Guilds of London Institute
CPVE	Certificate of Pre-Vocational Education
CSE	Certificate of Secondary Education
CSYS	Certificate of Sixth Year Studies (Scotland)
CTC	City Technology College
DES	Department of Education and Science
DFE	Department for Education
DfEE	Department for Education and Employment
DOVE	Diploma of Vocational Qualifications
ERA	Education Reform Act
FE	further education
FEFC	Further Education Funding Council
FEU	Further Education Unit
GCSE	General Certificate of Secondary Education
GNVQ	General National Vocational Qualifications
GSA	Girls' School Association
HE	higher education
HMC	Headmasters' and Headmistresses' Conference
HMI	Her Majesty's Inspectorate
IB	International Baccalaureate
ISIS	Independent Schools Information Service
LEA	local education authority
LMS	local management of schools
NC	National Curriculum
NCC	National Curriculum Council
NCVQ	National Council for Vocational Qualifications
NUT	National Union of Teachers
OFSTED	Office for Standards in Education

PRU	Pupil Referral Units
QCA	Qualifications and Curriculum Authority
RSA	Royal Society of Arts
SCAA	School Curriculum and Assessment Authority
SEAC	Schools Examinations and Assessment Authority
TEC	Training and Enterprise Council
TVEI	Technical and Vocational Education Initiative
UCAS	Universities and Colleges Admissions Service
UVP	Unified Vocational Preparation
YTS	Youth Training Scheme

Education 14–19: Divided and Divisive

Sally Tomlinson

Major challenges for those who shape educational policies are how to widen participation in education, how to inspire a national demand for learning and how to ensure a skilled, capable and knowledgeable workforce. Until the 1970s, even into the 1980s, these issues were not taken seriously. The historical divisions between those who were academically successful and moved into higher education and professional training, and those who left education early and undertook vocational training or unskilled employment still made some economic sense. Only a minority of young people were considered to need professional, executive, scientific or technological expertise (Crombie-White, *et al.* 1995) and only a few were considered able to benefit from a subject-centred curriculum beyond basic levels. By the 1980s it was apparent that global, economic, technical and social changes meant that it no longer made sense to educate elite 'thinking classes' and offer only basic education and early vocational training to the rest. There were choices to be made between preparing young people for a low-skilled, undereducated society or a highly skilled, informed, learning society which *educated* everyone.

The central theme of this book is that, in the 1990s, government made the wrong choices. Despite the unprecedented and serious efforts made over the past ten years to improve education and training and to encourage a majority of young people to participate, there has been an intensification of divisions between traditional liberal-academic education, vocational preparation and occupational training routes for young people post-14. A divided and divisive system is becoming embedded, just at the time when a unified framework is required.

Education 14–19 is not a cohesive system for the majority. It is fragmented in institutional, curricula, assessment, organisational and funding terms. It is hampered in development by a legal school-leaving age of 16; by competing qualifications offered by bodies with strong vested interests; and by a seemingly unbridgeable academic–vocational divide. Although there has been intensified support during the 1990s for a unified system, the choices have been made to reinforce fragmentation through a three-track system; the academic A-level track, a vocational or 'applied educational' track of General National Vocational Qualifications (GNVQs) and a continued occupationally specific route of youth training, associated with National Vocational Qualifications (see Figure 1.1). Legislative and other changes resulting from the government White Paper on *Education and Training for the 21st Century* (DES/DOE 1991) and the *Dearing Review of Qualifications for 16–19 Year Olds* (Dearing 1996) have cemented a divide widely recognised to be economically and socially damaging. The Department for Education and Employment asserts that young people today have better opportunities to learn than

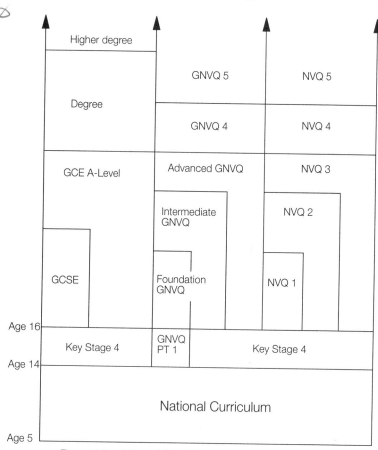

Figure 1.1   Adapted from NVQ Monitor, *1994, p. 19.*

in any previous generation through this divided and competitive system: 'Young people now have access to A-levels, GNVQs, NVQs and a range of competing Sixth Form Colleges, employers and other work-based training providers' (DfEE 1996a, p. 1).

But despite a rhetoric of parity of esteem between routes and courses in this divided system, there is no real intention to question historical assumptions about the status superiority of academic routes over vocational routes (Pring 1995, Edwards *et al.* 1997) and little recognition of the disparity in funding between routes or institutions.

A BRIEF HISTORY

A concern with post-14 education for the majority is relatively recent. Up to 1939, 88 per cent of young people had left school by 14. Upper- and middle-class children continued their liberal-academic education in private or grammar schools (see Walford below), sitting examinations validated by university-dominated boards, while the majority of young people went into unskilled employment, a minority taking up apprentice-ships and vocational training validated by such bodies as the City and Guilds of London Institute and the Royal Society of Arts. By 1959 there were still only 10 per cent of young people remaining in education until 17 (Crowther 1959), and it was in 1974, when the school-leaving age was raised to 16, that the first generation ever to experience a full 5–16 education left school.

While nineteenth-century education was deliberately and unambigu-ously designed to cater for different social classes (Simon 1974; 1991), in the twentieth century educational policy-makers drew on psychometric theories of intelligence and ability to rationalise the continued separ-ation of a minority into high-status academic education and a majority into early leaving and training. The restriction of educational opportun-ities and access to professional and managerial employment to those of proven 'high ability' nicely paralleled both perceived economic needs and the social class structure. It was ironic that during the Second World War, as Simon (1991, p. 35) has pointed out, young working-class people of supposed 'low ability' were rapidly trained as skilled engineer and electronic experts, while at the same time a secondary education system was being designed based on spurious notions of 'different types of mind'. The Norwood Committee grounded its proposals (Norwood Report 1943) for re-structuring secondary education into grammar, technical and modern schools on the assumption that a minority of students were capable of abstract thought, a minority interested in applied technical ideas and a majority in practical activities, although one critic even at that time was of the opinion that 'seldom has a more unscientific or unscholarly attitude disgraced the report of a public committee' (Curtis 1952). Divided schooling and curricula were supported by the Labour Government in 1946, which endorsed the lower status of modern schools, with their vocational and practical orientation, as for 'children whose future employment will not demand any measure of technical skill or knowledge' (Ministry of Education 1946). From the 1940s to the 1960s selection at 11+, a narrow subject-centred curriculum, early specialisation and an arts–science divide, characterised the education of the largely middle-class elite, with a practical and vocational curriculum for the rest.

The development of the curriculum in comprehensive schools, which by 1979 were educating 87 per cent of pupils, has been well documented (Simon 1991; Lawton, 1989). Most comprehensive schools incorporated academic and practical courses into their curriculum and from the mid-1960s to the 1980s, largely sorted pupils at 14 into O-level, Certificate of Secondary Education (CSE), or 'non-exam' with different curricula. Option choice at 13+ became crucial for future employment. Not surprisingly, academic courses were dominated by middle-class pupils; working-class and minority students were mainly directed towards technical, practical, creative, physical and remedial courses (Smith and Tomlinson 1989). Many of these courses were interesting and useful, but there was never any parity of esteem. The GCSE was an attempt to overcome the early division into the liberal versus the relevant, as was the Technical and Vocational Education Initiative (TVEI). One of the criteria for the funding of TVEI was the design of a four-year curriculum that stressed problem-solving, individual initiative and personal development. Pring has raised the question as to whether TVEI and other pre-vocational developments contained the seeds of an educational philosophy which bridges the academic–vocational divide (Pring 1995, p. 65).

The secondary curriculum became an arena for more acute political conflict in the 1980s. The HMI view of a common curriculum (HMI 1981), based on 'areas of experience', received much teacher support. Despite this, it was modified by Keith Joseph in *Better Schools* (DES 1985) and by 1988 the Baker National Curriculum had returned schools to a traditional subject-based agenda, plus 'new' technology.

By the end of the 1980s, post-16 education and training was still incoherent and confused, with competing courses and qualifications, exacerbated in the 1980s by competition between schools, sixth form and further education colleges. A-levels, with added A/S-levels, dominated the academic route, despite a 20 per cent failure rate in some subject areas, and the Higginson Report, which suggested a modest broadening of A-levels (1988), was rejected by the government as compromising the 'gold standard'. The National Council for Vocational Qualifications (NCVQ) had been created in 1986 to develop NVQs, originally work-based qualifications based on competences culled from behaviouristic psychology, and in 1991 the White Paper *Education and Training for the Twenty-first Century* (DES/DOE 1991) established the GNVQ (General National Vocational Qualifications) as a half-way house between the academic and the vocational.

The 1990s have seen the development of GNVQ in what will ultimately be 15 vocational areas studied at three levels. Figure1.1 illustrates the three-track system which is now in place from 14 to 19. A more elaborate version can be found in Pring (1995, p. 71), together with a critique of its lack of coherence, problems of programming, the nonsense of talk of parity or equivalence between tracks and qualifications, and the fragmented nature of a divided, competitive system which discourages co-operation between institutions.

THE DEARING REPORTS

By 1993 the National Curriculum was in sufficient disarray for Sir Ron Dearing to be invited to 'slim down' the subjects and simplify testing. Incorporated into his final report (Dearing 1994) was an acceptance of the three-track post-16 system:

- the craft or occupational – NVQ;
- the 'vocational' – a midway path between academic and vocational, leading to GNVQ;
- the 'academic' leading to A and A/S-levels (ibid. p. 19).

His report suggested extending a vocational/occupational element post-14 as an option to 'better develop some young people into capable and sensible men and women' (ibid., p. 20). Dearing's success at slimming the National Curriculum led to an invitation in 1995 to 'find ways to strengthen, consolidate and improve the framework for 16–19 qualifications' while maintaining the rigour of A-levels, improving participation in education and training and reducing wastage.

This report (Dearing 1996) ensured that a three-track system will remain in place in the foreseeable future. The report suggested renaming GNVQs as 'applied A-levels' – a suggestion rapidly rejected by government – and a continuation of experimental collaborative schemes offering common modules between A-levels and GNVQ, although research by Edwards and his colleagues (1997) has demonstrated the difficulties of co-ordinating the learning styles of the two routes. The report also proposed a new framework for national awards at entry, foundation, intermediate and advanced levels and an advanced National General Diploma, which would seem to further complicate rather than unify the qualifications system. There was also a proposal to allow 14-year-olds who are failing at school to leave and attend college courses – 'vocationally relevant activity' in the world of 'applied knowledge'. This particular proposal appealed to government, and in December 1996 a White Paper was published entitled *Learning to Compete: Education and Training for 14–19 year olds* (DfEE 1996b). In the competition for qualifications, some students will be offered the 'exciting development' of a new vocational qualification at 14 (GNVQ Part I), while others will be encouraged to leave education for new vocational options at 14, administered by employers and trainers, as well as schools and colleges (ibid. p. 23). It is safe to assume that those students offered these new courses will be from lower socio-economic and disadvantaged groups, the groups well known to be at risk of educational failure and targeted for low-level training as early as possible.

A-LEVEL TENACITY

While the rhetoric of the 1990s has been about bridging academic and vocational divides (Avis *et al.* 1996), it is clear that the A-level route is the preferred and most sought after route by large numbers of students. Few middle or aspirant middle-class parents will be satisfied with other routes. For his review of 16–19 qualifications, Dearing was instructed to 'maintain the rigour of "A"levels'. Subsequent government responses to the Dearing review centred on an intensification of the narrow specialist three A-level route into higher education and on reversing reforms which have broadened A-level syllabuses and teaching (DfEE 1996b). A political consensus across Left and Right emerged to protect this particular qualification as the major conduit into higher education. The qualification retains enormous influence with employers, who are still relatively ignorant of other qualifications, and almost all policy-makers and senior educationists have reached their present positions via A-levels. It will require a seismic shift in the thinking of politicians, employers, many educators and the general public, to change a culture which has become accustomed to thinking that the majority of young people should be encouraged on to vocational or occupational routes at 16, or even 14, while an expanded elite take a narrow specialist subject-centred route.

It is tempting to speculate that the three-track route is now becoming acceptable provision for young people post-14 precisely because it accords with the future society and economy envisaged by Galbraith (1992) and Hutton (1995). This scenario suggests a 40/30/30 society in which a contented majority (with A-levels and higher education) enjoy secure jobs and a comfortable life-style, a middle group (the GNVQ group?), even with their 'applied education' to high levels, undertake contract work and insecure employment, and the bottom group, despite NVQs, are fortunate to find any kind of employment or niche in the economy. It is not surprising that there has been an intensification of division and competition in the education and training system, and why discussion of different approaches, possibly via a unified curriculum and qualifications structure post-14, is only just beginning (Spours and Young 1996).

ISSUES AND CONSEQUENCES

In bringing together this collection of papers, the main purpose has been to examine some of the problems implicit in recent policy developments in education and training post-14, and some of the practical issues as they affect colleges, schools, teachers and students. The contributors have drawn on their own recent research to provide much evidence that government confidence in the post-14 three-track route to adult working life offered by the divided, divisive, competitive post-14 system may not be the best way to educate for a learning society, meet the skill needs of employers, or enhance the drive towards raised national targets for education and training.

Part I of this book focuses particularly on policy developments which have led to the divisions described above. There *is* an urgent need, recognised by all the contributors, to enhance and co-ordinate vocational aspects of the curriculum, but, as Richard Pring demonstrates in Chapter 2, there has been a conspicuous absence of debate about the *educational* aims of reforms. He points out that an uncritical association of education with preparation for economic life can foster a narrow, utilitarian educational programme. A focus on the economic requirements of the present day might not be the best preparation for an increasingly unpredictable future. The qualities, understandings, attitudes and skills young people need to acquire are not simply confined to the goals of economic success for themselves or the wider society. His chapter crucially points up the need to integrate the liberal-academic and the vocational tradition rather than endorse the three-track divide.

In Chapter 3 Geoff Stanton likens the design and implementation of the National Curriculum post-14, National Vocational Qualifications and General National Vocational Qualifications to a car company developing three new models. Each vehicle is designed by a different division in the company and complaints pour in from customers and garages. The company directors continue to drive the vintage (A-level) model preserved from change. Eventually the Dearing corporation is called in to review the whole range! The chapter nicely illustrates why developments in post-14 education since 1986 have proved so complex and unmanageable. Although the Chair of the first Review of Vocational Qualifications had in that year declared his intention to bridge the divide between vocational and academic learning (de Ville 1986), the failure of educators and trainers to communicate has led over the years to some bizarre consequences. For example, while the National Curriculum Council was designating numbers 1–4 for Key Stages and 1–10 to levels of attainment, NCVQ was already using 1–5 to represent vocational performance. Stanton considers that the post-14 reforms have suffered from *technical* failures – with reformers failing to recognise the relationship between learning programmes, learning outcomes and qualifications – and *managerial* failure, as policy-makers have consistently refused to think in terms of a system, rather than isolated initiatives. He also notes the fear of informed debate which seems to have characterised post-14 reforms and which has led to a lack of knowledge and much confusion on the part of employers, parents, students, teachers and the general public.

In Chapter 4, Alan Smithers, who served on both the National Curriculum Council and the 1995 Beaumont Committee which reviewed vocational qualifications, offers a stringent critique of the development of National Vocational Qualifications. He points out that the National Council for Vocational Qualifications rightly emphasised employer-led requirements for standards of competence, but the attempt to turn every performance standard into a *competence* has led to 'an orgy of analysis resulting in highly fragmented and incomprehensible qualifications'.

Furthermore, he thinks that, since NVQs turned out not to be a good way of preparing people for work, it was bizarre that the government gave NCVQ the job of developing 'applied education' in schools and colleges. However, if NCVQ 'went down the wrong path', the new Qualifications and Curriculum Authority (QCA) may put things right. Unlike most other contributors to this book, Smithers supports separate but coherent pathways for young people 14–19, although with a 'truly national system' of vocational awards.

Teachers' views of policy on the education of young people post-14 have seldom been sought, despite the fact that the success or otherwise of policy implementation depends on secondary school and post-16 college teachers. In Chapter 5, Sally Tomlinson reports on a pilot project, commissioned by the National Union of Teachers in 1994, to enquire into teachers' views of 14–19 education. Teachers in a small but geographically representative group of schools were asked what they thought a coherent 14–19 curriculum should encompass, what kind of assessment was most appropriate, how they viewed the separation of academic and vocational courses, and whether they thought equal opportunities for all students could be enhanced. The findings from this study have been incorporated into the National Union of Teachers' 14–19 policy (NUT 1996). The teachers interviewed for this research were working hard to incorporate new vocational courses and qualifications, but were not happy with the divided qualifications system that is emerging and would prefer reform which worked towards a unified curriculum and assessment system. They also questioned the necessity for a formal break in education for *any* student at 16, and the use of the GCSE as a 'terminal' exam. The teachers were supportive of modular courses with credit accumulation, and saw many possibilities for modularising courses 14–19. They were very aware that social class, race and gender issues could not be ignored in debating post-14 education and training. Much previous evidence has pointed to the academic– vocational divide being a middle-class – working-class divide, with racial minority students and (until quite recently) girls less likely to move on to high-status courses. Although generalisation from small samples must be undertaken with care, this study suggests that many teachers may now be questioning or opposed to policies for separate tracks for young people, regard an academic–vocational divide as artificial, and disagree with the idea that narrow vocational courses should be offered to those deemed 'less academic' at 14.

The consequences of divisions in educational provision post-16 are well-documented in Chapter 6. Sheila Macrae, Meg Maguire and Stephen Ball report on their research into the effects of the imposition of market forces on secondary school and post-16 education. The post-16 sector is a stratified and hierarchical system, with intense competition for different kinds of students developing between further education colleges, school sixth forms and sixth form colleges. Students are very much aware post-16, if not post-14, that they are making choices about their future in a three-track system which carries different messages about desirability and exchange value in the labour market, and that in any case their choices are constrained, since successful institutions will usually be doing the 'choosing'. The view that 'staying in education, especially on the premier A-level route, remains fundamentally a select-ive process with markers of likely success or failure laid down early on' (Banks *et al.* 1992, p. 49) was borne out in this research. There is an increased polarity between the well-behaved middle-class student who proceeds through a high-status route, and the disaffected or 'less able' working-class students who are steered firmly towards vocational or work-based routes. Class and race act as a filter, as students are allocated to courses, although in the competitive guerrilla warfare that has developed between institutions, some are able to exploit niche markets and attract racial minorities or special needs students on to particular courses. This chapter vividly illustrates the point that post-16 provision is attempting to cater for the first time in the history of educational provision in the UK for all school-leavers. As a consequence of the competitive market some institutions are able to cream and select 'high fliers', while others are forced to enrol the 'less desirable' and those previously unsuccessful in education.

In contrast to the complexity involved in the socio-economic repro-duction by class and race which accompanies the schooling of the edu-cationally unsuccessful, Walford examines an area where educational failure is inadmissible – private schooling. In Chapter 7 he reviews the seamless educational experiences of the 14–19 curriculum in schools outside the state system, which do however, via 'invisible pedagogies', enable students to be prepared for their future occupations. The expectations and the reality in fee-paying schools is that most students will stay at school after GCSE and move after A-levels into higher education. However, while there is no overt academic–vocational divide in the private school curriculum, headteachers of these schools have been in the forefront of support for a unified (but differentiated) system of qualifications post-16. Walford reports that in 1994 the Headmasters' Conference condemned the academic–vocational divide as 'misleading and damaging' and supported a single universal qualification at 18 and the development of modular A-levels.

Part II of the book is concerned with the effects of current and proposed post-14 policies on different groups of students. How are those groups previously known to be disadvantaged by selective and discriminatory policies and practices faring as separate post-14 pathways, curriculum differentiation and a divided qualifications structure become embedded in institutional arrangements and educational thinking?

David Gillborn, in a chapter discussing race and ethnicity in post-14 education, begins with a quotation by Kenneth Baker, architect of the 1988 Education Reform Act, which illustrates the increasingly acceptable view on both the Right and the Left, that 14 rather than 11 is the 'natural break' for selection onto different pathways – one being the academic route leading to higher education and one the practical, technical and vocational route. As always with those who propose this kind of separation, Baker stresses that the vocational pathway is not inferior, just different. Gillborn points out that this separation supports and reiterates the assumptions of the 1930s, expressed in the 1943 Norwood Committee report (Norwood 1943), that there are different 'types' of students with different 'types' of mind – beliefs which led inexorably to the Eleven Plus examination and secondary modern schools. Gillborn expresses the concern that the Dearing reviews of the National Curriculum and post-16 qualifications (Dearing 1994; 1996) simply endorse out-dated legitimations for the separation of students on to academic and vocational courses. On past record, it has overwhelmingly been the case that students from lower socio-economic groups (girls and boys), racial and ethnic minorities, and those with disabilities and special educational needs, were found disproportionately on vocational tracks. What is the situation now and in the foreseeable future?

Gillborn uses his own recent research to explore the situation of racial minority students post-14. He uses data on educational achievements at GCSE level from 1992 to 1996 to demonstrate that, despite general improvements in examination performance, 'black inequalities in educational achievement are persisting at a significant level', and that this applies to black female students as well as male. Indian students achieve well at 16, but Bangladeshi and Pakistani students do less well. Almost all minority students stay on at school or college post-16, but already on different tracks. White and Asian students opt more for academic tracks GSCE and A-levels, and also for retakes of GCSEs post-16. Black students are more likely to take vocational courses. Gillborn points to the already existing option choice and exam entry process at 14 which result in curriculum stratification. Existing selection processes provide additional hurdles for racial minority students, and the evidence suggests that in the future these students may be subject to increasing disadvantage. Issues of race and ethnicity no longer feature prominently in education debates, and in the three paragraphs on ethnic issues mentioned in the Dearing review of qualifications (Dearing 1996, pp. 130–2), lower-level or vocational choices are blamed on to students themselves who hold 'stereotypes of ways forward'.

By contrast girls, particularly white girls from manual working-class backgrounds, have over the past five years improved their examination performance at GCSE level, on average out-performing boys. This 'out-performance' does not apply at A-level, where male students still do better. There is also a continuing sharp arts–science divide, with girls far more likely to opt for arts and humanities, but university undergraduate intakes are now around 50 per cent female. Improved girls' educational achievements have led to a focus on 'boys underachievement' (Woodhead 1996), in particular the 'underachievement' of white working-class boys. In Chapter 9, Tamsyn Imison, headteacher of a co-educational comprehensive school, offers an intriguing insight into girls' views of changed educational practices, and demonstrates the raised expectations and aspirations of girls. In a structured conversation with two sixth-form students who had completed A-levels and were about to take a year out before university, she explores their views of the purposes of education, the improved performance of girls *vis-à-vis* boys, and the academic–vocational divide. The girls, one (self-styled) working class and one middle class, had positive and sophisticated perceptions of education, seeing it as far more than preparation for economic activity, and they were aware of and deplored the academic–vocational divide created by A-level and GNVQ courses. They held very positive views about their own education which did appear to be influenced by the school ethos and its commitment to equal opportunities and equal respect for all students. The students considered that, despite such a commitment, a two-track system led to A-level students 'feeling superior'. Although they were aware that boys' achievements were problematic, these two young women were confident that their own success had been achieved by motivation and merit.

There is still little chance of students with disabilities or learning difficulties being allowed to 'feel superior'. Jenny Corbett in Chapter 10 explores four elements in the 14–19 education of young people with special educational needs. These include the transition of the students from school to college, training or community living; their specialised curriculum; the attitudes of their teachers and trainers; and the issue of inclusion in the mainstream – an issue which is now a civil rights concern. While disabled students who do not exhibit learning difficulties or problem behaviour are more likely to be integrated into mainstream school and college courses, unmanageable and problematic students are more likely to remain in segregated special schools and on special college courses. Colleges increasingly offer courses for those who choose to identify themselves as having a specific learning difficulty (dyslexia) and for the larger groups of young people who leave school with poor levels of literacy and numeracy. Corbett's chapter vividly illustrates the realities for those students, whether 'statemented' as having special needs, or non-statemented low achievers, in a competitive education system and economy in which qualifications are crucial in gaining even unskilled employment. Students whose disabilities disbar them from undertaking assessment for NVQs and those disaffected students from Pupil Referral Units already to be found post-14 on college courses, are at the bottom of the heap in the current qualifications scramble. Dearing's recommendation (Dearing 1994, p. 20) that more disaffected school students should leave to attend college courses will lead more students on to low-level courses with subsequent unemployment prospects, in addition to changing the culture in colleges in certain areas. Corbett regards the Dearing proposals as a continuation of programmes set up during the 1980s to contain and control potentially troublesome or disaffected young people, who might otherwise swell the crime figures and the prison population, but she does consider that Dearing is 'confronting reality' by suggesting the adaptation of vocational courses to persuade these young people to stay on in some form of education. For a large minority of young people post-14, becoming an independent 'good citizen' is at odds with a competitive job situation and restricted funding for courses geared to qualification outcomes. There is also a potential for escape from the work ethic by young people who do question 'the dubious honour of becoming a member of a community they disregard and even despise'.

The post-14 education of students regarded as disruptive and disaffected is taken up by Roger Slee in Chapter 11. Using examples from Australia, he reminds us that in every country where education and economic free-market policies have been adopted, school for many young people has become a conduit to long-term unemployment. This has inevitably led to detachment and disruption by some students. Current moral panics in both the UK and Australia blame students, their parents, schools and teachers for disaffection and disruptive behaviour. Quick-fix solutions include punishing and excluding students, and labelling the schools and teachers as failing. Slee demonstrates that disruptive behaviour is much more than student pathology. It is better understood as a result of interactions between the political economy (who gets jobs and why), the teaching and learning processes in schools, changing patterns of authority and youth cultures and identities. Traditional approaches to disciplining young people are increasingly useless. The identification and removal of problem students may 'deliver schools from disruption' and allow 'good' students to work unimpeded, and it may deliver the tough message that schools are only for the serious student. But it does nothing to engage the disaffected students with education. Using his own research, Slee shows that improvements in behaviour can be achieved through curriculum reform – easier to implement in Australia than the UK. The provision of a comprehensive academic and vocational curriculum, with decision-making involving the students, their parents and the business community, did improve behaviour and achievement in the institutions he studied. Radical rethinking in education is required to rescue students from a potential educational wasteland.

The above analyses have presented a depressing view of the impact of current and future suggested policies on many young people post-14. However, the final contribution to the book is positive. In Chapter 12 Crombie-White describes and celebrates the Award Scheme Development and Accreditation Network – ASDAN Youth Award Scheme – which is a remarkable success story in post-14 education. Developed in 1986 in one school, this scheme, offering a progressive series of awards at bronze, silver, gold and platinum level, now operates in 1,800 schools and colleges in 84 local education authorities, and 100,000 students were enrolled in 1995. Crombie-White had a personal involvement with this scheme, developed at a time when teachers still had some professional input into the school curriculum, and it was largely due to his efforts that so many students have had enriched curriculum experiences, with the awards now recognised by universities and by employers. This chapter also returns to the questions raised by Richard Pring in Chapter 2. What are we trying to achieve through our education system and for whom? What qualities do we want to develop and celebrate in young people? What knowledge, skills and competences will be most useful in the next century and will our current divided and divisive system achieve what we want?

FUTURE DIRECTIONS

As the three-track system becomes more firmly embedded, and the academic–vocational divide widens in schools and colleges, the hopes of a unified 14–19 curriculum leading to a unified qualification are diminishing. Yet, from the late 1980s, an astonishing number of associations called for an end to divisions and reform at this crucial period in the education of young people.

Sources as diverse as the Confederation of British Industry, the Institute of Directors, the Trades Union Congress, the Royal Society, the Royal Society of Arts, the Advisory Council on Science and Mathematics, the National Commission on Education, the Association of Sixth-Form Principals, the Committee of Vice-Chancellors and Principals, and (jointly) the Association for Colleges, the Girls' School Association, the Headmasters' Conference, the Sixth Form College Association and the Society of Heads in Independent Schools (Joint Statement 1944), have urged a reformed post-14 curriculum, with flexibility and breadth and a merging of the academic and vocational. The IPPR publication *A British Baccalaureate* (Finegold *et al.* 1990), was of particular importance, as it argued for a single award at 18 and a unified framework of modular academic and vocational courses. This was partly inspired by the example of Scotland, where a single national certificate for vocational studies had been developed, and the Scottish system has been subject to further unifying reform. In 1996 the Institute of Welsh Affairs published proposals for a Welsh Baccalaureate 'advocated as a corrective to the damaging academic–vocational split endemic in Welsh education' (Bellin 1996).

The Labour and Liberal parties have also supported curriculum unification. In the run-up to the 1992 election, the Labour Party committed itself to a unified Advanced General Certificate of Education, and one Shadow Minister suggested the abolition of GCSE and a 14–19 curriculum offered to all in non-selective community colleges (Fatchett 1992). In 1994 Labour was still supporting an integrated academic–vocational system, with GCSE courses developed as modules with credit accumulation for a final award of a General Certificate of Further Education (Labour 1994). However, by 1996, all party political support seem to have moved to an acceptance of the three-track system. The House of Commons Education Committee in that year supported the Dearing 16–19 proposals and 'looked to the DfEE' to find ways 'which will best enhance the rigour of assessment of A-levels, GNVQs and NVQs' (House of Commons Education Committee 1996).

A schizophrenic situation has developed whereby politicians repeat mantras of a learning society in which all are educated enough to want lifelong learning, while cementing a system that cuts off large numbers of young people from education at 16, and perpetuates the notion that there are separate types of students suitable for separate tracks.

Although many business leaders and industrialists remain largely unaware of recent developments in schools, it may be the case that divisions will soon be more firmly challenged by employers and the business community. Edexel, the foundation which incorporated the Business and Technology Education Council and London Examinations, now offers awards to 'employers and teachers who have taken innovative steps with regard to bridging the gap between academic and vocational training' (Edexcel 1996). The Council for Industry and Higher Education, in its submission of evidence to yet another Dearing committee, this one examining the future of higher education, sees higher education as part of a continuum of learning which is neither narrowly vocational nor narrowly academic, and suggests collaboration and partnership between families of institutions – schools, colleges, libraries, enterprise agencies and universities (Council for Industry and Higher Education 1996).

Breaking down the physical barriers between institutions and allowing young people post-14 more choice from a modularised curriculum incorporating academic, vocational and work experience for all students, with credit accumulation towards a unified qualification, *is* one way forward. But it will be a difficult way, as all institutions now have such strong competitive interests in their own survival. Moving from a three-track to a unified system will also be difficult, although Spours and Young, in their project *Learning for the Future* have made proposals as to how this could happen (1996). Their conclusion at that time was that reform will 'have to wait for a government with a very different policy' (Spours and Young 1996).

It would be a salutary exercise for politicians and policy-makers to ask themselves what kind of education they would want for their own children. The answer, on current evidence, would be that they wanted their own children to be educated to 18 and beyond, and preferably not guided into early vocational or occupational training. In a society that valued all its young people there would be a desire to devise an education system that incorporated academic, vocational and work-experience aspects for all students. The three-track system currently becoming embedded is leading to a situation where young people are not educated to be equal citizens in the society or even members of the same economy.

REFERENCES

Avis, J., Bloomer, M., Esland, G., Gleeson, D. and Hodkinson, P. (1996) *Knowledge and Nation – Education, Politics and Work*. London: Cassell.

Banks, M., Bates, I., Breakwell, G., Bynner, J. and Elmer, N. (1992) *Career Identities*. Milton Keynes: Open University Press.

Bellin, W. (1996) *The Welsh Baccalaureate: Proposed by the Institute of Welsh Affairs*. Cardiff: School of Education, University of Wales.

Council for Industry and Higher Education (1996) *A Learning Nation – Submission to the National Committee of Enquiry into Higher Education*. London: IHE.

Crombie-White, R., Pring, R. and Brockington, R. (1995) *14–19 Education and Training: Implementing a Unified System of Learning*. London: Royal Society of Arts.

Crowther Report (1959) *15–18: A Report of the Central Advisory Council for Education (England)*. London: HMSO.

Curtis, S.J. (1952) *Education in Britain Since 1900*. London: Hodder and Stoughton.

Dearing, R. (1994) *The National Curriculum and its Assessment*. London: Schools Curriculum and Assessment Authority.

Dearing, R. (1996) *Review of Qualifications for 16–19 Year Olds*. London: School Curriculum and Assessment Authority.

DES (Department of Education and Science) (1985) *Better Schools*, Cmd. 9469. London: HMSO.

DES/DOE (Department of Employment) (1991) *Education and Training for the 21st Century*, Cmnd. 1536. London: HMSO.

De Ville, O. (1986) *Review of Vocational Qualifications in England and Wales*. London HMSO.

DfEE (1996a) *Choice and Opportunity – A Learning Future for 14-19 year olds.* London: Department for Education and Employment.

DfEE (1996b) *Learning to Compete – Education and Training for 14-19 Year Olds.* London: Department for Education and Employment.

Edexcel Foundation (1996) *Foundation Awards for Academic Excellence.* London: Edexcel.

Edwards, T., Fitz-Gibbon, C., Hardman, F., Haywood, R. and Meaghan, N. (1997) *Separate but Equal? A-levels and Advanced GNVQs.* London: Routledge.

Fatchett, D. (1992) 'Count on the comprehensive', *The Guardian*, 10 June.

Finegold, D., Keep, E., Miliband, D., Raffe, D., Spours, K. and Young, M. (1990) *A British Baccalaureate.* London: Institute for Public Policy Research.

Galbraith, J.K. (1992) *The Culture of Contentment.* London: Sinclair-Stevenson.

Higginson Report (1988) *Advancing 'A' levels.* London: HMSO.

HMI (1981) *The School Curriculum.* London: HMSO.

House of Commons Education Committee (1996) *Education and Training for 14-19 Year Olds: First Report.* London: House of Commons.

Hutton, W. (1995) *The State We're In.* London: Vintage.

Joint Statement by Headmasters' Conference (1994) *Post-Compulsory Education and Training.* London: HMC.

Labour Party (1994) *Aiming Higher: Labour's Plans for Reform of the 14-19 Curriculum.* London: Labour Party.

Lawton, D. (1989) *Education, Culture and the National Curriculum.* London: Hodder and Stoughton.

Ministry of Education (1946) *The Nation's Schools*, Pamphlet no. 1. London: Ministry of Education.

Norwood Report (1943) *Curriculum and Examinations in Secondary Schools.* London: Ministry of Education.

NUT (1996) *14-19 Strategy for the Future – The Road to Equality.* London: National Union of Teachers.

Pring, R.A. (1995) *Closing the Gap: Liberal Education and Vocational Preparation.* London: Hodder and Stoughton.

Simon, B. (1974) *The Two Nations and the Educational Structure, 1780-1870.* London: Lawrence and Wishart.

Simon, B. (1991) *Education and the Social Order: 1940-1990.* London: Lawrence and Wishart.

Smith, D.J. and Tomlinson, S. (1989) *The School Effect: A Study of Multi-Racial Comprehensives.* London: Policy Studies Institute.

Spours, K. and Young, M. (1996) *Dearing and Beyond: Steps and Stages to a Unified System*, British Journal of Education and Work, vol. 9, no. 3, pp. 5-18. Dearing and Beyond; Steps and Stages to a Unified 14-19 qualification system.

Woodhead, C. (1996) 'Boys who learn to be losers', *The Times*, 6 March.

PART I

Analysis: Policy Developments

2

Aims, Values and the Curriculum
Richard Pring

INTRODUCTION

One common, but rarely noticed, feature of recent recommendations for post-14 reform is the lack of any examination in depth of the *educational* aims of such reforms. There is, of course, much said about the economic aims – the need for a well-educated and trained workforce if we are to compete successfully with our economic competitors. Indeed, it seems to be such economic imperatives which finally have persuaded those who govern us that all young people need to be educated (or at least trained) to a high level – not any concern for the intrinsic merit of that education. Thus, the otherwise excellent report by the National Commission on Education, *Learning to Succeed*, devotes a chapter (and many other references) to economic needs arising from international competition, but gives only a rare glimpse of its *educational* values; the Commission refers to information technology on 27 pages, but to the arts on only two (National Commission on Education 1993). Again and again, the reports and documents that have influenced policy (for example, the CBI (1989) report on skills shortage, Ball's brief but effective documents on schools and higher education, (1990 and 1991) have brought public and political attention to the economic needs of a country within a very competitive world.

That this should be the case is not surprising. It has been necessary to change rapidly a culture in which only a relative few need to be educated – indeed, in which only a relative few are deemed *educable* in any broad sense of that term. The educational system has always, even in its more meritocratic form, been characterised by a series of tests which prevented the majority from proceeding to the next stage of education. And that might be said to reflect a particular economic context, one which was characterised by a very large number of unskilled workers or by skilled workers who could receive their training in the workplace, needing very little education broadly conceived.

Nonetheless, there are three interconnected concerns which I wish to address. The first is the frequent *equation* of 'education' with preparation for the economic needs of society. I do not wish to deny the connection: indeed, I wish to delineate that connection all the more clearly. But I wish to deny the *equation*. 'Education' refers to a set of values, which may be compatible with the economic needs as they are perceived, but are not reducible to these.

Second, there is a danger that an uncritical association of education with preparation for economic life might foster a rather narrow and utilitarian educational programme. Qualities and understandings which we would wish to associate with the educated person might receive lower priority than they deserve. The quality of life worth living, which should be the constant concern of education, might receive but cursory examination – and, surely, 'the unexamined life is not worth living'.

Third, too close a focus upon the economic benefits of education might not provide an adequate preparation, either economically or personally, for the increasingly unpredictable future. Too close a focus on economic necessities of today might not meet the economic necessities of tomorrow. The curriculum consequences of this need to be spelt out.

EDUCATION: AIMS AND VALUES

We talk about an educational system in the sense of those institutions and arrangements whereby we enable or compel people to learn. *In that sense*, 'education' is a neutral term – it does not evaluate that system of learning, simply *describes* it. There is no necessary sense of valuing it as educational. Indeed, it may be the case that the educational system in this *descriptive* sense is picked out for educational criticism. But in the *evaluative* sense of education, such a system might be regarded as an educational disaster.

Thus, the educational system may be described by reference to the different kinds of schools and funding arrangements, to the different stages of transfer, to the examinations, and so on. But it may then be criticised from an educational point of view. Such criticisms would point to the kinds of understandings and qualities which such a system neglected or even undermined (for example, through the content of what was taught or through the social processes which developed particular attitudes). For example, the system of education which we have inherited has been criticised for not developing economic understanding, and for not developing qualities and dispositions such as entrepreneurship, which provide an educational base for entrance into the world of work. It is important to bear in mind this distinction between the descriptive and the evaluative sense of 'education' – particularly as the descriptive sense seems to be parasitic upon the evaluative sense. In either case education refers to learning. The *raison d'être* of an educational system is to enable people to *learn* – but, nonetheless, to learn those things which society, or its guardians, believe to be worthwhile. The educational system is so organised as to enable all young people between the ages of 5 and 16 to learn those things (now defined in the National Curriculum) which the government and its advisers believe to be valuable – literacy, numeracy, a second language, and so on. Every so often the content and the process of learning are changed in the light of further discussion about what is worthwhile. Thus, 'economic awareness' is introduced (though half-heartedly) as a cross-curricular theme, work experience is made compulsory before the age of 16, careers advice is encouraged, and information technology has come to permeate the curriculum.

It is possible to condemn an education *system* as not *educationally* valuable. For example, one might say of a particular system that it was indoctrinatory, the very opposite of what *educationally* we should be aiming at. But the apparent contradiction here is easily dealt with. Such a system of learning would be judged by those internal to the system as worthwhile. The Nazi educational system would be seen by the Nazis themselves as encouraging the right qualities and understandings. Those outside the system, however, deny it to have educational quality. The nature of the argument would be essentially ethical: namely, that the particular qualities and understandings which were fostered by the Nazis were not worthwhile ones. They lacked, indeed subverted, the qualities and understandings which we would wish to associate with 'the educated person'. One could interpret Wiener's (1985) critique of our educational system as *educational* arguments in this evaluative sense. Past emphasis on such subjects as the classics or the location of schools in 'places set apart' had encouraged attitudes which were inimical to the kinds of understandings and qualities which should be expected of a person living and working in this day and age.

This evaluative sense of education cannot be avoided. What are the qualities, the understandings, the skills, the attitudes that we want young people to acquire? The answers to such questions may well point to the requirements for them to be employed or for the wider society to be economically successful. But it would be strange if the answers were confined to the requirements of economic success, because there is surely much more to being a person and to living successfully within society than economic accomplishment. Indeed, it is difficult to think of educating persons without attending to what it *means* to be a person and to achieve personal fulfilment.

There is nothing new in this – only a reminder of what schools and teachers have, for the most part, always recognised. As teachers introduce pupils to a literature not obviously connected to being a successful business person, or as they focus upon the key concepts of physical science for those who do not intend to be scientists, or as they in history initiate the next generation into the peculiarities of feudal power, they are selecting from a cultural heritage, the merits of which are only partially related to economic success.

Those merits are based on a view, often implicit, of what is worth learning or of what powers of the mind are worth developing or of what qualities of person are worth nurturing if one is to live a distinctively human life. Economic success has, of course, a part to play in that distinctively human life – both in making it possible and in being part of the understandings without which each of us is handicapped in an important sense. But economic success – or the understanding of it – is but a part. And that is obvious upon reflection. It is quite feasible that a person's economic success might lead to a distinctively inhuman existence – to one bereft of moral or aesthetic value. There is, in other words, something odd about *educational* arrangements and institutions being dominated by economic considerations. There are more basic questions to be asked about the quality of life which such economic success will either bring or not bring about.

To be educated, therefore, is to be able to look beyond the immediate economic imperative. It is to be able to explore, from many perspectives, the sort of life which is worth aspiring to, and to do so in the light of evidence, argument and deliberations of other people, as these are expressed in art, literature, history and science. At the centre of any educational programme must be those 'humane' studies whereby young people are helped (to use Bruner's words) to explore what it means to be human, how they became so, and how they might become more so (Bruner 1965). In other words, education values understandings, dispositions, knowledge, skills, attitudes which reflect a distinctively human form of life. And, in an age where there is little consensus on such important matters, 'education' values particularly the understandings which enable the young person to take such questions seriously and to engage in a personal search for value.

To be equipped to engage in that search for value the young person needs first to be enabled to understand the physical world, at least to the extent to which he or she is able to act intelligently within it. That may not require being a scientist in any professional or sophisticated sense. It does require an acquisition of those concepts and theories which inform our everyday understanding of the physical universe. It requires in particular a technical know-how and understanding of those processes (for example, in information technology) which extend the human capacities. Second, young persons need to have a basic grasp of the economic and social world which, if, through ignorance, they are not able to shape, they will be shaped by. How can one live intelligently without a basic understanding of the economic and political context in which one lives? Third, they must be enabled to grasp, and to work intelligently within, the moral world, inspired by ideals and sustained by values which give direction in what is so often a confusing world of different fashions and influence. Such a moral world – a world of loyalties, obligations, responsibilities, promises, commitments, relationships – is by no means foreign to the vast majority of young people. But to be educated requires the refinement of such a world, the subjection of it to critical examination, its internalisation and serious adoption, its extension to new and unforeseen circumstances. Finally, education initiates the young person into the aesthetic world, through which pleasure, appreciation and satisfaction are found in the physical world.

This might be put rather differently. Each of us inhabits a world of ideas through which experience is sieved and organised. Such a world of ideas is the product of a cultural history – of what Oakeshott (1972) refers to as the 'conversations which have taken place between the generations of mankind'. That world of ideas might, if not fully grasped, be an impoverished thing. The aim of the teacher is to initiate the young learner into that world – or, more precisely, into the physical, social, moral and aesthetic worlds through which we experience, understand, think about the present and the future, and find value. That initiation will require the often systematic introduction to what others have said and argued, or produced – the books and the artefacts. And it will require helping the young initiates to make sense of all that – not necessarily to accept, but to make sense and to come to a considered view.

There is, of course, a perennial argument over exactly what, from the world of ideas, should be selected for the benefit of the young learner – what, exactly, should inform those personal attempts to make sense of, and to find value in, experience. To that extent, there is no consensus on what exactly counts as the educated person within our society or what exactly should be the core of learnings that everyone should be acquainted with. The National Curriculum tried, unsuccessfully, to prescribe a canon of good literature. But such a failure does not undermine the general point that education is centrally concerned with those learnings which we find ultimately to be of value – the acquisition of the skills, understandings, knowledge, attitudes which help each and every one to discover what is a worthwhile form of life, and empower each to pursue it.

Part of those learnings will, of course, be the economic grasp of the world which we inhabit, and also the practical know-how to live within it intelligently and creatively. But it necessarily goes much beyond that. There is much more to a distinctively human life than economics.

THE UTILITARIAN DANGER

These general considerations are relevant to what is happening in the reforms of education and training, particularly at the upper end of the school, in further education and in the universities. Many have been the warnings that the curriculum is not as relevant as it should be to the economic needs of the learners themselves or to the society that they are to live in. 'Relevance' is the rallying cry of the reformers. That requires a change not simply in what is learnt, but also in who should control what is learnt, in how that learning should be assessed and indeed in the very language of learning and education.

First, with regard to the change of control, education is expensive. It is a major national investment. It is natural, therefore, that people will ask what the economic return is on such an investment. This especially is likely when it is believed that standards are slipping or when the 'products' of the education system do not have the knowledge, skills and attitudes required for economic success in a highly competitive world. And, indeed, there has been a systematic criticism of both the standards and the economic relevance of education at every level. This concerns not just the standards of literacy and numeracy of a large minority of school 'failures', but also the lack of social and economic awareness even amongst the successful learners within the system. It concerns the mismatch between the skills and knowledge required by business and those fostered by a liberal tradition in education which, as far as the more able are concerned, has been rather disdainful of the practical and the useful.

The consequence has been a range of initiatives by the government in which money is put into education on condition that it becomes more vocationalised and that people from industry and commerce play a more active role in determining the goals as well as the means of learning. For example, the government invested millions of pounds in the Technical and Vocational Education Initiative (TVEI) to make the school curriculum more relevant to the world of work; one condition of receiving this money was that the curriculum should become more vocational and, because of the changes affecting industry, more technical. Again, changes in the composition of governing bodies of schools were legislated so that there had to be a 25 per cent representation from the community, especially the community of industry and commerce. Or, again, all schools now have to incorporate work experience into the curriculum. Again, still, there is a growth of mini-enterprise schemes in which school students set up businesses as part of their school activities. One can point, too, to the government-established City Technology Colleges which attempted to harness industrial and commercial interest through investment in schools and participation in the curriculum. In further education, money that was normally fed into colleges through the local education authorities has been placed instead in the hands of the newly established Training and Enterprise Councils under the control of business people. Business people play an important role in government-appointed bodies which make recommendations about the curriculum – in history, say, or in teacher training. And in higher education, the TVEI principles developed in schools were extended to universities through the Enterprise in Higher Education scheme. It is as though education cannot be left to the teachers, the lecturers or their employers. Their aims, purposes and values are thought to be too 'narrowly liberal', too taken up with what is intrinsically worthwhile, not related sufficiently to the 'real world' of business and commerce.

Secondly, 'relevance' is seen to require a reform of how learning should be assessed – and, indeed, what should be assessed. There has been a massive change in the organisation and form of assessment. This has required the bringing together of the many kinds of vocational qualification into a system of National Vocational Qualifications which shape rather than reflect what is learnt – an assessment-led rather than curriculum-led system. The criticism levelled against traditional modes of assessment is that they do not spell out what exactly the successfully assessed person can do. It is not possible, say, to deduce from the fact that someone received an A grade in History at GCSE what skills or knowledge have been acquired. But that is precisely what employers, we are told, want to know. How, then, might one change a system of assessment based on judgement into one focused upon precise statements of what needs to be assessed?

The answer, most articulately put by Jessup (1991), was to list the range of competences – the 'can do's – which are derived from an analysis of the tasks to be done. Driving a car or installing a central heating system is a complex activity which can be analysed into a range of very specific skills and bits of knowledge, and these in turn can be translated into a finite (though lengthy) list of observable behaviours. In this way, one is able to be freed from the often vague and general aims which characterise so much assessment and which depend upon the apparently subjective judgement of the many examiners.

The consequence of this shift in assessment approach has been a bureaucratic listing of specific competences for every aspect of learning seen to be relevant to subsequent employment — or indeed 'life' as one acquires 'life skills' and 'parent competences'. The result has been a recent re-examination of such a competence based approach (see Capey 1996). But the problems, as in the case of shifting modes of control, lie deeper.

Thirdly (but partly under the influence of changing modes of control and of assessment), relevance has required a change in the language through which education is described and thereby evaluated. Increasingly the language is taken from the world of business. Education becomes a commodity or an investment, no longer a transaction between teacher and learner. The value of that commodity is measured quantitatively by 'cost effectiveness' and 'value addedness', rather than by the quality of learning and intellectual experience. That commodity is bought by a consumer, no longer enjoyed by a learner. Standards of effectiveness and of 'value-addedness' are determined by usefulness to extrinsic goals – 'fitness for purpose' – not by intrinsic worth. Those standards are spelt out in a limited range of 'performance indicators', not left implicit within academic judgement. And standards are preserved by systems of 'quality control' and 'quality assurance', checked by regular 'audits' – no longer by the judgements of those who, by reason of their initiation into the traditions of learning, have internalised the criteria by which intellectual excellence is to be assessed. There is, therefore, an emphasis upon explicit goals. Subject-matter is broken down into independent modules of learning. 'Relevance' becomes a criterion of value. Teaching requires explicit objectives, and such objectives enable unambiguous assessment. Clarity, sharpness, precision, sureness of judgement, explicitness of assessment replace the uncertainty over worthwhile outcomes and the fuzziness of standards. And of course this is the language of management and control.

The danger of this three-pronged attack on traditional learning and its arrangement – namely, the greater control of education and training by those from outside the academic and educational world, combined with an assessment system which provides the tools of control and a language borrowed from management and business – is that it subverts the very aims of education which I outlined in the previous section. It is essentially a 'means-end' model of education – a system which is valid or worthwhile or of value in so far as it leads effectively to particular goals which are formed outside the educational debate and community. The government or business or industry sets the goals – and the assessment and language reflect those goals. Education becomes a descriptive term applied to those activities which most effectively help people to reach those goals.

The 'liberal tradition', by contrast, however much it is open to criticism for being too narrowly disdainful of the practical and the useful or for being dismissive of so many young people as ineducable or for ignoring the voices of those who do not fit easily into mainstream educational thinking, does point to the total inadequacy of the narrowly utilitarian view which lies behind so many recent developments. That liberal tradition emphasises those distinctively human capacities for acting intelligently and critically in the physical, social, moral and aesthetic worlds that one inhabits. It is concerned with the goals or ends of human activity as much as with the means. Above all it is centrally concerned with the values which permeate our understanding of the world and of the ideas through which we understand it. In such an *educational* world and in such *liberal* discourse there can be no authority or control except from within the tradition itself – the tradition of critical debate, of verification and argument determined by the intellectual or social or moral or aesthetic discourse itself.

The question then is: how might such liberal values be reconciled with the legitimate desire for more vocational relevance?

THE PRE-VOCATIONAL RESPONSE

The liberal tradition is correct in pointing to the fact that we do live in a world of ideas, that those ideas constitute our capacity to think and to argue, to appreciate and to value, to understand and to set ourselves ideals. Without basic concepts of science we cannot understand the world about us; without a grasp of religious ideas, a whole dimension of experience is closed to us; without an historical perspective, we have but a limited sense of what we are and of the contingency of the conditions in which we live; without an acquaintance with literature and with poetry, we are denied access to the 'best that has been thought and said' about the quality of life.

It is the job of the teacher to initiate the learner into that world – to liberate the learner from ignorance through the possession of the different forms of knowledge through which they are enabled to think, to criticise, to appreciate and to value. Moreover, in entering critically into the different forms of knowledge, they are introduced to the never ending discussions about the quality of life worth pursuing. The excitement of literature, for example, lies in the way it changes the perceptions of the reader about the value and understanding of human situations.

And there is no predetermined end to such enquiry. For that reason, teachers have reason to be suspicious of educational planners who, under the banner of vocationalism, state the precise objectives of learning and derive from them the 'performance indicators' according to which the quality of learning might be judged. Furthermore, they have a right to be suspicious of those who, having derived the goals of education from an analysis of industrial or social needs, see education and training to be no more than the acquisition of the knowledge and skills which will lead to those ends. For the ends themselves belong to the world of values which are the object of educational enquiry within the arts and the humanities, in particular, but also anywhere within a curriculum where young people are encouraged to enquire and to think. The questioning pupil or apprentice, as much as the academic, will want to understand the economic and social values which permeate the course of study. Economic efficiency is only efficiency for certain ends, and those ends might be morally questionable. But to see that, and to make one's voice heard, requires not only the intellectual tools that lie within the liberal tradition, but also the freedom of the teacher to engage in the transaction with the learner in a way that is not constrained by external demands. The freedom to think, to enjoy the argument wherever it might lead, to criticise and to question, is intrinsic to the educational enterprise. That liberal tradition is already being eroded, as government, in pursuit of economic and social ends, encroaches upon the authority of the teacher.

On the other hand, much of education has treated some learners as ineducable – excluded from the 'conversation' which has chosen to value parts of our culture to which they cannot relate. It is as though what they have to learn at school is of no importance to them. Their concerns, the knowledge that they need and the problems that they want to solve, have no place on the curriculum. It is as though, not fitting into the framework of those who decide what is of educational value, they have no minds to be nurtured, no emotions to be refined, no interests to be developed. Too many, therefore, have been relegated to a narrow form of vocational training.

Furthermore, education, liberally conceived, has ignored economic relevance – as though one can assume that the educated person will have understanding and intellectual versatility to turn his or her mind to whatever subsequent employment demands. But that is not true. The academically successful may prove to be technically and practically useless; the person initiated into the pursuit of disinterested enquiry may be disdainful of what is studied for the sake of its usefulness; the person who is acquainted with 'the best that has been thought and said' may lack economic and social awareness.

To resolve this problem requires both a respect for the liberal tradition and yet a recognition of the importance of economic relevance both for the learner and for the society in which the learner is to live and work. And this brings us back once again to the aims and values inherent in education, given the particular social and economic context in which it is to take place. Teachers are but part of the debate about the aims of education. It is, of course, an important part: they introduce the young learner to those ideas from literature, from history, from science and so on, through which they are able to appreciate what is worthwhile. But there are others who have a part to play: employers who understand the economic basis of the life we lead, government which has responsibility for reconciling the many different demands upon limited resources, the wider community which has a view about the kind of society which education prepares the next generation for, and the young people themselves whose voices are too often ignored. And in engaging in this essentially ethical debate, which brings representatives of the liberal and the vocational traditions together, there is a constant need to reflect upon what it means to be an educated person.

To be an educated person requires the nurturing of those qualities of mind and of feeling which are distinctive of being a person and of living a full and satisfying life. At the centre of that would be the entry into that world of ideas which the liberal tradition emphasises. But it would also attend to the capabilities and skills which enable one to work and live effectively in the changing economic circumstances. It would include the moral commitment and the social skills which fitted one to be a responsible member of the community. It would provide the capacity to enjoy and to create artefacts within the world of music and the arts. It would above all teach people to be human – and in defining what it means, all have a part to play.

Such considerations have not been absent from recent thinking about the programmes of learning and the qualifications within our schools and colleges – although it is surprising how quickly those who exercise control of education forget. When the Further Education Unit (FEU) was established within the Department of Education and Science (DES) in the late 1970s, its first task concerned what to do with the growing number of young people who, unable to get jobs, were knocking at the doors of colleges demanding further education. And yet neither the academic tradition, represented by A-levels or repeat O-levels, nor the vocational tradition, represented by training for specific jobs, was appropriate. More often than not these young people were the school failures, those deemed unsuited for academic study. At the same time, they were not clear about the jobs or careers they wanted to be trained for. The FEU was left with the question: What counts as a continuing general education for a growing number of young people, alienated by past failure, disillusioned with education as it had been experienced, ignorant of what future employment had in store – but recognising that learning mattered?

The FEU produced *A Basis for Choice*, which set out principles addressing the problems of diversity in a time of economic and social change. In so doing, it challenged many of the preconceptions about educational purposes and about processes of learning that dominated the curriculum. Furthermore, it had far reaching effects upon developments which were then to take place both in further education and in schools – but which have so sadly been neglected in recent standardisations of the curriculum. Those principles encapsulated the *tacit* understandings of teachers as they grappled with the problems of educating young people, often reluctant learners, frequently those who by traditional standards were failures. Hence, the swift adoption, by colleges and schools, of the City and Guilds of London Institute (CGLI) 365 courses, the rapid take-up of the Certificate of Pre-Vocational Education (CPVE), the immediate transformation in 1982 of the Technical and Vocational Education Initiative from the narrowly vocational prescription of Lord Young into something exciting and educationally defensible. This 'pre-vocational' approach became embodied in the best of the Business and Technology Education Council (BTEC) and Royal Society of the Arts (RSA) qualifications and in the CGLI Diploma of Vocational Education. It was captured in the RSA's Declaration of Capability in 1980:

> There exists in its own right a culture which is concerned with doing and making and organising and the creative arts. This culture emphasises the day to day management of affairs, the formulation and solution of problems, and the design, manufacture and marketing of goods and services

A Basis for Choice addressed two questions. What sort of learning do these young people personally need to prepare for adult life? Secondly, what skills and knowledge does society need from these young people if it is to survive? It was a two-way movement arriving eventually at the same place – at the quality of the transaction between teacher and learner. One move came from a concern about the person – the skills, knowledge, understanding and attitudes necessary for him or her to live a worthwhile life. The other move came from consideration of what the society needed – economically and socially – from the next generation of adults. The analysis did not start from the 'given' of most educational thinking – from the list of subjects which are normally to be found in schools. Perhaps the end point *might* be the same; the starting point was different.

The principles of learning, spelt out and developed in the practices of teachers through various pre-vocational qualifications and projects such as TVEI, might be summarised as follows. First, there was a focus on the process of learning – on the practical mode through which many people profitably learn, but which is barely recognised in the academic ways to which they had been exposed. 'Knowing how', which can be engaged in critically, needed equal recognition with 'knowing that'; practical knowledge could be as demanding as propositional knowledge; 'able to *do*' required as much intelligence as 'able to *say*'.

Second, there was emphasis upon personal guidance – on helping each person to know his or herself in relation to the aspirations and fears for the future. Careers guidance and counselling were given a central place on the curriculum. Should not vocational guidance – what Dewey referred to as enabling the young person to sort out the life he or she wished to lead, in which the quality of employment played a significant part – be central to the *education* of all young people? Part of getting the right job is 'knowing thyself'.

Third, there was stress on personal development – on enabling young people to develop, through achievement and mutual support, the sense of dignity and personal worth which too often had eluded them, but which was crucial if they were to face an unpredictable future with confidence. Part of that preparation would lie in the development of a defensible set of moral values – of *respect* for themselves and of others whatever the background, class, gender or race, of *responsibility* for the consequences of their actions, of *commitment* to social and political engagement, of *caring* for equal opportunities.

Fourth, the importance of communication skills was highlighted – that is, being able and confident in articulating what one wants to say in different audiences and contexts.

Fifth, in the preparation for adult life, serious attention was given to the capacity to participate in decision-making at different levels – hence, the importance of social, political and economic awareness, but an awareness gained as much through 'doing it' as from reading about it.

Sixth, the significance of information technology was recognised not simply as a new set of skills to be acquired but as a challenge to existing organisations of learning. It opened up possibilities of young people setting their own agendas and being less dependent on institutional arrangements.

Seventh, there was reappraisal of the role of the wider community, including employers, in the shared contribution to young people's learning – especially regarding the different resources and expertise which could be put at their service.

These principles established broad criteria according to which the teachers themselves might engage educationally with young people as they, the students, prepared both personally and economically for an unpredictable future. The subsequent TVEI arrangements of the Department of Employment, and the vocational preparation of both BTEC and RSA, refrained from specifying syllabuses. The professional job of the teacher – faced with learners of such diverse achievement, background and aspiration – was, within a framework of broadly con-ceived criteria, to help young people to be more intelligently engaged in the self-knowledge, the practical know-how, the social and political awareness, the moral sensitivities, the technical skills which would enable *them* to make responsible decisions about a future which, because of social and economic change, could not be based simply on past knowledge and understandings.

Furthermore, when economic changes are so rapid yet unpredictable, then the future adult needs the personal qualities and generic skills to face those changes with confidence and equanimity. When past know-ledge is inadequate for future practice, then the process and styles of learning are as important as the content that has been learnt. When new relationships between teachers, industry and the community are estab-lished for relating resources to the process of learning, then old insti-tutional arrangements will be found wanting. These, at least, are the lessons to be learnt from the many attempts to readdress the aims of education in the context of diversity and change. How sad, therefore, that the £1 billion invested by the Department of Employment in TVEI should have received but two grudging mentions from the Department of Education in its 1987 consultative document on the National Curric-ulum. In facing diversity and on managing change, there were different agendas from different departments of state.

This pre-vocational tradition by no means eschews the subject-matter normally associated with liberal education. Indeed, such learning is the resource upon which it must draw. But it is critical of the unexamined tradition. Therefore, concentrating on the process and quality of learn-ing and focusing on the personal formation of the learner, it might be contrasted with both the academic and the vocational.

The academic tradition starts, not with the needs of the learner, but with the nature of the intellectual disciplines – with the subjects from which the curriculum is traditionally built. Its aim is to initiate the learner into those subjects which are regarded as intrinsically worthwhile, requiring no justification in terms of utility or personal relevance. It tends to be rather disdainful of the practical, seeing that to be the prov-ince of the less able. The vocational similarly starts not with the needs of the learner. But there the similarity ends. It starts with an analysis of what is needed to do a job well. Its aim is to be useful, economically useful in particular. Its language is concerned with competence and 'can do's' – with practical and specific skills rather than with theoretical understanding. Personal development becomes personal effectiveness.

The danger that we face, as we try to address, in educational terms, both diversity of economic and personal needs and the massive social changes which exacerbate that diversity, is that we leave the academic and vocational divide as it is and simply add a third track to a two-track system.

REFERENCES

Ball, C. (1990) *More Means Different: Widening Access to Higher Education.* London: RSA.

Ball, C. (1991) *Learning Pays: the Role of Post-Compulsory Education and Training.* Interim Report. London: RSA and Ball.

Bruner, J. (1965) *Towards a Theory of Instruction.* Boston: Harvard University Press.

Capey Report (1996) *Assessment of GNVQ.* London: NCVQ.

CBI (1989) *Towards a Skills Revolution.* London: CBI.

Dewey, J. (1916) *Democracy and Education.* New York: Free Press.

FEU (1979) *A Basis for Choice.* London: HMSO.

Jessup, G. (1991) *Outcomes: NVQs and the Emerging Model of Education and Training.* London: Falmer Press.

National Commission on Education (1993) *Learning to Succeed.* London: Heinemann.

Oakeshott, M. (1972) 'Education: the engagement and its frustration', in T. Fuller (ed.) *Michael Oakeshott and Education.* London: Yale University Press.

Pring, R. (1995) *Closing the Gap: Liberal Education and Vocational Preparation.* London: Hodder and Stoughton.

RSA (1980) *Manifesto for Capability.* London: RSA.

Wiener, M. (1985) *English Culture and the Decline of the Industrial Spirit 1850–1980.* Harmondsworth: Penguin.

3

Patterns in Development
Geoff Stanton

Imagine a situation in which a car company decides that its model range requires completely revamping. Its vehicles still sell, and are being continually if gradually improved, but international competition is showing them up. The company therefore commissions three new models, each of which is intended to mark a departure from the past. They come on stream at different times but each embodies innovative design features, and aims to provide a step change in performance.

Unfortunately, events do not develop as intended. Complaints pour in, not only from customers, but also from the garages that sell and maintain the vehicles. Each vehicle has been designed and produced by a different division of the company, and each division struggles to put things right. The divisional heads are replaced, and in some cases the divisions themselves are reorganised. It is argued (whether by the divisions or by the parent company it is not altogether clear) that the new models are basically fine, and that the problems derive from users being reluctant to change or failing to understand the innovative features. However, attempts to improve the marketing of each model do not stem the complaints.

The task of the marketing people is not helped by the fact that the company directors and their families themselves continue to use a vintage model which is preserved from change, and does not adopt the innovative approaches which are causing some of the problems.

Finally, the parent company calls in third parties to undertake fundamental reviews of each of the new products. This leads to their recall and redesign. While this process is still under-way, it is realised that there is also a more general problem, resulting from the fact that each model has been designed independently, and that the vintage model continues in production. Customers cannot understand how they relate, or how their characteristics and purposes differ, and the garages find that even parts that perform identical functions have different designs and even names. Eventually, the most high profile of the third parties, the Dearing corporation, is given the task of reviewing the whole range.

Had this all indeed happened in a commercial context, the company would not have been satisfied simply to remedy the problems, it would have wanted to know what was going wrong and why it kept happening. Was it to do with the mismanagement of change? Did all three new models share similar design faults?

This chapter attempts to undertake this analysis with regard to the design and implementation of three initiatives:

- the National Curriculum (NC), and especially Key Stage Four (KS4);
- National Vocational Qualifications (NVQs);
- General National Vocational Qualifications (GNVQs).

In other words, I shall be asking "Why is it that three of the most significant developments in post-14 education and training in the last decade proved to be unmanageable when first introduced?" To have this happen once might be thought to be a misfortune. Three times looks like a systems fault from and about which we are failing to learn.

INITIATIVES IN THE 1980s

There were, of course, other initiatives which made considerable impact on 14–19 provision during the 1980s. These included the Certificate of Pre-Vocational Education (CPVE), introduced in 1983 to rationalise and improve courses for the increasing number of young people who wished to stay on in education beyond the end of the compulsory schooling at 16, the Youth Opportunities Programme (1978) and its successor from 1983 onwards, the Youth Training Scheme (YTS). In the current employment market it is salutary to recall that there was also a scheme which started in 1978 for those many 16-year-olds who were employed but who received no systematic education or training. These schemes of Unified Vocational Preparation (UVP) were thought by many of those involved to embody a range of exciting and effective approaches to the needs of a difficult target group. Interestingly, in view of the more recent preoccupation with qualifications and testing, UVP focused on new approaches to the learning *process*, and to the role of teachers, youth workers, workplace supervisors – and the learners themselves – within it.

The most comprehensive and well resourced initiative was TVEI – the Technical and Vocational Education Initiative – which was intended to affect all 14–19 year-olds in time – and which continued in reduced form until 1997.

It is worth taking a slightly closer look at TVEI, because of the way it set about promoting change. Despite the fact that it was aimed at full-time students, TVEI was administered by the Ministry concerned with employment and training, rather than the Ministry concerned with education. This may have been partly because the officials and ministers concerned were thought to have the right kind of initiative in more senses than one, but it was also for a very good constitutional reason. The education ministers administered a system in which crucial decision-making was devolved to local education authorities (LEAs). They could indicate that an element of the local authority grant was intended for a given purpose, but they could not ensure that LEAs spent it that way, or even that it all reached the education budget. The local council might have other pressing priorities.

Any other Ministry, by contrast, could enter into contracts with LEAs, and, just as with any provider of services to them, they had the legal power to see that the money was spent as the contract specified. In the light of later developments, it is interesting to recall how this was handled. There was no centrally devised master plan at an operational level. Instead, those responsible for TVEI specified the aims they wished to see achieved, and invited schools, colleges and LEAs to propose ways of achieving them. This empowered energetic and imaginative practitioners. Indeed, some comparatively junior staff achieved local significance very quickly because of their ability firstly to construct plans which the funding body recognised as having potential, and secondly to deliver them effectively.

Therefore, although there were common national objectives, differing schemes were designed to achieve them locally. In order to be approved for funding, a scheme was required show how staff and organisational development was being introduced to support curriculum changes, how changes were to be evaluated, and to explain how any innovation fitted into and would permanently enhance the local pattern of provision.

The philosophy and power of the TVEI approach was perhaps best encapsulated in the annual planning and review meetings, at which representatives of a local scheme would meet with central officials to review the working of the contract and consider the terms of its renewal. Local managers would be held to account for the achievement or otherwise of the objectives they themselves had proposed a year earlier, but they would also have a chance to raise technical and policy issues for the central officials to tackle.

This was a powerful and effective mechanism for change, and for balancing national priorities with the use of local innovation and special facilities. TVEI also recognised the importance of evaluation, and of balancing curriculum development, staff development and organisational development.

However, there were also problems. In particular, change appeared to be rather slow and somewhat messy, and there were difficulties in matching new learning programmes with existing qualification systems. Perhaps as a result, the pendulum swung, and we entered an era in which educational reform became equated with qualifications reform, and initiatives took the form of detailed schemes drawn up by central government or its agencies.

This was made possible by the Education Reform Act of 1988, which gave the Department of Education and Science the right to specify what was provided in the state sector of education for children of 5 to 16, whether with its money or that of the LEA.[1] Unfortunately, these new powers were then deployed without sufficient attention being paid to what was already known, not least from schemes such as TVEI, about:

- mechanisms for the effective management of educational developments;
- the need to be clear about the relationship between qualifications and the curriculum;
- the importance of any initiative as part of a larger system.

Finally, mention should be made of the introduction of the General Certificate of Secondary Education (GCSE) from 1986 onwards, although it had been under discussion for many years previously. Possibly because of these extended discussions between practitioners and policy-makers, and the parallel development of staff and materials, it has proved a remarkably effective innovation. However, the inability of policy-makers to consider education as a system produced problems about the interface between GCSE and post-16 qualifications and – as we shall see – between GCSE and the overall National Curriculum.

THE NATIONAL CURRICULUM

The government's consultation document on the National Curriculum 5–16 was issued in July 1987, and required responses by the end of September. The National Curriculum was implemented by the Education Reform Act 1988, and the National Curriculum Council (NCC) was established in August 1988.[2] Even before that, two subject working groups, on mathematics and science, had been meeting. Their final reports coincided with the formation of the Council.

Therefore, before the Council even existed it had been decided that the curriculum was to be developed, and phased in, subject-by-subject. This meant that some of the later subject working groups could benefit from the difficulties of the earlier ones, but it is likely that this subject by subject approach derived less from a considered decision than from the fact that many of the politicians, officials and subject specialists involved could conceive of no other way of proceeding. For them, it was obvious that attainment targets, teaching schemes and testing all had to be subject-based. That was their personal experience, and how else could it be?

The schedule provided for the first of the ten national curriculum subjects to be introduced for 5-year-olds (Key Stage One) in 1989, and the last ones for the same age group in 1992. For 14-year-olds (Key Stage Four) all ten subjects would be phased in between 1992 and 1995.

The first Chairman and Chief Executive of the NCC, Duncan Graham, had previously chaired the mathematic working group, and has noted:

> We were conscious that the science group was also meeting but we were all far too busy to meet each other. This was most unfortunate. A sharing of knowledge and some jointly formulated definitions of attainment targets would have reduced the incompatibilities which surfaced later. (Graham and Tytler 1993)

Many responses to the original consultation document had advised strongly that the curriculum should be planned as a whole rather than being designed a subject at a time. A few years earlier Her Majesty's Inspectorate (HMI) had published a report on the whole curriculum which analysed it in terms of areas of knowledge, but government appeared to be in no mood to pay great heed to those who were responsible for the current system, and tended – perhaps understandably in the light of some of their previous experiences – to interpret arguments about things being more difficult than they seemed as delaying tactics.

The subject-based approach may have worked for secondary schools, where cynics said that only the pupils had to engage in and understand the curriculum as a whole, but primary school staff found themselves at the receiving end of what seemed like a never ending series of subject-based National Curriculum orders, each of which took its own line and few of which acknowledged the potential and problems deriving from the fact that the staff and students were dealing with other subjects in parallel. As Sir Ron Dearing pointed out, referring to the assessment requirements for 7-year-olds:

> A classroom teacher at Key Stage 1 with 35 pupils . . . would (need to) make and record some 8,000 judgements. Statistics like these illustrate why many teachers feel that the current approach causes administrative overload (Dearing 1993a).

If the problem for primary schools came in part from a failure to see the National Curriculum itself as a system, the problem at Key Stage Four (the curriculum for 14–16 year olds) came from a failure to relate the National Curriculum to other systems.

Duncan Graham has stated that his deputy Peter Watkins (who had been a secondary school head) persuaded him of the incompatibility of the ten-subject National Curriculum and the GCSE examinations as early as June 1988. He also claims that their initial attempts to raise the problem with civil servants met with ' the most discourteous reception, the first indication that no matter how justified proposals were they would not get very far if they were out of tune with current official thinking' (Graham and Tytler 1993, p. 83). According to Graham's admittedly partial view, this thinking had at least two aspects: that they were 'rocking the boat' by questioning the 'fundamentals of something which was perfect in origin'; and that there was plenty of time before Key Stage Four was to be introduced, whereas Graham and Watkins were all too aware of the lead time required for educational change.

After a number of interim solutions were put forward by NCC and ministers (who differed), the issue was addressed in Sir Ron Dearing's wide-ranging review of the National Curriculum and its assessment in 1993.

Dearing's final report commented that 'despite action already taken by the Government, more flexibility was needed in Key Stage 4' (Dearing 1993b para. 5.1). Dearing identified policy issues as well as an implementation problem. Two of them were:

- whether Key Stage Four was to be seen not as an 'educational terminus' but rather as 'the beginning of a distinct phase which runs through to 19' (para. 5.7);
- whether the ten-level scale was compatible with the GCSE grading system (paras 7.61–7.64).

The fact that these questions were being asked in 1993, six years after the first consultation document on the National Curriculum, and one year after Key Stage Four was implemented, is powerful evidence of the original failure to see KS4 as part of a wider system. Even in 1993, the problem was only seen in terms of the problems which had arisen within KS4 itself. Although there was discussion of how to incorporate elements of the newly introduced GNVQs, there was no real mention of how KS4 related to A-levels and NVQs. It was not until the next Dearing Report, in 1996, that there was talk of a framework within which to place all national qualifications (Dearing, 1996a).

NATIONAL VOCATIONAL QUALIFICATIONS (NVQs)

The development of NVQs roughly parallelled that of the National Curriculum in terms of dates, but not in terms of all of its approach or assumptions.

The National Council for Vocational Qualifications was set up in 1986, two years earlier than the NCC, as a result of a Review of Vocational Qualifications chaired by Oscar de Ville. In his introduction to the report, he said: 'I believe that the 14–19 age group should increasingly be seen as a whole . . . and that the "divide" between vocational and academic learning should be bridged' (de Ville 1986). However, his brief was confined to vocational qualifications, for which he proposed a national framework with five levels. The levels spanned from operative through craft and technician functions to junior and senior management. As with the National Curriculum two years later, each level was to be given a number. So at the very time that the National Curriculum was designating (for instance) level three as representing the achievement of an average 7-year-old, NCVQ was already using the same number to represent vocational performance approximately equivalent to that reached by 18-year-olds gaining a couple of A-levels.

There were other similarities which were nevertheless presented in crucially different ways. As with the National Curriculum two years later, NVQs were to offer greater clarity about the intended outcomes of learning. However, whereas for NVQs these outcomes were called *standards of competence*, in the NC they were *statements of attainment*. There were also important differences. NVQ competences were grouped into *units*, reflecting occupational functions, whereas the National Curriculum was strongly subject-based. Whereas the National Curriculum placed for the first time a legal obligation on all state schools to implement a certain curriculum, the introduction of NVQs followed a period during which government had disbanded most Training Boards, which had imposed a compulsory levy of firms above a certain size in order to fund training. NVQs were to be adopted voluntarily, and, in order to encourage this, 'Lead Bodies' representing sectors of employment were to be given the right to specify what they wanted to see as the required standards. The 1986 White Paper specified that the first qualifications designated as NVQs should be available by summer 1987, and that the framework for the first four levels should be operational by 1991 (HMSO 1986).

Although everyone now refers to NVQs as (radically) new qualifications, both the de Ville Report and the subsequent White Paper apply the label 'NVQ' to the national *framework*. Qualifications were intended to become NVQs, rather than an NVQ becoming a new qualification. As the White Paper said 'this framework should be designed to incorporate and embrace existing qualifications'. This would have meant setting the criteria for inclusion in the framework rather loosely at first, tightening them up in order to bring greater coherence as quickly as experience, and perhaps the market, allowed. In fact, the reverse happened, with initially very strict conditions having to be relaxed as problems of implementation were encountered.

Although, in the early years, some existing qualifications were provisionally accredited as NVQs, for the most part the requirements were so detailed and so strictly applied that brand new qualifications had to be designed. This produced a situation in which innovative but untried qualifications found themselves in competition with others which might have required updating but already had recognition and currency.

Partly because of this, and the need to develop standards for each occupation, the new qualifications came on stream more slowly than anticipated, and some of the initial awareness-raising amongst employers and colleges fell rather flat when the relevant qualifications turned out to be not yet available.

However, by 1990 there were about 130 Lead Bodies, with a further 20 in the process of being set up. They varied immensely in size and scope (from engineering to envelope manufacture, and from hairdressing to museums) and they had considerable freedom with regard to *what* they defined as standards of competence for their sectors. There was, however, considerably rigidity about *how* standards were to be defined, and the related qualifications were required to test every element of the standards, no more and no less.

This rigidity with regard to technical matters extended to other things. For instance, it was decided by NCVQ officials that

- requirements for knowledge and understanding did not need to be separately specified, since they were implied by the ability to perform competently;
- the written specifications could be made so precise that competent performance would be reliably interpreted by all assessors, as long as they had the relevant NVQ assessors qualification;
- in order to ensure that no candidate would be barred from gaining a qualification because of an inability to access a formal course, no syllabus or learning processes would be specified;
- since an employee was either competent or not, the qualification should be pass/fail, with no grading.

This has resulted in standards written in a way which employers and employees find difficult to understand, qualifications which can fail to correspond to the differing 'shapes' of similar jobs with different employers, and certification which does not always facilitate progression. Possibly as a result, take-up continues to give rise to concern.

It was intended that by 1995 NVQs would have largely replaced traditional vocational qualifications, as well as having filled the gaps where no qualifications were available. In fact, in 1995, City and Guilds, the awarding body which had certificated the majority of NVQs, was expressing disappointment in the 'continuing slow growth of NVQs, in which we have invested heavily' (City and Guilds 1995). At the same time, the market for C&G's traditional qualifications remained buoyant. Similarly, in 1991 the then Junior Minister was saying: 'In a very short space of time, NVQs will dominate the vocational provision offered by FE Colleges' (Eggar 1991a). However, in 1995 the Further Education Funding Council (FEFC) was reporting that of the qualifications it funded in English colleges only 8 per cent were NVQs, compared (for instance) to 18 per cent A-levels and even 9 per cent GCSEs. GNVQs were only 4 per cent at that time. It was estimated that the majority of the remaining 60 per cent of qualifications funded were other vocational qualifications (see Association for Colleges 1996). The market, which NVQs were designed to satisfy, seemed to be signalling that something was wrong.

This was the background against which the review of 100 of the most used NVQs and SVQs was commissioned from Gordon Beaumont in 1995–96 (Beaumont 1996). It was noticeable, however, that the report did not fully admit or quantify the problem. Indeed, the evidence from NCVQ reported 'significant rates of expansion across all occupational areas and at all levels' (NCVQ/SCOTVEC 1996). It was not pointed out that the rate of growth was slowing down. Mention of take-up varying between sectors concealed the fact that 43 NVQs (out of 734) accounted for over 80 per cent of all awards,[3] and that the majority of NVQs were awarded in service occupations, such as hairdressing (where one NVQ accounted for almost 8 per cent of all NVQs ever awarded) and retail distribution, where previously many employees had been unqualified (see Robinson, 1996). Though important in themselves, such occupations make little contribution to the oft-mentioned matter of the UK's international competitiveness.

On the other hand, employers and others clearly like the outcomes-based approach, and the grouping of them into units. Beaumont's suggestion that NVQs should increasingly be composed of core units plus a choice of optional units will certainly make the product more flexible and attractive. He is also right to require that standards should be written in plain language, but seems to assume that present problems derive simply from unnecessary use of jargon, rather than from the attempt to make the specifications completely unambiguous.

GENERAL NATIONAL VOCATIONAL QUALIFICATIONS

In the late 1980s it was being assumed that the National Curriculum would provide a uniform diet for all of compulsory school age, and that all post-16 qualifications that were not GCSEs or A-levels would become NVQs. By the early 1990s, it was being realised that not all vocational provision could meet the NVQ criteria, particularly if the learners were not yet employed. Such learners needed a broad vocational preparation, whereas NVQs were occupationally specific, and many NVQs required access to the workplace for the valid assessment of the specified standards.

The need to develop a coherent range of *general* vocational qualifications was flagged up in the 1991 White Paper (HMSO 1991). In May 1991 ministers wrote to NCVQ to ask them to co-ordinate the necessary work. NCVQ issued a consultation paper in October, in the following September the first five vocational areas were piloted, at two levels, and they were fully implemented from September 1993.

It does not take much thought to see how strenuous (some might say ludicrous) this schedule was. Colleges, for instance, start recruiting students for the following September early in the calendar year. In order to offer applicants proper guidance, the general shape of any new provision has to be known by then, and for quality provision the teaching plans and learning materials have to be drawn up, and the course timetabled and staffed, between Easter and the summer break. In the case of GNVQs, the pilot schemes could not even be designed by NCVQ until the close of the consultation period in December, and the schemes proper had to be planned before the pilot period which followed was half completed.

There might have been some chance of this working if NCVQ had stuck to the original brief which was to 'design the framework and the criteria for GNVQs . . . and to invite . . . awarding bodies to develop GNVQs which meet these criteria'. Although it was requested by ministers that the first GNVQs should be accredited in time to be available in colleges and schools from September 1992 it was suggested by them that 'it should be possible to make rapid progress towards modifying some existing qualifications to bring them in line with the new criteria very quickly, and accrediting them' (Eggar 1991b).

What happened was that, once again, NCVQ set about designing a radically new qualification from scratch, adapting the approach which was already giving rise to unacknowledged problems with NVQs. Problems were exacerbated by ministers' requirement for external testing, which was added to the normal NVQ-type continuous assessment. Not only was the resulting assessment system unmanageable, but teachers found themselves having to start the course without knowing what the assessment criteria were to be, and without sample test papers. When the first test papers did arrive there had been no time to put them through the usual process of piloting. Errors and anomalies were therefore discovered via the experiences of the first generation of students. There are ominous echoes here of the situation with regard to the first generation of National Curriculum Tests.

Even as late as 1995, the FEFC Inspectorate was reporting: 'Many of the changes to assessment and grading practices which have occurred so far have resulted in only piecemeal improvements. The system remains too unwieldy to be either efficient or effective and further work is required' (FEFC 1995, p.24).

The same report was more positive about other aspects of GNVQs: 'The quality of teaching and the promoting of learning is rising . . . (though) . . . after one or two years of operating GNVQs . . . the quality of teaching on advanced GNVQs still compares unfavourably with that found on A-level.' (p. 1). 'Standards of work for students who are successful on Advanced GNVQs are broadly equivalent to those achieved by students on comparable vocational courses, or those achieved by students on GCE A-levels studying two subjects.' (p. 3).

In other words, the Inspectors failed the *assessment/qualifications* regime, said that the *teaching/learning* programmes could be better, and gave a pass mark to the *standards* being achieved. It is important to distinguish between these three aspects of provision. The failure to take due account of each of these at the design stage of GNVQs contributed to the implementation difficulties. In effect, NCVQ issued a comprehensive set of standards[4] by the deadline, as if these represented all that was required for quality provision. The design of an assessment regime to measure the achievement of the standards, and of learning programmes to enable students to reach the standards, had to follow. Not only did this not allow time for the assessment regime to be de-bugged, it did not provide for the standards to be amended in the light of insights gained through attempts to assess against them. Also, many teachers, particularly those in schools which had not offered the predecessor courses, needed much more guidance.

As OFSTED reported, 'some teachers . . . found it difficult to devise programmes of learning which enabled their students to achieve all the outcomes required for the GNVQ, particularly in the newer areas of study', and 'course design has been impeded by the continuing absence of clear guidance and insufficient exemplar materials'. The starkest illustration of the problem was with regard to time allocation: 'The average was 14 hours per week, but some allocations were as low as 4 hours per week, quite inadequate to cover the necessary work.' (OFSTED 1994)

The problems were not all caused by the unrealistic schedule for implementation, but this certainly did not help. Some would argue that the fact that ministers agreed to and even required this rate of change was itself an illustration of the academic–vocational divide. It would never have been allowed for A-levels.

It is instructive to compare the implementation schedule proposed by the Higginson Committee, whose proposals for A-level reform were rejected by the government as being too radical. The proposals were made in 1988, subject groups were to have reported by early 1990, teacher training programmes should have been under development by mid-1990, and the new syllabuses were to be in use in schools and colleges by September 1992.

The GNVQ proposals were *really* radical, and were:

• made by NCVQ in October 1991
• piloted in September 1992
• implemented in September 1993.

It is therefore not surprising that there followed:

• a six point 'agenda for action' to ensure rigour and quality set by ministers in March 1994;
• a fundamental review of GNVQ assessment under Dr John Capey in the autumn of 1995 (Capey 1995).

A classic case of 'more haste, less speed'!

THE DEARING REVIEW OF 16–19 QUALIFICATIONS

The remit given to Sir Ron by the Secretary of State in April 1995 was to advise on how to 'strengthen, consolidate and improve the framework of 16 to 19 qualifications'. Cynics said that he was actually being asked to *devise* a framework for the three types of 'route' – A-levels, NVQs and GNVQs – which had formed the basis of government policy since the 1991 White Paper. Within this overall task he was asked to 'ensure that the rigour and standards of GCE A-levels are maintained' (Dearing 1996a). The review took place in parallel with the Capey Review of GNVQs, and the Beaumont review of NVQs.

Continuing the 'route' metaphor, Dearing was being asked to create a more coherent road network whilst keeping the most elderly route unchanged, and whilst the two most recently designed were already under repair. Also, although the remit only made mention of three routes, a large number of students in the age group, and the majority of FE students, were taking qualifications which fell outside these routes.[5]

To his credit, Dearing went some way to recognising these issues. In his final report, the first of his 198 recommendations is that *there should be* a national framework of qualifications, and he recognises that 'there are legitimate claims that some of the existing (vocational) qualifications cater for need that are not met either by an NVQ that required the candidate to have access to relevant employment, or by the broadly based GNVQ. . . . The time is ripe for drawing these other qualifications into a more coherent framework that better meets the needs of candidates and employers' (Dearing 1996b, para. 6.20).

Dearing also made recommendations to do with *improving* the uniformity and clarity of A-level standards. He argued that clarity could be improved through making the intended outcomes of A-levels – that knowledge, understanding and skills a candidate would be expected to demonstrate for the award of a particular grade – more explicit.

Such a statement of outcomes is, of course, what is *meant* by the word 'standards' in the NVQ and GNVQ sense. We hit here one of the many differences of approach which bedevil our qualifications, and make it difficult to make them more coherent. When the Secretary of State asks that 'A-level standards should be maintained' she does not mean that, for instance, the learning outcomes of A-level Physics should be the same now as they were in 1945, or as they should become by the year 2005. She means that – whatever the developments in the subject over time – its level of intellectual demand should remain equivalent.

In my view, Dearing only partially recognises the importance of clearing up some technical questions if his recommendation about a national framework is to be effectively implemented – or even constructively debated. For instance, if we were all to use the NCVQ definition of 'standards', it would allow people to argue for the maintenance of standards which make the same level of demand whilst querying the narrowness of a total programme for A-level students which delivers these standards through the study of only three subjects. Seeing academic subjects as the primary *source* of these learning outcomes or standards, as opposed to the only means of delivering them, is extremely liberating, both to our thinking and to our timetabling.

Dearing recognises that clarity about the standards they embody is a strength of vocational qualifications, but in merely requiring that 'the (A-level) regulatory bodies should examine the extent to which it is practical and advantageous to take further the specifications of A-levels in terms of required learning outcomes' (Dearing 1996b) para. 10.65) he underestimates the importance of this for the rest of what he wants.

For instance, he argues that the distinguishing characteristics of each of the three 'routes' should be made clear, and these should reflect their underlying purposes. As part of this he advocates that there should be identified 'broad principles for allocating subject areas to pathways'. But *is* it the nature of a 'subject area' which distinguishes one pathway from another – or is it the nature of the learning outcomes (standards), or the learning programme, or the assessment method, or the purpose to which the qualification is put?

It is difficult to see how to decide whether 'economics' or even physics or English are academic or vocational in purpose, without comparing the intended learning outcomes of particular courses which have these titles. And how can these outcomes be compared if A-levels do not state them, or if they state them in an idiosyncratic way which makes comparisons with other qualifications difficult?

At the same time as saying that the distinctiveness of each route should be preserved, Dearing argued for easier progression and transfer between them. This apparent paradox can be resolved as long as we are clear about whether their differences lie in:

- the nature of their intended learning outcomes (or standards)
- the source of the standards (e.g. the requirements of an academic subject, a vocational area, or a specific occupation)
- the structure of the learning programme
- the assessment regime.

This clarity cannot be achieved if outcomes are stated in different ways for no good reason, or are not stated at all, or if it is assumed that everything needs to be subject-based. It is not only Dearing who made this assumption about subjects. A linked report into the extent to which A-levels and GNVQs can be taught together describes a GNVQ as being one 'subject', and suggests that an A-level programme is broader because it contains three subjects (Coates and Hamilton 1996). In fact, of course, two A-level subjects may have overlapping outcomes (standards), and a single GNVQ may contain units which cover many different types of outcome.

Therefore we also need to make the necessary comparisons at the unit level, where a unit is a coherent group of outcomes. As the Scots[6] and the New Zealanders[7] are showing, it is possible to analyse academic as well as vocational qualifications into units, which clarifies rather than changes their distinctiveness. Analysis at unit level also helps to check that qualifications are equivalent in terms of the amount and level of achievement they require. As Dearing himself implies, this check is essential if other vocational qualifications and courses leading to Open College accreditation are also to be brought within the new framework.

In the end, Dearing fought shy of reference to *units*, probably because of political and practical concerns about *modularisation*. However, units describe what is being assessed in qualifications, and are relatively unproblematic, whereas modularisation is a method of structuring learning programmes which has risks as well as advantages.

This is an example of apparently simple proposals (about pathways, transfers and frameworks) being in reality technically problematic, whilst other approaches (making use of learning outcomes grouped into units) are avoided because of an overestimation of their difficulty.

CONCLUSIONS

While it is true that each of these initiatives had difficulties which were special to itself, there are others which they had in common, and which we are at risk of repeating. This risk arises not least because we have failed to identify the patterns in these developments.

Worse than this, we may be on the verge of misinterpreting the history. The myth being created is that the 'professionals' involved first produce an over-complex proposal, which is so difficult to implement that a pragmatic outsider has to be brought in to simplify matters in a commonsense way. My thesis is that the difficulties are created by a combination of technical and managerial fallacies.

Because the 'pragmatic' approach of the various Capey, Beaumont and Dearing Reports of 1993–96 tends to avoid going back over the past, they have not identified the theoretical and policy assumptions which proved to have been dubious, and the managerial/political techniques which were unhelpful or obstructive.

On the technical level, there has been a failure to understand the relationship between the necessary learning *programmes*, the learning *outcomes (standards)* being sought, and the *qualifications* required to test their achievement.

With regard to the management of change, there has been a failure to use an identified development model, and to ensure that the right balance is kept between:

- *curriculum development* (meaning standards, qualifications and learning programmes)
- *staff development* (meaning skills, knowledge and understanding awareness)
- *organisational development* (meaning school and college structures, financial support, learning materials, record-keeping systems, and so on.)

In policy terms, there has been a tendency to see each initiative in isolation from others, even though each could affect the success or failure of the rest: an unwillingness to think in terms of systems. All of this has been overlaid by a fear of informed public debate, which has meant that crucial assumptions have not been examined and the impact of initiatives has been reported via assertions rather than in the form of more objective evaluations.

There are three things that could help make a reality of such a debate, and thus to make educational initiatives an ongoing part of a 'learning society', as opposed to a political football. These are:

1 A *shared language* in which to define achievement of all kinds, so that standards, learning programmes and qualifications can be compared and contrasted – not least for the benefit of the learners;
2 An open *forum for debate,* in which are represented those who need to influence standards, such as employers, unions and universities, those who are responsible for assessment and certification (awarding and examining bodies), and those who are tasked to provide accessible, challenging and motivating learning programmes.
3 Clarity about the appropriate *roles of the centre and the periphery.* In particular, we need a Government which resists the temptation to interfere with operational details, but accepts the responsibility for strategic management of the system as a whole and the boundaries between its constituent parts. It is in attempting to cross these boundaries that so many of our more vulnerable learners fall by the wayside.

Central government is increasingly and rightly requiring overt and good quality strategic planning and management from those it funds. Perhaps there should be a tax-payers' charter which demands the same from government with regard to the increasing number of central initiatives.

NOTES

1 It also gave it the reserve power to specify what qualifications could be taken by 16–18-year-olds on state-funded courses.
2 Along with the Schools Examinations and Assessment Authority (SEAC).
3 A significant number of the available NVQs remained entirely unused.
4 'Standards' are a description of the learning outcomes to be achieved.
5 See the section on NVQs.
6 The Scottish Higher Still Initiative plans to create all 16–19 full-time provision from a bank of some 3,000 units.
7 New Zealand is designing a unit-based qualification system covering all secondary further and higher education. See Robson (1996).

REFERENCES

Association for Colleges, (1996) *FE Now*, March.
Beaumont, G. (1996)) *Review of 100 NVQs and SVQs.* London: NCVQ.
Capey, Dr J. (1995) *Review of the Assessment of GNVQs.* London: NCVQ.
City and Guilds (1995) The Director General in *C&G's Annual Review, 1994–95.*
Coates, P. and Hamilton, J. (1996) *16–19: Coherence Project Review of 16–19 Qualifications.* London. Gatsby Foundation and SCAA.
Dearing, Sir Ron (1993a) *The National Curriculum and its Assessment, Interim Report*, July. London: NCC/SEAC.
Dearing, Sir Ron (1993b) *The National Curriculum and its Assessment, Final Report*, December. London: NCC/SEAC.
Dearing, Sir Ron (1996a) *Review of Qualifications for 16–19 Year Olds*, March. London: SCAA.
Dearing, Sir Ron (1996b) *Review of Qualifications for 16–19 Year Olds*; full report, section 16. London: SCAA.
De Ville, Sir Oscar (1986) *Review of Vocational Qualifications*, April. London: Manpower Services Commission/DES.
Eggar, Tim (1991a) in *DES Press Release*, 21 March 1991.
Eggar Tim (1991b) letter to Sir Bryan Nicholson (Chairman NCVQ). DES, May 1991.
FEFC (1995) *General NVQs in Further Education Sector in England*, National Survey Report, FEFC Inspectorate.
Graham, D. and Tytler, D. (1993) *A Lesson for us All.* London: Routledge.
HMSO (1986), *Working Together – Education and Training.* London: HMSO.
HMSO (1991), *Education and Training for the 21st Century.* London: HMSO.
NCVQ/SCOTVEC (1996) *Review of 100 NVQs SVQs: A Report on the Findings.* London: NCVQ.
OFSTED (1994) *GNVQs in Schools 1993/94*, London: HMSO.
Robinson, Peter (1996) *NVQs, Rhetoric and Reality.* London: Centre for Economic Performance, LSE.
Robson J. (1996) 'The New Zealand Qualifications Authority and the universities: progress towards a unified framework' *Journal of Vocational Education and Training*, vol.46.

4

A Critique of NVQs and GNVQs

Alan Smithers

Ten years ago vocational education was like the scattered pieces of many different jigsaws. Although some of the individual qualifications were widely respected, they did not belong to any coherent picture. There were several hundred awarding bodies offering a great variety of qualifications, many of which led nowhere. The Rev George Tolley,[1] Principal of what was then Sheffield Polytechnic, was at the forefront of a campaign to introduce a national framework to rival the well-established academic ladder of O-levels, A-levels and degrees. The government heard the cry, set up the De Ville Committee (De Ville 1986), and accepted its recommendations for a National Council for Vocational Qualifications to oversee a national system.

A decade later, with at least £107 million of public money spent (see Robinson 1996), there is not only the former confusion, but adding to it we have NVQs and GNVQs. NVQs which were intended to be National Vocational Qualifications are at best Niche Vocational Qualifications, suitable mainly for assessing prior learning in the workplace. General National Vocational Qualifications are an odd variant of them for schools and colleges. Over two-thirds of vocational qualifications currently awarded are the old-style awards outside the ambit of NCVQ.[2] Both the school and further education inspectors[3] have severely criticised the contribution of NVQs and GNVQs to education 14–19. What went wrong?

It is clear – and not only with hindsight – that the fault lies in the way NCVQ interpreted its brief. The 1986 White Paper called, somewhat unfortunately in view of what happened, *Working Together – Education and Training* (DES 1986) put in train de Ville's recommendation that: 'a new National Council for Vocational Qualifications (NCVQ) should be set up to secure necessary changes, to develop the NVQ framework and to ensure standards of competence are set.'

The emphasis on standards was to ensure, quite rightly, that the system was to be employer-led, geared to the nature and levels of performance required by them. A qualification to be a qualification must be *in* and/or *for* something. Since the *raison d'etre* of vocational education is to prepare for, or enhance performance in, work, it is essential that employers be involved in specifying what a particular qualification is to be about.

The National Council for Vocational Qualifications (NCVQ), however, interpreted 'standards of competence' literally and tried to turn every standard into a statement of competence. This led to an orgy of analysis resulting in highly fragmented, almost incomprehensible, qualifications. What NCVQ lamentably failed to do was to distinguish between, on the one hand, setting standards and, on the other, designing qualifications to enable those standards to be met. It tried to turn one directly into the other, missing out the vital stages of settling what was to be covered and the tests by which we would know that the standards had been reached.

This was no mere oversight however. In Bees and Swords (1990), Gilbert Jessup, the chief architect of NVQs, proudly wrote of doing away with 'the syllabuses, the courses or the training programmes, i.e. the specification of the learning opportunities provided.' He also had particular views on assessment. In his book, *Outcomes: NVQs and the Emerging Model of Education and Training* (Jessup 1991) he wrote, 'what I am proposing is that we forget about reliability altogether and concentrate on validity, which is ultimately all that matters', seemingly unaware that assessments which are not reliable cannot be valid. As might be expected, with foundations like these, the qualifications that emerged were idiosyncratic, but within NCVQ the approach became elevated to almost a religious faith, with all attempts at constructive criticism being brutally rebuffed.[4].

Belatedly, the government, through Dearing,[5] Beaumont[6] and Capey,[7] is trying to get to grips with the problem, but the flaw runs so deep that it will require a radical re-think to get us back on track. The extent of the damage can be gauged from the consequences of NCVQ's approach for the content and assessment of qualifications.

CONTENT AND ASSESSMENT

Qualifications to be recognised by NCVQ have had to conform to its model. This involves breaking down the award into 'units' which are further subdivided into 'elements' which are based on lists of 'performance criteria'. The candidate has to collect 'evidence', usually in the form of a 'portfolio', that the performance criteria have been met over certain 'ranges'. Although superficially plausible, setting out the requirements in this way means that the content of the qualifications is not clearly specified, nor is there any assessment of overall performance. More specifically, as regards content, the approach lacks precision, is fragmentary, does not prioritise, and devalues knowledge and understanding. Assessment is atomised, internal and bureaucratic, and is not robust enough to withstand payment by results.

PRECISION

NCVQ's analytical approach becomes in practice a search for the elusive irreducible building blocks of competence. The NVQ Level 2 Care (Residential/Hospital Support), for example, is set out as 11 units, 39 elements and 338 performance criteria. Although this detail is assumed to give precision, in fact the performance criteria come out as very generalised. In the unit 'Enable clients to eat and drink' the first element is 'Enable clients to choose appropriate food and drink', of which the first performance criterion is, 'The support required by the client is established with him/her.' Similarly, in the NVQ Level 3 in Engineering Assembly, the unit, 'Produce assembled output by joining and fastening operations' contains the element 'Process materials to produce assembled output', which has as a performance criterion, 'Materials presented to the assembly operation are completely compliant with operational specification'.

Not only are the performance criteria generalised, but they hang in the air and are addressed to no one. If they had been written for candidates they would have said something like, 'In order to get this qualification you will have to show you can . . .', or if for employers, 'A person holding this qualification is able to . . .'. But they are written in an odd abstract language which has been shown to break the rules of grammar and therefore be very difficult to read (see Channell and St John 1996).

FRAGMENTATION

The fault is, however, more than technical; it is fundamental. There is no guarantee that numerous individual competences – even if they could be identified, and simply and unambiguously stated – would amount to skilled overall performance. Being able to dribble and do headers do not make a footballer. It is the way they fit together that matters.

PRIORITISATION

NCVQ's lists of performance criteria are not only not integrated, they are not prioritised. In the NVQ Level 2 in Bus and Coach Driving and Customer Care, for example, the minutiae of customer care are treated on par with keeping the vehicle safely on the road. NVQs take no account of time, and thus difficult decisions as to what is essential as opposed to being merely desirable do not have to be faced. This is claimed as a virtue (see Jessup 1991), an escape from the time-serving basis of old apprenticeships, but discounting time altogether conveniently side-steps difficult decisions about what can be fitted in.

KNOWLEDGE AND UNDERSTANDING

The telephone directory approach also has profound consequences for the way knowledge and understanding is treated. It was first considered to be embedded in the performance criteria and implied by them. But even in the Revised Criteria[8] (January 1995), which are intended to lay greater stress on knowledge and understanding, it comes out as itemised and disparate 'knowledge specifications'. This means that NVQs are virtually useless as qualifications for 14 to 19-year-olds, or indeed adults preparing *for* work, since there is no coherent statement of content. Nor is there a reservoir of knowledge and understanding to enable people to cope with a changing working world or provide a platform for progression.

ASSESSMENT

The unsuitability of NVQs as qualifications *for* work, as opposed to accrediting prior learning *in* work, is underlined by the way they are assessed. NVQs were said to have been devised on the driving test model. That is, it does not matter how you have learned to drive – through a school or from a spouse or friend or any other way – what is important is that you can do it, and satisfy an independent examiner that you can. However, as they have emerged, NVQs have no equivalent of the driving test, but consist of long lists of performance criteria that have to be signed off. Given that there may be several hundred of them, the only practicable way of achieving this is to leave it to the teachers/trainers whose main task becomes signing their name. There is some check through external verification, but that is based on inspecting portfolios of evidence rather than observing the candidate in action. Moreover, because the requirements are loose, the external verifiers are to some extent able to invent the qualifications by insisting that in the portfolio the candidate does or does not include printed material, uses 'I' or 'we' and so on. Some private providers for the sake of their candidates are having to deploy a member of staff specifically to get to know the foibles of particular verifiers.

NVQ assessment, instead of being based on tests of skilled overall performance, depends on collecting evidence in relation to checklists. It lacks the fairness, reliability and authenticity that would make it believable. Without trust the qualification cannot act as a passport between the training provider and employer. Increasingly, the only training that an employer can have confidence in is that provided in-house. Far from enabling education and training to work together, NVQs have driven a wedge between them.

OUTPUT-RELATED FUNDING
Not only is the assessment of NVQs intrinsically flawed, but it is not strong enough to bear the weight of the payment by results that is increasingly being adopted by Training and Enterprise Councils and, to a lesser extent, by the Further Education Funding Council. As the instances of malpractice that surface from time to time in the press illustrate,[9] the assessment arrangements leave a lot to be desired. There is ample scope to, in effect, sell NVQs or give them away if the state is paying. What NVQ assessment amounts to, in practice, is a bit like your driving being assessed by your trainer, with each item – gear changing for example – signed off as you achieve it, and the trainer only being paid if he/she passes you. No wonder most employers do not find NVQs credible.

GENERAL NATIONAL VOCATIONAL QUALIFICATIONS

At best NVQs accredit prior learning in the workplace. As such, they are claimed to have a motivational value for people who missed out on education first time around (see Jessup 1991). But there is also a dark side. The Beaumont Committee heard evidence that some employers have been using NVQs as part of their downsizing process by setting requirements for existing employees, in terms of being able to read and write, that they cannot meet and so leave to avoid embarrassment.

However, whatever their merits for accrediting people for the job they already have, NVQs are not, as we have seen, a good way of preparing people for work. This makes it even more bizarre that, in 1991, the government should give NCVQ the job of developing applied education in schools and colleges. The White Paper *Education and Training for the 21st Century* (HMSO 1991) introducing the new qualifications reads as if the original intention was to build on the success of qualifications like those of the Business and Technology Education Council, but what emerged in response to the NCVQ credo was something quite different (NCVQ 1993).

The General National Vocational Qualification in Health and Social Care at intermediate level (said to be equivalent to five GCSEs at grades A–C) came out as four mandatory units, two optional units, and three core skill units comprising 31 elements and 129 performance criteria (for example, 'Key social factors which influence well-being are identified and explained'; 'Key lifestyle patterns which affect individuals are identified'). The advanced GNVQ in Leisure and Tourism (said to be equivalent to two A-levels) has eight mandatory units, four optional and three core skill units consisting of 52 elements and 310 performance criteria (for example, 'Situations when customer contact or service is commonly needed are correctly identified').

Originally NCVQ intended GNVQs to be assessed on a pass/fail basis through evidence collection in the way NVQs are, but the government insisted on some external testing, and grading of performance. Reluctantly NCVQ introduced one-hour multiple choice tests into the mandatory units, but side-lined them from contributing to the grading which was carried out by inspecting the portfolios against the themes of data handling and evaluation, with quality only becoming a criterion later.

The weaknesses of the approach, well understood by bodies like BTEC[10], were brought into sharp focus when NCVQ was obliged to co-operate with the School Curriculum and Assessment Authority (SCAA) in developing GNVQ Part Is. These were mooted by Sir Ron Dearing in his review of the national curriculum (Dearing 1993) to make vocational education available to 14–16-year-olds in the time of two GCSEs. The two halves of the joint SCAA/NCVQ committee found themselves speaking very different languages. At one stage, each pilot GNVQ Part I was drafted with a line down the middle of the page with NCVQ's performance criteria, range statements and evidence indicators on the left, and, on the right, SCAA's amplification which amounted to a syllabus and test arrangements. It was only through SCAA's approach that it was realised that most of the biology was missing from the intermediate GNVQ in Health and Social Care.

Gradually, the SCAA view prevailed and it is beginning to suffuse the whole GNVQ structure, not just Part Is. In the latest thinking, the GNVQ requirements will include some specification of content and assessment involving substantial tests of knowledge and depth of understanding and externally set assignments. But what a lot of time has been wasted through starting in the wrong place.

TAKE-UP

What has really forced a reappraisal of both NVQs and GNVQs has been the growing realisation that the people for whom they are intended are not using them and, even if they do, they drop out in unacceptable numbers. The Confederation of British Industry, a strong supporter of the vocational reforms, in 1994 published a report exposing the low take-up and high cost, and making 68 recommendations for improvement which amounted to a complete redesign (CBI 1994).

While John Hillier, the Chief Executive of NCVQ, was comfortingly reassuring the Education Committee of the House of Commons in January 1996:

> To refer to the low uptake of a qualification that has only existed since 1990, now has in excess of a million people holding the qualification, and over three million working towards it, and whose uptake has been increasing steadily at the rate of 30 percent per year and is continuing to do so, does seem to me simply to fly in the face of the facts.[11]

Peter Robinson of the London School of Economics was beavering away checking all the publicly available figures. He found (Robinson 1996):

- 660,000 *not* 3 million working towards NVQs;
- against a target of 50 per cent of the workforce to be working towards NVQ Level 3 by 1996, only 2 per cent were doing so by spring 1995;
- of 794 NVQs on the books, 364 had not been completed by anyone and 43 had been completed by only one person;
- the NVQs that are taken are in the internationally sheltered service occupations – clerical, secretarial, personal service and sales;
- over two-thirds of vocational qualifications currently awarded are the old-style pre-NVQ awards;

• NVQs do not appear to have added to the total training taken but have increased the complexity of provision.

John Hillier has once more responded by attacking the messenger.[12]

Similarly, GNVQs have officially been presented as a great success story. In August 1995 the National Awarding Bodies brought out a confident press release[13] claiming, '100,000 GNVQs successes and still growing'. However, contained within the notice were figures which showed:

• the 100,000 was based on 61,604 completions and 41,378 who had only passed some units;
• the completions were only about a third of the students who had registered to take the award;
• that of the 13,165 advanced passes (compared with 64,000 BTEC National Diplomas), 6,651 were in business and 1,669 in art and design (compared with the 21,818 and 31,534 at A-level respectively); only Health and Social Care (1,936) and Leisure and Tourism (2,340) seemed to be breaking new ground.

The Joint Council of National Vocational Awarding Bodies followed up their '100,000 successes' a year later with a press release[14] in August 1996 proclaiming 'Record numbers of GNVQ awards'. But this time the registration figures were conspicuously absent. However, comparing the 1996 completions for the advanced GNVQ with the 1994 registrations (since the courses could be expected to take two years) shows at best a pass rate of about 40 per cent. Over 90 per cent of those awards were in business, leisure and tourism, health and social care, and art and design. Manufacturing, engineering, construction and the built environment, information technology and science contributed only 1,749 awards between them.

The existence of advanced GNVQs alongside A-levels in business studies, art and design, the sciences and technology does raise the question of their respective roles. Why should a student do an advanced GNVQ rather than an A-level in, say, science? Is it a case of those who can – do A-levels; those who can't – do GNVQs? Or do the awards serve different purposes? If so, what are they? These were some of the issues addressed by Dearing's review of qualifications for 16–19-year-olds.

REVIEWS

In spite of the generally rosy picture of the progress of NVQs and GNVQs presented by NCVQ, the system has come under intense government scrutiny. Gordon Beaumont (1996), recently retired Corporate Development Director of Alfred MacAlpine plc, and former Chairman of the CBI Training Policy Panel, was asked to review the top 100 NVQs. Dr John Capey (1995), Principal of Exeter Further Education College, was asked to review the GNVQ assessment system. The ubiquitous Sir Ron Dearing (1996), on completing his review of the National Curriculum, was asked to consider and report on qualifications for 16–19 year-olds. But perhaps most important of all for the future of vocational education, NCVQ itself was subject to a quinquennial review.[15]

BEAUMONT

Beaumont's review of NVQs was originally intended to be an in-house affair, with NCVQ operating under a contract from the then Employment Department, Beaumont advised by NCVQ's Evaluation and Advisory Group and his report to go first to NCVQ Council. In the event, Beaumont was encouraged by ministers to be more independent and several new members were added to the committee, including myself. His report also went directly to the government with NCVQ Council allowed to comment on it subsequently.

Beaumont produced a potentially hard-hitting report:

- It suggested that setting standards and designing qualifications should be separated. (p.5: '*It is proposed that standards are written for employers. Qualifications, training and the development of assessment needs should be separately specified.*')
- It recognised that NVQs as presently framed are all but incomprehensible. (p.13: '*Standards are marred by complex jargon ridden language.*' p.28: '*The complex and jargon ridden language used is universally condemned.*')
- It identified a number of problems with assessment. (p.13: '*Assessors and verifiers are unsure of the standards they are judging and their views differ.*' p.19: '*External verifiers suffer from combining incompatible roles.*')
- It found that the assessment system is not robust enough to withstand output-related funding. (p.7: '*Funding programmes and*

policy should be harmonised with qualification systems.' p.40: *'Funding by outputs brings a potential for conflicts of interest.'*)
- It recognised that NVQs do not provide a training route for unemployed young people or adults. (p.26: *'The fact that NVQs are work-based prevents those not in work from obtaining the qualifications.'*

But the edge is taken off of it by the claim, 'There is widespread support for the NVQ concept'. There is certainly widespread support for introducing good occupational awards but it is not clear that this is for NVQs as they stand.

For example, 'competence' is defined in the Consultation Document as 'The ability to apply knowledge and understanding in performing to the standards required in employment, including solving problems and meeting changing demands.' ('Skills' was added later). Most people, myself included, would have no difficulty in signing up to this.

But it is different from 'competence' as it is used in devising NVQs where 'functional analysis' seeks to arrive at numerous (often several hundred) 'competences'. Beaumont himself used competence in this sense on p.13 where he wrote 'Candidates are unsure of the competences they are trying to achieve.' So just what is 'the concept' for which there is apparently widespread support – capability or a competence catalogue?

The claim in the report that most employers are in favour of NVQs (the percentage variously put at between 80 and 90 per cent) is based on a very shaky sample. In fact, fewer than one in five of the employers contacted bothered to respond in spite of boosting the sample and frequent follow-ups. Neither of the claims tally with the CBI report (CBI 1994) expressing concern at the low take-up of NVQs. If employers were using them there would be no problem. They are not, so there is.

It gradually dawned on Beaumont that NVQs were not working, but what he saw as a language problem is a concept problem. This will become increasingly apparent as attempts are made to get NVQs into plain English (or plain Welsh as Beaumont disarmingly reiterates). So long as NVQs are frozen at the stage of fragmenting into competences there will be problems.

CAPEY
Capey had a specific remit: 'to review GNVQ assessment and grading'. Its findings as encapsulated on page 22 were 'the evidence presented to the review group was unequivocal in identifying the need for a further

simplification of the GNVQ assessment and recording requirements'. But the recommendations are disappointing in that the review group seems to have got bogged down in NCVQ-speak rather than going to the heart of the matter.

Capey recognises (page 23): 'the GNVQ differs significantly from the NVQ in its broader purpose and range . . . this in itself is sufficient to justify a different approach to the assessment of outcomes'. But this is not followed through by asking what good applied education should consist of, and how it should be assessed. NCVQ-speak tends to cause people, including Capey, to take their eye off the ball. Essentially with applied education it matters *what* is being learned not *how* it is being learned. Curiously this was one of the early tenets of NCVQ which seems to have got lost in the keenness to prescribe particular styles of learning.

Capey becomes enmeshed in learning styles and goes beyond his remit when in the executive summary he contends (page 7): 'Many students are being motivated by the independent approach to learning that the GNVQ offers'. This does not square with the failure of two-thirds of registered students to complete. Moreover, the style of learning is largely irrelevant if the focus is outcomes. Crucial here is the credibility of the assessment process. This is likely to involve some external practical and written tests: just what Capey was set up to advise on and where notably he fails to give a clear lead.

NCVQ has attempted to put a gloss on both Capey and Beaumont. In the NCVQ's foreword to Capey it claims to have support for 'the characteristics of GNVQ' and 'the philosophy and structure' when neither was part of the remit. Nor are these claims sustainable when so many of those attempting to deliver GNVQs are gagged from commenting on them.[16]

DEARING

Dearing asked Capey to consider some specific issues including:

- modifying the tests so that they contribute to grading
- introducing standard assignments
- the use of end-of-course externally set examinations or projects through which students could show they had integrated the knowledge and skills from the course

which indicate the kind of improvements to GNVQs that were being looked for. But Dearing's remit was far wider: to consider the whole range of qualifications for 16–19-year-olds. In doing so he addressed the thorny question of the respective roles of A-levels, GNVQs and NVQs. Dearing recommended that:

- A-levels and GCSE should be for 'where the primary purpose is to develop knowledge, understanding and skills associated with a subject or discipline'.
- GNVQs should be for Applied Education 'where the primary purpose is to develop and apply knowledge, understanding and skills relevant to broad areas of employment'.
- NVQs should be for Vocational Training 'where the primary purpose is to develop and recognise mastery of a trade or profession at the relevant level'.

To underline the importance of the applied pathway he recommended renaming advanced GNVQs, 'Applied A-levels', and transferring A-levels like business studies to become flagships of the new route. But this is seen by some as threatening the gold standard of A-levels and it may not be accepted by the government.

QUINQUENNIAL REVIEW
The largely unsung and unheralded review of NCVQ itself conducted by the Department for Education and Employment has thrown the future of the body into the melting pot. Although it was brought about as a regular five-yearly monitoring exercise 'a prior options review' was added to determine 'whether the functions delegated to NCVQ remain essential to Government and Department objectives' and, if so, 'whether there is scope for merger with or transferring some or all of the functions to another body'. In other words, the future of NCVQ was up for grabs.

The review reported in two parts, in November 1995 and February 1996, with an Executive Summary added later (May 1996). It concluded that NCVQ 'has not been able to establish a national framework for all, or even a majority, of vocational awards', and 'despite all its achievements, there remains a negative perception of the organisation from some quarters'. The Executive Summary notes that, 'The Review Team thought that NCVQ's marketing function might lend itself to separate contracting out. This would provide the solution to what some saw as a fundamental problem, that of the incompatibility of NCVQ's regulatory and promotional roles.'

Sir Ron Dearing, in his review of qualifications for 16–19-year-olds, considered regulation (the rough equivalent of Ofwat or Ofgas – Ofqual perhaps) and put forward two options:

- setting up two new bodies, one responsible for qualifications from 14+, the other responsible for the curriculum and for statutory assessment by national tests;
- replacing SCAA and NCVQ with one body to oversee qualifications, the curriculum and statutory assessment.

The government consulted on the two options in May 1996 DfEE 1996), expressing a preference for a single body. This led, not unexpectedly, on the basis of about 75 votes for and 25 against, to a proposal[17] to establish a Qualifications and National Curriculum Authority (QNCA) to bring together the work of SCAA and NCVQ. It is intended to be in place for September 1997 but it will require legislation. In 1997 the 'national' was dropped.

At best, the new authority could be just the shake-up vocational education needs. With NCVQ gone there would be room for fresh thinking. At worst, however, it could mean the take-over of SCAA and an undermining of the academic ladder through competence-speak.

WHAT NEXT?

Assuming that QCA comes into being it will have the vital task of driving forward the follow-up to Dearing, Beaumont and Capey. The central issue facing it will be how to establish a truly national system of awards. The model devised by NCVQ became a Procrustean bed on which all other awards were going to be forced to lie: 'the Government intends that GNVQs, together with National Vocational Qualifications (NVQs), will replace other vocational qualifications and become the main national provision for vocational education and training.'[18]

In order to achieve a national framework, QCA will have to adopt a set of criteria for vocational awards which can accommodate the qualifications that employers value, whether old or new. The key to this is probably the distinction that Beaumont makes between setting standards and designing qualifications. It is for employers through their Lead Bodies to set the standards, and for the vocational awarding bodies to design appropriate qualifications. The role of the regulatory body then becomes to check that the award meets the standards.

It should not however attempt to do this through criteria which imply one-to-one correspondence, as with present NVQs, but by making sure that vocational qualifications have:

• appropriate content
• appropriate assessment.

It is likely, as Capey and Beaumont suggested, that there will be different models for preparing *for* work and upskilling *in* work.

GNVQs need to be properly designed as applied education. They are, if anything, further back than NVQs. At least with NVQs employers did attempt to set the standards even if they did not always recognise what the consultants wrote for them. But GNVQs have been largely left to the people contracted to write the specifications, without any high-level thought being given as to what their organising principles should be (as the organising principle of a subject is a distinctive way of making sense of the world).

Applied education is about practical organisations of understanding. The organising principle of a GNVQ should be the class of practical problems that it addresses, in the way that medicine in higher education is organised about health. Not enough thought has gone into the defining core of GNVQs. Leisure and tourism, for example, sit uneasily together, with would-be travel agents and swimming pool attendants sometimes unhappily getting their wires crossed.

Unless significant progress is made in the meantime, QCA will have to consider what distinguishes GNVQs from A-levels and GCSEs, what to call them, how they are to be set out and how they are to be tested.

CONCLUSION

Just over ten years ago the government took some bold decisions. It recognised that a crucial problem was how was Britain going to pay its way in the world and it has come to see an improved system of vocational education as making a major contribution towards increased competitiveness. It has also accepted that in countries like Germany, Switzerland and Hungary, many young people who do not happen to like learning for its own sake are able to reach high levels of attainment in mathematics and their mother tongue through applied learning and vocational training. These aims are no less important today. The fact that NCVQ went down the wrong path has set us back, but QCA gives us a chance to put things right. But will the government be prepared to grasp the nettle? It was aware that something was seriously amiss five years ago, but attempted to tough it out through the appointment of John Hillier as Chief Executive of NCVQ. It is to be fervently hoped that this time the realities will be faced and we will at last get a coherent set of pathways for 14–19-year-olds and a truly national system of vocational awards.

NOTES

1 G. Tolley, 'Putting labels on people: the qualifications business'. *RSA Journal*, no. 5363, October 1986.

2 DFEE, *Awards of Vocational Qualifications 1991/2– 1994/5*, Statistical Bulletin 4, 1996.

3 FEFC, *NVQs in the Further Education Sector in England – National Survey: Report from the Inspectorate*, September 1994; FEFC, *GNVQs in the Further Education Sector in England – National Survey: Report from the Inspectorate*, November 1994; OFSTED, *GNVQs in Schools: Quality and Standards of General National Vocational Qualifications, 1993/4*, November 1994; OFSTED, *Assessment of General National Vocational Qualifications*, June 1996; Her Majesty's Chief Inspector, *Annual Report*, June 1996.

4 See, for example, 'Lecturers in row over academic freedom', *Financial Times*, 19 April 1996. 'Developing a framework for vocational qualifications is always going to be expensive', Letter from John Hillier, *TES*, 18 October 1996.

5 R. Dearing, *Review of Qualifications for 16–19 Year Olds.* London: SCAA, 1996.

6 G. Beaumont, *Review of 100 NVQs and SVQs.* London: NCVQ, 1996.

7 J. Capey, J. *GNVQ Assessment Review.* London: NCVQ, 1996.

8 NVQ Criteria and Guidance.London: NCVQ, January 1995.

9 See, for example, 'Colleges in scandal of exam passes', *Observer*, 27 March 1994; 'Inquiry set up into worthless qualifications', *Observer*, 3 April 1994; 'Second training scam alleged', *Guardian*, 27 May 1994; 'A vocational charter for cheats', *Daily Telegraph*, 14 December 1994; 'Sleaze and loathing in the classes of conflict', *Observer*, 12 March 1995; 'Fraud squads to root out phantom studies', *Independent on Sunday*, 28 May 1995; 'Minister acts on exams for cash scandal', *Evening News*, 2 May 1996; 'Arrests in £1m NVQ "fraud"', *TES*, 18 October 1996.

10 P. Rogers, *Chairman's Speech*, Launch of BTEC Annual Report, 27 May 1992.

11 J. Hillier, Oral evidence to the Education Committee of the House of Commons, 17 January 1996.

12 J. Hillier, 'Misleading view of NVQ progress'. Letter to *Financial Times*, 9 October 1996.

13 National Vocational Awarding Bodies, '100,000 GNVQ successes and growing'. Press release, 21 August 1995.

14 Joint Council of National Vocational Awarding Bodies, *Record Number of GNVQ Awards in 1995/96*, press release, 28 August 1996.

15 DfEE, *NCVQ 1995 Quinquennial Review*, Stage One Report, November 1995; DfEE, *NCVQ 1995–96 Quinquennial Review*, Stage Two Report, February 1996; DfEE, *NCVQ 1996 Quinquennial Review*, Executive Summary, May 1996.

16 See, for example, 'Lecturers loath to report on GNVQs'. Letter to *THES*, 11 November, 1994; 'Colleges impose sound of silence'. *Guardian*, 15 November 1994; 'Quango blunders'. Letter to *Guardian*, 29 November 1994.

17 DfEE, 'Top advisers join forces to raise standards'. *DfEE News*, 281, September 1996.

18 *GNVQ Information Note*. London: NCVQ, 1993.

REFERENCES

Beaumont, G. (1996) *Review of 100 NVQs and SVQs*. NCVQ.

Bees, M. and Swords, M. (1990) *National Vocational Qualifications and Further Education*, London: Kogan Page and NCVQ.

Capey, J. (1995) *GNVQ Assessment Review*. London: NCVQ.

CBI (1994) *Quality Assessed: The CBI Review of NVQs and SVQs*. London: Confederation of British Industry.

Channell, J. and St John, M. J. (1996) 'The language of standards', *Competence and Assessment*, no. 31, February.

Dearing, R. (1993). *The National Curriculum and its Assessment: Final Report*. London: SCAA.

Dearing, R. (1996) *Review of Qualifications for 16–19 Year Olds*. London: SCAA.

DES (1986) *Working Together: Education and Training*, Cmnd, 9823. London: HMSO.

DfEE (1996) *Building the Framework. A Consultation Paper on Bringing Together the Work of NCVQ and SCAA*. London: DfEE.

De Ville, H.G. (1986). *Review of Vocational Qualifications in England and Wales: A Report by the Working Group*. London: HMSO.

HMSO (1991) *Education and Training for the 21st Century*, Cmnd 1536, vol. 1. London: HMSO.

Jessup, G. (1991). *Outcomes: NVQs and the Emerging Model of Education and Training*. Lewes: The Falmer Press.

NCVQ (1993) *GNVQ Information Note*. London: NCVQ.

Robinson, P. (1996). *Rhetoric and Reality: Britain's New Vocational Qualifications*. London: Centre for Economic Performance, London School of Economics.

5

Teachers' Views of 14–19 Education

Sally Tomlinson

In current debates about the education of young people post-14 the views and opinions of teachers are seldom sought. Yet it is secondary school teachers, and their colleagues in post-16 colleges, who are required to teach and assess new vocational courses, and who are compelled to work within a system that continues to divide post-14 education into academic, vocational and training pathways (School Curriculum Assessment Authority 1994) and retains a legal school-leaving age of 16.

The National Union of Teachers (NUT) has long expressed concern that policies directed towards post-14-year-old students remain polarised by a gulf between academic and vocational routes, with a minority considered able to follow the route of a broad liberal education – a majority being regarded as possible candidates for narrower vocational training.

In 1994 the NUT commissioned a small pilot project to enquire into secondary teachers' views of 14–19 education. The project was based at Goldsmiths College, University of London, and involved interviewing teachers in a geographically representative group of schools to ask what they considered a coherent 14–19 curriculum should encompass, what assessment and examinations they thought were most appropriate, how they perceived the separation of academic and vocational courses, and how they viewed the issue of equal opportunities for all students (Tomlinson 1995). The findings from the study have been incorporated into NUT policy on 14–19 education (National Union of Teachers 1996). This chapter reports on the findings from the study, the teachers being interviewed over the winter of 1994–95.

THE SCHOOLS AND TEACHERS

The project worked with six co-educational comprehensive schools which were selected on an opportunity sampling basis to represent geographical diversity. Two schools were in the south of England, two in the north, one in the Midlands and one in Wales. The schools were different in their age-ranges. Two were urban schools, one taking students 11–16, one 11–18; two were rural schools: one a grant-maintained school 11–18;, one an 11–18 community college; two schools were in mixed areas, one 14–18, one 13–18. This diversity of schools in one small project matched the diversity of comprehensive schools found by Benn and Chitty (1996) in their large survey of comprehensive schooling carried out in 1994. Comprehensive schooling has never led to the uniformity its critics have claimed. Yet, despite the diversity of schools, one of the most interesting findings from the project was the similarity of views about 14–19 education expressed by the teachers.

School A is a large 11–18 comprehensive school, describing itself as a college, and situated in a small southern country town. In addition to National Curriculum subjects, its curriculum includes drama, media studies, business studies, extra foreign languages, child care, community and agricultural studies, physical education to examination level and, like all the schools, personal and social education. Students can enter for GCSE, A and A/S levels, intermediate GNVQ, and the ASDAN youth award. School B, a medium-sized 11–18 comprehensive school in a south Midlands town, serves a widespread rural area. Although the school went grant maintained because of extra funding offered, the staff are firmly committed to comprehensive education. Indeed the school acts as a focus for local community activities, including offering the use of sports facilities and the swimming pool. In addition to the national curriculum, School B offers drama, home economics, textiles, A-level law and business studies, leisure and recreational studies. Students enter for GCSE, A and A/S levels. School C operates on a split site as a 11–18 inner city school, taking pupils from local council estates. It offers drama, sociology, child development courses, government and politics to A-level, in addition to the National Curriculum, and students enter for GCSE, A and A/S levels, GNVQ at intermediate levels, RSA, the ASDAN youth award and a computing award. The school works in a consortium with other schools and the local further education college to share post-16 facilities. School D, a 14–18 community school, has an intake from two 11–14 schools. Its curriculum includes drama and community studies, and students enter for GCSE, A and A/S levels, GNVQ at advanced and intermediate levels, RSA, a Certificate in Information Technology and the Welsh Certificate of Education. School E is a northern inner-city 11–16 comprehensive offering drama, dance, sculpture, photography, a home and family course and courses in health and safety and hygiene. Students take GCSE exams and an NVQ in catering is popular. School F is a large 13–18 school in a small Midlands town, offering drama, home economics, business studies and classics, and students enter for GCSE, A and A/S levels, GNVQ at intermediate level and a certificate in pre-vocational education. All the schools offer personal and social education and are committed to serving their local communities. To that extent they have begun to blur the distinction between schooling and continuing education.

The intention of the project was to interview senior and junior staff, but headteachers mainly selected teachers for interview and the sample was skewed towards senior teachers – the average number of years of teaching of the 48 respondents being 19 years, and the average time spent teaching in their present school over 10 years. It was noteworthy that in an opportunity sample of schools around the country there was a core of experienced, long-serving staff. All the teachers had a professional qualification: 90 per cent had a first degree; and 15 per cent an additional higher degree. An interview schedule was prepared and piloted in the autumn of 1994. Questions probed teachers' views on what they thought constituted a broad balanced curriculum 14–19, and what they thought a national curriculum should include. Teachers also gave their views on comprehensive schooling, diversity and selection for different schools and courses, assessment 14–19, the introduction of GNVQs and the academic–vocational divide in the curriculum. Final questioning asked for views on special needs education, race and gender issues and counselling, in an 11–19 curriculum.

TEACHERS' VIEWS OF THE CURRICULUM

Although from the mid-1970s comprehensive school teachers, among others, had begun to argue seriously for a common curriculum to 16, there was no government imposition of even a common core of subjects until 1988 when a National Curriculum was imposed. A ten-subject curriculum was introduced in haste and with very little consultation with those who had to implement it. The failure of the original National Curriculum proved a costly operation in money, time and teacher stress. By 1994 the content of the curriculum had been 'slimmed down' on the recommendations of the first Dearing Report (School Curriculum and Assessment Authority 1994) but the aims of the curriculum and the rationale for its span of 5–16 remained unclear. By contrast, the Scottish National Curriculum covers 5–14 which ensures a more coherent post-14 phase.

The teachers in the project were all of the opinion that wider consultation and more cautious implementation of a National Curriculum would have prevented many problems. They were also concerned at the minimal input that teachers had as the curriculum was developed. However, contrary to views that teachers wish to 'capture' and control the curriculum, they were very clear that they would want an input from a wide variety of people, including employers, parents, local as well as national government, local communities and even students themselves. Over half the teachers regretted that with the introduction of a 5–16 curriculum the opportunity for developing a coherent 14–18 curriculum had been compromised. Teachers wanted progression and continuity in a 14–19 curriculum and would wish the majority of young people to stay in full-time education until 18 or 19. They were, however, unsure how this could happen as long as the present school-leaving age remained in place, and 60 per cent supported an end to leaving at 16.

The characteristics of a broad balanced curriculum post-14 were defined by the teachers as:

- a range of subjects and experiences
- a breadth of knowledge and skills
- the development of critical abilities
- scope for independent learning
- equal opportunities for all students
- no arts–science divide
- no academic–vocational divide.

Some of their views were expressed as follows:

Pupils should have a range of experiences including scientific, practical, physical, humanities, creative, and aesthetic experiences.

We need a curriculum which develops the whole individual emphasising a range of skills, including an ability to think critically about the world we live in.

A broad curriculum means not specialising early – keeping all options open; we are educating the whole person; it is important to balance practical, academic and social areas.

The teachers' views of a balanced curriculum and the emphasis on educating the whole person are reminiscent of the American educator John Dewey's writing,[1] and is much broader than the current qualification-oriented view of education. Indeed the teachers' views are also more in line with the requirements of employers (CBI 1990) that all young people should experience a broad general education, with an end to divisions that lead to early specialisation.

SUBJECTS IN THE CURRICULUM

Teachers were concerned that the present subject-centred 14–16 curriculum was too narrowly academic – particularly for students with learning difficulties. They were aware that the National Curriculum was based on the model of traditional discrete subjects, but only two teachers favoured this model. They generally favoured the kind of 'areas of experience' model suggested as early as 1977 by Her Majesty's School Inspectors (DES 1977). Areas that all students should experience for as long as possible included humanities, science and maths, technology, aesthetic areas (which included art, music and drama), physical and practical areas. Half the teachers recorded their preference for teaching in combined or integrated ways rather than discrete subjects, and expressed frustration that there was a lack of official support for integrated teaching. As one teacher noted:

> I am involved in a Science across Europe project, and communicate with many countries, the course is taught in collaboration with different science teachers and geography teachers.

Another noted that in his school modular courses and cross-curricular themes were a way of combining subjects.

Teachers had clear views about religious education and technology, only 22 per cent thinking that the former should be compulsory after 14, while 88 per cent thought the latter should be an integral part of the curriculum. However, between them the teachers included 27 areas of knowledge and skills as 'technology'.[2]

Although it is undoubtedly easier in the 1990s to combine arts and science subjects, this 'divide' still worried some teachers, and the 'scientist ignorant of humanities' (and vice versa) still causes concern.

The provision of a broad balanced curriculum for all students was firmly linked by the teachers to equal opportunities. Ideally, they wanted all students to have access to all areas of the curriculum regardless of personal characteristics. Equal opportunities means equal access – but not necessarily equality of outcome – to the whole curriculum, fair resourcing, and no denial of opportunity or resource on the grounds of race, gender, disability or learning difficulties of any kind. Teachers were, however, aware that merely asserting belief in equal opportunities did not solve problems of curriculum content, organisation or methods.

A 16–19 CURRICULUM

The reality of existing arrangements for teaching and learning is that there is a division between a pre- and post-16 curriculum. By 1994 a competitive model of schooling, in which as many students as possible were to be brought to a 'standard' of five GCSE passes at A–C characterised the pre-16 period. While the major rationale for this policy appeared to be the publication of school league tables, the educational value of a terminal subject-centred exam at 16, followed by narrow specialisation post-16 has seldom been raised (Benn and Chitty 1996, p. 373).

The teachers interviewed in this project were very concerned that curriculum arrangements and discussion were polarised into 14–16 and 16–19. This was regarded as a major stumbling block to a coherent 14–19 curriculum. Anxieties over early specialisation had become more acute by the end of 1994 when the Dearing review of the National Curriculum suggested that troublesome students should leave schools post-14 and take vocational courses at college (Schools Curriculum and Assessment Authority 1994, p. 20). While teachers acknowledged that disaffected young people could be motivated by vocational courses, there was a general view that familiar patterns of the social exclusion of lower-class children excluded from broad general education would persist.

Where the curriculum was experienced post-16 was less important than openness and access for all. Despite the encouragement of competition between schools and colleges for students post-16, teachers were concerned that students should be committed and their interests should be paramount. As one teacher noted:

> Some students like the idea of college, but can't cope and come back . . . others do better in a college atmosphere.

Two schools in this project had already created formal links and shared courses with local further education colleges.

SELECTION AND DIVERSITY

For supporters of comprehensive schooling, the teachers in this project provided heartening news. They overwhelmingly believed in comprehensive schooling – and this included comprehensive grant-maintained schools. Only two teachers – both former grammar school teachers, favoured the retention of existing grammar schools. Comprehensive schools were described as places where:

- all abilities could be catered for
- a broad curriculum with a range of specialisms could be offered
- there were equal opportunities for all students to share facilities and resources
- the local community was served
- social integration was facilitated.

Comments illustrating these characteristics were as follows:

> Comprehensive schools take in the whole span of ability and social strata and can be geared to individual needs.

> They are schools where each child can work at their own level in each subject, and be brilliant in some areas yet get remedial help in others.

> They should be schools with a strong sense of community, caring and catering for the needs of all students regardless of ability, background, race, gender or class – a school where all kinds of achievement are valued.

The teachers in the grant-maintained school were firmly committed to the comprehensive ideal, even though a local competitor was a well-known independent school. There was little evidence in this study of apprehension over the concept of a 'neighbourhood school' and any resulting social integration that Benn and Chitty suggest characterises much of the debate about comprehensive schooling in recent years (Benn and Chitty 1996, p. 35).

The development of a coherent 14–19 curriculum for all students does mean a commitment to comprehensive education in comprehensive schools or colleges and the teachers were opposed to selection for different institutions at 11 and 14. However, those teachers wanting some form of selection for courses at 14 had a sophisticated view of how this might take place. They noted pupil choice, guided choice with teachers and parents advising, testing including continuous assessment, and setting or option blocks. They also supported the notion of an individualised curriculum post-14, one teacher commenting that 'courses should be customised for each pupil', and there was some support for special courses for students demonstrating particular skills or talents.

ASSESSMENT PRACTICES

Given current debate over post-14 assessment and examinations, teachers were asked for their views on public examinations, especially the retention of GCSE and A-level in their present forms, the extent of coursework in examinations and the role of teacher assessment.

Teachers were very much aware that in 1994–95 the government was still strongly committed to A-level as a 'gold standard' while expressing hopes that there would be 'parity of esteem' for GNVQ qualifications and that universities would begin to accept these as an equal entry qualification. Indeed the University Committee of Vice-Chancellors and Principals had by 1994 argued for a reform of A-levels and access to universities via other routes (CVCP 1994). Also, as Nicolle (1995) points out, 'A-levels have adapted to the market place more than most of their critics understand', citing the introduction of modular A-level courses and the introduction of A-levels in business studies, theatre, media studies and government and politics as 'relevant' A-levels. However, this does beg the question as to differences in A-level and GNVQ curricula in similar areas if both are to lead on to the same higher education courses.

At GCSE level the 1994 report by the Chief Inspector of Schools criticises assessment procedures in secondary schools generally, but notes that 'GCSE coursework criteria provides a helpful framework for teacher assessment in the 14–16 curriculum' (OFSTED 1994, p. 29). However, by 1994–95 teachers interviewed in this project were questioning the retention of GCSE, fewer than half wanting it to be retained in its present form. One teacher commented that:

GCSE could be replaced by teacher assessment especially as most children now continue into further education. The money saved could be spent on resourcing schools properly.

By 1996 these views were finding more support, the President of the Secondary Heads Association noting that:

> In the long term, a sensible 14 to 18 system of qualifications would not have a major national exam at 16 (Pyke 1996).

The teachers were not in favour of the reduction of coursework in GCSEs and over 80 per cent favoured more rather than less coursework if GCSE was retained, particularly in English and the humanities. One of the major problems with the current GCSE was perceived as the 'kitemark' effect of grades A–C. Since published league tables of school performance were based on these grades teachers felt that students achieving lower grades were demotivated and that employers did not take either lower GCSE grades or alternative forms of assessment seriously. One teacher commented that:

> Industrialists are sceptical of lower level NVQs, and do not take them seriously. Neither do they take seriously GSCE grades D, E or F or Records of Achievement.

Teachers were asked whether there should be more teacher assessment than external assessment in the 14–16 curriculum, and a majority replied that they valued both! There was no antagonism to external assessment, but the teachers would prefer all GCSE syllabuses to retain an option whereby they could be examined either by coursework, or externally, or a mixture.

The teachers at the Welsh school were enthusiastic about the Welsh Certificate of Education which entails 80 per cent coursework, 20 per cent examination and 'is designed to emphasise pupil achievement, not failure'. They felt that, if an examination for 16-year-olds was retained, this certificate could provide a positive model.

In discussion of A-levels, half the teachers interviewed wanted some form of different assessment at 18 or 19, while the rest wanted to retain some kind of reformed A-level. The different forms specified by those wishing to retain A-levels included:

- a broader base with more subjects studied
- modularised courses

* modernised flexible courses
* more coursework.

The plea for a broader-based A-level with students required to study more than three or four subjects echoed the recommendations of the Higginson Report (Higginson 1988) which the Government rejected. In addition the teachers were enthusiastic about modularising A-levels,[3] and there was also support for modernising A-levels, and moving away from the 'traditional' learning skills to develop research skills and knowledge application. Interestingly, these are criteria for the advanced GNVQ level. Teachers wanting to retain A-levels also wanted more flexibility so that they were regarded as a part of a qualifications system, not separate. One teacher noted that:

> To allow flexibility in a mix and match scenario, A-levels should be constructed so that they can interlock with other qualifications.

Teachers who were familiar with the International Baccalaureate were enthusiastic for this kind of examination at 18 or 19. They noted that the Baccalaureate retains a broad base of subject study – seven or eight subjects – but offers choices to students, was thus not over-specialised, retained compulsory foreign language study, and had high status and reputation in European countries.

At the time of the interviews the teachers tended to blame universities for insisting on A-levels for entrance and did not think that GNVQs would be acceptable to universities as alternative entry qualifications. By 1996 there was evidence that universities were accepting the GNVQ qualifications for some courses. However, over half the teachers interviewed had begun to consider some form of credit accumulation from 14 for access to higher education. The credits would be accumulated via modular courses and, as one teacher noted 'could do away with arguments over labels for exams'.

THE ACADEMIC–VOCATIONAL DIVIDE

The teachers were well aware that the intention of the government from the 1980s had been to entrench divisions between academic and vocational courses. The White Paper on *Education and Training for the 21st Century* (DES 1991) had clearly specified the government's intentions to establish three broad qualification pathways for young people –

the A-level system, NVQs and the new GNVQ. This division is illustrated in Figure 1.1 (p. 2) adapted from the National Vocational Qualifications *Monitor*, published in the autumn of 1994, and at the turn of the year the Dearing Committee endorsed a three-track system of:

- craft or occupational – NVQ
- vocational – a midway path between academic and vocational
- academic – leading to A and A/S levels
        (School Curriculum and Assessment Authority 1994, p. 19).

Discussion with teachers about academic and vocational education did reveal a series of dilemmas. By and large the teachers were not in favour of dividing students up into those who 'can do' academic work and those suited to the vocational – although they admit that the divide has such a strong tradition in English schooling that it is difficult to overcome. All the teachers thought that at 14 all students should be entitled to a mixture of academic, vocational and work-related courses rather than being set on different tracks. This is an important finding in this small project as the teachers views *do* conflict with government policy.

Teachers were increasingly regarding the academic–vocational divide as artificial. As one teacher remarked, 'doctors are vocational as well as plumbers', and they disagreed with the proposals that narrow vocational courses should be offered to those judged 'less academic' at 14. However, they were also well aware that some students had become disaffected with traditional school courses by 14, and could be motivated by job-related courses.

GNVQs

By 1994–95 General National Vocational Qualifications were available in eight areas at intermediate and advanced levels, with six more areas due to come on stream by 1996–97. The teachers were asked whether, given that government policy was to retain divisions rather than implement a unified curriculum, GNVQs were the right way to bring a vocational element into the curricula. While 77 per cent felt they were, the overall approval of GNVQ courses was accompanied by the view that the introduction of courses had been too hasty, teachers had not been sufficiently informed or consulted, the courses were not properly funded and could intensify an academic–vocational divide. Teachers' knowledge of which GNVQs were currently being offered or piloted depended, in 1994, on what each school currently offered. There was some vagueness as to actual titles. The Leisure and Tourism course was described on occasions as Travel and Tourism, Health and Social Care as Health and Society, Information Technology as Office Technology – and one teacher described a course in land-based industry not piloted until 1996.

There was also some confusion as to which bodies actually awarded GNVQs. Teachers who were not involved in teaching or co-ordinating GNVQ courses had not been given up-to-date information or consulted over the introduction of the courses.

There was also confusion over the aims of GNVQ, 26 per cent of teachers declining to attempt to define aims. Those that did attempt a description were largely conversant with the official aims – a broad route to employment or to higher education, of equal standing with academic qualifications – but several teachers wrongly thought that GNVQs *were* an actual training qualification to offer an employer. GNVQ courses were described as:

a preparation for the world of work

an alternative qualification comparable to A-levels – they have an integrated rather than a subject-based approach

an introduction to work-related areas and skills beyond the spoon-feeding security of the normal school curriculum.

The teachers were less clear about the aims of NVQs, except those in one school which offered an NVQ Level 1 in Catering, and where teachers were enthusiastic that 'job-related courses give openings to the job market'. There was, however, a general consensus that NVQs were not appropriate in schools as they were work-based and job-specific. One teacher commented that they were 'all about getting faster tractor drivers', and another expressed frustration that, while he wanted to help prepare his students to find work, he did not want 'degrees in shelf-filling'.

SPECIAL EDUCATIONAL NEEDS

The 1988 Education Act, while promising an entitlement to a National Curriculum for all students, nevertheless allows for the modification or disapplication of the National Curriculum for children considered to have special educational needs. The creation of a market in education from 1988 has led to an increase in the segregation and exclusion of children with learning and behavioural difficulties. For this reason teachers felt they had been placed in a dilemma not of their making. The teachers interviewed were unequivocal in their view that all students with special educational needs should be entitled to all National Curriculum subjects, and they did not want to segregate or exclude. However, they did want resources, especially staff, to offer a broad curriculum.

We need resources to make sure equal time is devoted to all. This ensures support for those with lower abilities and the enhancement of higher abilities.

The teachers were clear that students with special needs cannot be catered for merely by recommendations for 'good practice' and they thought that schools would probably continue to exclude the 'special' and the 'difficult' until a broad modular curriculum, with access to all at different levels, was developed.

RACE AND GENDER

Early in the interviews teachers were asked for their views on how to ensure equal opportunities for all in a National Curriculum and a curriculum 14–19, and most touched on issues of race, gender and special needs. Despite evidence that some government ministers and their advisers were determined to remove issues of race and gender equality from the educational agenda in the 1990s (Tomlinson 1993, Lawton 1995), this study indicates that teachers do consider race and gender issues to be of the utmost importance to schools. It was significant that in an opportunity sample of schools around the country *all* schools considered that the education of the next generation should incorporate deliberate policies and practices to eradicate race and gender discrimination, raise awareness of the issues involved, and promote positive action.

Ways in which awareness of race and gender issues could be promoted were noted as follows:

- whole school policies on equal opportunities
- open discussion between staff, students and parents
- curriculum planning to incorporate issues
- personal and social education
- good school ethos and sensitive teaching
- appropriate school organisation and administration
- the presentation of role models
- proper representation on school committees and decision-making bodies
- good government policies.

Teachers were clear that any policies developed by the school must have the support of students, parents and the whole community, that policies needed support from senior management and that with such policies not only equality of opportunity but equality of value of all students should be part of a school ethos.

GUIDING AND COUNSELLING

The 14–19 curriculum will undoubtedly continue to change and develop, and guidance and counselling systems will become more important to help students through their schooling and into further education, training and adult life. Teachers suggested that the best ways of counselling students were through a good pastoral staff and pastoral system, with year heads and tutors taking a lead. All teachers, however, should have some training in guidance and counselling and should know how to make links with parents. Careers teachers and the Careers Service were essential, but guiding students through the complex choices to be made in education should be the responsibility of all teachers. Some teachers were more concerned with pastoral care – guidelines on drugs, sex education and diet – others with providing academic guidance and individual support, and others stressed provision of careers information and parental links. From discussion in this area it did appear that, if there are to be changes in curriculum and assessment – through modularising courses, changing coursework balances, integrating courses or even abolishing GCSE or A-levels – schools will need to develop more structured guidance systems to inform and assist students than presently exist.

CONCLUSIONS

This small pilot research project investigated teachers' views of the 14–19 curriculum with reference to curriculum content, assessment and organisation, within an educational structure that still encourages an academic–vocational divide, early specialisation and early leaving. While small-scale project information must be interpreted with care, the teachers' views do represent a valid contribution to the debate.

It was clear from this study that, while teachers are working hard to incorporate new vocational courses and qualifications they were not, in 1994–95, particularly happy with the divided qualifications system that is emerging and would prefer reforms which worked towards a more unified curriculum and assessment system 14–19.

Teachers were also questioning the break at 16 and the 'final' examination. They were prepared to question the necessity for a school-leaving age of 16 and a GCSE-type examination. The teachers were supportive of modular courses and suggested that there are many possibilities for modularising existing courses 14–19. There were in this study, and in subsequent developments, indications that current government policies are not in line with the views of teachers. It is certainly questionable how long a separation of A-levels and GNVQs can continue, despite the recommendations in 1996 for the retention of separate courses, renaming GNVQs as 'applied' A-Levels (School Curriculum and Assessment Authority 1996).

Teachers were certainly at odds with Conservative Government policy in their overwhelming support for comprehensive schools, rather than selective schools, and they are clear as to the educational, social and community benefits of comprehensive schooling. They are also at odds with Conservative Government policies in their overwhelming support for equal opportunities policies, their concern that race and gender issues should be taken seriously, and that students with special educational needs should have access to all curriculum subjects. Despite their views that policies in the 1980s and 1990s have led to inadequately resourced education and that the pace of change and lack of consultation has been detrimental to some aspects of schooling, the teachers in this study did not wish to act as a professional interest group imposing their views on others. They were very clear that in matters of curriculum and assessment reform, partnerships should be created, and central and local government, parents, employers, governors, local communities and students should all be able to influence the education and training of 14–19-year-olds.

NOTES

1 J. Dewey, *Education and Democracy*. New York: Free Press, 1916. Dewey's writings on education were the subject of derogatory comments by the Prime Minister's Office in the early 1990s. See Jarvis (1993).
2 Areas mentioned by teachers as comprising technology: computer skills and application; design; graphic design; textiles/sewing/fabrics; business technology; manufacturing; creative use of materials/tools; maintenance skills; food; food technology; home economics; cooking; engineering; agriculture; horticulture; building; building; electronics; financial budgets; problem-solving; planning/working with adults; control technology; moral and environmental; aspects of technology; decision-making; team-work.
3 By 1996 over half of A-level courses were offered in modular form. Debates centred on whether modular courses lowered A-level standards.

REFERENCES

Benn, C. and Chitty, C. (1996) *Thirty Years On: Is Comprehensive Education Alive and Well or is it Struggling to Survive?* London: David Fulton.
CBI (1990 *Towards a Skills Revolution*. London: Confederation of British Industry.
CVCP (1994) *Reform of Post-Compulsory Education for 14–19 Year Olds*. London: Committee of Vice-Chancellors and Principals.
DES (1977) *Education in Schools – A Consultative Document*. London: HMSO.
DES (1991) *Education and Training in the 21st Century*. London: HMSO.
Dewey, J. (1916) *Education and Democracy*. New York: Free Press.
Higginson Report (1988) *Advancing A-levels*. London HMSO.
Jarvis, F. (1993) *Education and Mr Major*. London: Tufnell.
Lawton, D. (1995) *The Tory Mind on Education 1972–1992*. London: Falmer.
National Union of Teachers (1996) *14–19: Strategy for the Future: The Road to Equality*. London: NUT.
NVQ Monitor (1994) London: National Council for Vocational Qualifications.
Nicolle, H. (1995) 'Respite from curriculum madness', *Education*, 20 January, p. 7.
OFSTED (1994) *Annual Report of Her Majesty's Chief Inspector*. London: OFSTED.

Pyke, N. (1996) 'Heads seek death of GCSE', *Times Educational Supplement*, 23 August, p. 1.

Schools Curriculum and Assessment Authority (1994) *The National Curriculum and its Assessment*. London: SCAA (First Dearing Report).

School Curriculum and Assessment Authority (1996) *Review of Qualifications for 16–19 year olds*. London: SCAA (Second Dearing Report).

Tomlinson, S. (1993) 'The Multicultural Task Group – the group that never was' in A. King and M. Reiss (eds), *The Multicultural Dimension of the National Curriculum*. London: Falmer.

Tomlinson, S. (1995) *Teachers' Views of the 14–19 Curriculum*, Report for the National Union of Teachers, London: NUT.

6

Competition, 'Choice' and Hierarchy in a Post-16 Market

Sheila Macrae, Meg Maguire and Stephen J. Ball

THE POST-16 CONTEXT: TURBULENT CHANGE

Contemporary post-16 education provision is constructed out of, and in response to, a myriad of interweaving policy shifts, accelerating student aspirations and changing demographic patterns, as well as changes in the structure and dynamics of the labour market or, more accurately, a variety of very different local labour markets. In the UK, as elsewhere in the West, there is a shortage of skilled labour and a 'need' for a flexible labour force, capable of retraining perhaps three or four times in a working lifetime; at least this is the argument presented in the public rhetorics of employers and policy-makers. Higher education (HE) is shifting from being an elite to a mass system; currently over 30 per cent of young people move into some form of HE, and the acquisition of a first degree is no longer limited to the white middle class. Thus, for a variety of reasons, more people in the UK, from wider non-traditional backgrounds, now participate in post-compulsory education and training and for longer periods than at any other time (Foskett and Hesketh 1995). According to the Department for Education (DfE) (1994), the proportion of 16-year-olds in full-time or part-time education has risen from 70 per cent to 80 per cent in the last five years. In 1993–4, 73 per cent of 16-year-olds stayed on full-time, as did 58 per cent of 17-year-olds and 37 per cent of 18-year-olds. In part, this expansion and reorientation of post-16 education is directly related to individual and community aspirations. However, high levels of unemployment and what is now called 'serial redundancy' (Hutton 1996) also encourage the view that educational credentials provide some bulwark against the current uncertainties of the labour market. At the same time, changes in social policy have coerced many 16-year-olds (and others) into continuing their education and training: state benefits having been largely withdrawn for this age group. All this has resulted in a massive expansion in the number and range of courses offered in the post-16 sector.

STAYING ON – HORSES FOR COURSES OR COURSES FOR ANYONE?

There are compelling reasons why the majority of school students in their final year of compulsory schooling now see a need to continue their education and training. They make a 'choice' within and between what is essentially a 'three-track system' of separate progression routes as follows:

- a general education track leading to GCSEs and A and A/S levels;
- a vocational education track leading to General National Vocational Qualifications (GNVQs) at foundation, intermediate or advanced level;
- a work-based track marked by the occupationally based National Vocational Qualifications (NVQs).

These different routes carry very different messages of desirability, currency and exchange value in the labour market. The post-16 sector is a stratified and hierarchical system. The various routes carry different degrees of status, and command particular labour market responses: A-levels become the gold card, while courses in caring, hairdressing or basic skills seem to assign their 'clients' to a limited range of insecure and low paid occupations: 'Staying on in education, especially on the premier A-level route, remains fundamentally a selective process with markers of likely success and failure laid down fairly early on' (Banks *et al.* 1992, p.49).

The situation is complicated by the fact that parents as well as employers are most familiar with A-levels as credentials: after all, these qualifications have persisted over a long period of time and provide established and validated routes into higher education and 'better' opportunities in the labour market. By implication, any other route may well be seen as second-rate and second best.

Against this background there are now two key aspects of policy which structure and reproduce the post-16 sector: patterns of 'choice' and the market-based system of funding for colleges and schools. 'The market provides a mechanism for the reinvention and legitimation of hierarchy and differentiation via the ideology of diversity, competition and choice' (Ball 1993, p.8). Briefly, students can 'choose' to stay on at school (if the school is 11–18), transfer to a sixth form, tertiary or further education college, undertake various forms of vocational training or look for employment. (They can also 'choose' to do none of these things but will not be eligible for benefits.) However, not all choices are available to all students. Choice as such is constrained in two ways. Some routes will be more or less available in relation to the academic profile of students at GCSE level. At the same time, although 'providers' will aim to recruit above their target numbers (to increase the likelihood of achieving their quota), popular and successful institutions will actually be in the position of doing the 'choosing' from among those who apply. 'The orientations of schools, colleges and employers are still fundamentally selective rather than facilitative' (Banks *et al.* 1992, p.188).

STRATIFICATION AND HIERARCHY IN THE POST-16 MARKET

In what follows we draw on data collected in one urban setting.[1] Briefly, we are tracking the 'progress' of one cohort of Year 11 students from Northwark Park Secondary School (11–18 years) as well as a cohort of students from two branches of the local Pupil Referral Unit (PRU) as they choose whether and where to continue in full-time education and training. In our locale there is a wide variety of post-16 provision: sixth form colleges, FE colleges, school sixth forms and the local Training and Enterprise Council (TEC) all in competition to recruit students.

Some post-16 institutions have strong local reputations for particular kinds of provision while others are generally less well regarded and less popular. Reputation and popularity, as in the 11–16 sector, are, in good part, a reflection and reproduction of the educational and social profile of the intake. As in other education markets some students are highly 'valued' and strongly competed for by providers and thus have considerable freedom of choice; others are less 'desirable' and find their 'choices' constrained. This is not simply a recent phenomenon but may be becoming more stark:

> The post statutory sector has always been stratified and hierarchised in its provisions and in its outcomes. The FE curriculum is stratified and this stratification is limited to the nature of the employment market. The curriculum is organised to a large extent into courses which have ostensibly different target groups and purposes (Sullivan 1989, p. 53).

Institutions located in the post-16 market are increasingly driven by expediency: the need to recruit in general terms to maintain or maximise income, and the need to recruit 'good' students who will maintain, if not enhance, the institution's reputation and market position. Institutions are positioned differently in the market by virtue of their reputation and potential to select:

> I suppose we are lucky in that I can be a bit choosy. I mean, there are a number of people who don't even get as far as an interview: either their report is not satisfactory—If they are from our partner schools, yes, but I think, why should our staff – who are really hassled – why should they take on other people's problems? I will just say that we are full, there are no places. (Vice-Principal, St Faith's Sixth Form College)

Some 'providers' have to manage and cope with the least desirable (and more costly) school-leavers:

> We do tend to get the reputation of our provision being for low achievers and it is not, you know. We are fighting hard to say it is not. It is for young people for whom a work-based vocation is more appropriate. The fact that we do have to deal with young people who may have few skills, a low level of education – and they may have social problems and an attitude problem – the fact that we also have to deal with them makes it difficult for us to attract a higher level client group. (Young People and Training Adviser, Rushworth TEC)

As more and more school-leavers 'postpone' their entry to the labour market, the post-16 sector (or more accurately, some segments of it) has had to respond to a new and non-traditional client group. Raffe (1994) has described a move towards 'polarisation' in the post-16 cohort: there are more students who have increased aspirations and there are more students who experience increased disadvantage who are now in the system. Some courses are now no more than underemployment-relief while others are routes into relative advantage and esteem: for example, A-levels provide a form of conservative credentialism. 'The corollary of conservative credentialism is stigmatisation: programmes designed to give dropouts or disadvantaged students a second chance' (Raffe 1994, p.47). (In our research, these students were referred to as the 'returned empties' by one provider.) Currently, post-16 provision is attempting to cater for a broader swathe of young school leavers (perhaps *all* school-leavers), including those with learning difficulties and 'the disaffected'. As a consequence of the drive to survive, expand, compete or close, many institutions are forced to enrol 'less desirable' students with little or no previous experience of educational success, while others are able to cream off and select the 'high fliers' (as above).

However, this creaming-off process is not only managed through constructs of 'ability' or 'aptitude'. Social class and 'race' become filters through which desirability/undesirability is constructed while concomitantly, and in some ways paradoxically, social deprivation, special needs and 'race' become categories for niche marketing or course-filling.

STRUCTURING INEQUITY IN THE POST-16 SETTING

As already noted, post-16 education and training has historically been segmented and fragmented with key routes and key institutions being recognised as class appropriate. In addition, the inter-relatedness and complexities of the processes of inequality work to reinforce older structures of segregation and stratification in the post-compulsory market:

> I think, traditionally, Further Education was generally working class in its clientele in that, certainly within the sixteen to nineteen group, if they go to schools with sixth forms then they will tend to stay on there and quite often we get people, second chance people, people who maybe didn't get any qualifications in school the first time around and are then coming back to do them again. (Deputy Head of Humanities Faculty, Bracebridge College)

In this situation, colleges inhabit a 'place' in their locality and develop their reputation. In many ways this can become a self-fulfilling discourse of availability/suitability which is difficult to deconstruct in the imaginings of the community as well as the mission of the institution:

> I don't think that the middle class parents would see this as the sort of college their children would come to. It's perceived, I think, as being working class. Places get reputations and it's difficult to change a reputation. Even when it isn't deserved, it lives on. (Deputy Head of Humanities Faculty, Bracebridge College)

'Reputation' does lead certain families and students to gravitate towards, or shy away from, specific institutions. It also results in different sorts of courses becoming popular and oversubscribed. In this way, the intake, courses and cultural habitus of the college become articulated through social class.

'Middle-class schools and colleges' and 'working-class schools and colleges' work with different concerns and considerations in the post-16 market. First, it is more likely that the 'middle-class' institutions will be targeting parents rather than students. The beliefs and values of the parents have to be acknowledged and their fears and concerns allayed. Assurances of support and guarantees of achievement must be given:

> The parents have got to make the youngster talk to you. You know it [Open Evening] is very parent dominated. I know that is not the case in some colleges where the youngsters go along on their own, but that is not the case here. So we do all we can to appeal to parents who need to know that we'll look after their youngsters, ensure they'll attend lessons, support them if the going gets rough, plug our good results, you know. (Marketing Manager, Burbley College)

The middle-class parents who visit a variety of institutions to select the most appropriate place for their youngster, assess and judge colleges by a number of criteria.[2] For some of these parents issues of class are a part of their assessment of the institution and are clearly intersected with issues of 'race'. Racist stereotypes come into play. In our study setting, the further away from the city centre, the higher the numbers of white students and the lower the intake of minority students, particularly on the high status courses and routes:

> Burbley is seen as a much more middle class and quite frankly much whiter college. So a lot of white, middle class parents want their kids to go there instead of Bracebridge College, so there are class issues and race issues even in the competition between colleges. There is also the perception that Burbley is less inner city, more rural. (Student Counsellor, Bracebridge College)

Class and 'race' become unspoken but powerful filters through which students are allocated and distributed across the spread of routes and courses. In relation to the over-representation of black and other minority students on low-status courses and training routes, it is evident that two crucial elements are at play in this context. First, Cross and Smith (1987) have provided compelling evidence that bias and stereotyping adversely affect the assessment of 'abilities' in respect of minority students. Their aspirations are seen as 'unrealistic'. Second, there is evidence which suggests that the careers 'service or disservice' limits and 'cools out' the choices and opportunities for minority groups (Cross and Wrench 1990). For example, in spite of all the evidence which demonstrates that African-Caribbean girls do very well in school, they face the same debilitating experience of being 'cooled out' and reconstructed in some part through the myths of 'under achievement' which persist to restrict their post-school opportunities (Safia-Mirza 1992; Mirza 1995). Nonetheless, for minority students, further education away from the school setting in an institution which may not be as regulating or all-invasive as that of the school might have more to offer. For some institutions this may afford a degree of niche marketing as well as an opportunity to disrupt the specific negative stereotypes which surround minority students and young black males in particular:

> We are perceived in the community as a black college. We are about 50 per cent black. Black people are over represented in this college, but then black people are twice as likely to be unemployed as their white counterparts. So it isn't surprising that they stay on in education and they stay on in education more strongly than their white counterparts. Perceived as a black college, and with that goes a whole range of stuff around drugs, violence and all matter of undesirable stuff. (Vice-Principal, Mainwaring College)

> I am saying these young black guys aren't the problem, because that was what they were being identified as, problems to be got rid of. They are not our problem, they are a very valuable asset and if we could get a reputation for providing them with an excellent service we would never be short of students because they are a pretty disenfranchised lot. Schools don't want them in the main, schools will just turn a blind eye to their truancy, hope that they will just sort of disappear. (Student Care Manager, Bracebridge College)

Currently in many urban locales the structures of 'raced'/classed inequalities are further compounded and intersected with issues of citizenship. Some institutions (inner-city, traditionally working-class intake) now provide specific courses for refugees and asylum seekers which again can be seen as a form of niche marketing or as an egalitarian impulse; or, more likely, a combination of both. However, these forms of specialisation may well contribute towards a more distinct delineation of institutional mission, as well as reputation and status, in the wider social setting. For middle-class aspiring consumers, developments such as these may not always be an attractive proposition:

> We have done some special provision in terms of setting aside some of

our hardship funds and access funds given that asylum seekers receive reduced rate income support, given that they are often living in the worst housing conditions and are not always recruited locally. For various reasons they come from quite a spread. So to help with travel expenses and other expenses we have targeted specifically refugees and asylum seekers. (Student Counsellor, Bracebridge College, 1 November 1995)

There are also contradictions in the position of and opportunities for female students. Currently females make up more than half the undergraduate cohort in UK universities (Lewis 1993; Acker 1994). Girls, it seems, are doing well. As Ball and Gewirtz (1996, p.20) have recently demonstrated, girls are relatively privileged in the school marketplace but 'the issues related to girls. . .are decisively cross-cut by ethnic and social class differences – not all girls are of equal value in the educational market'. However it is well established that 'young women's academic attainments are marginally better than young men's' (Felstead 1996, p. 40). This may well mean that high-flying girls have the most choice in the post-16 market and it appears that they are the most 'choosy':

> Some of the girls from our partner schools go to other places. They are certainly not the less able students – they are the most able students, but maybe there are other places that only want the most able students and therefore will only accept them. (Vice-Principal, St Faith's Sixth Form College)

In the post-16, post-compulsory sector, girls are not only valuable because 'their performance in traditional academic public examinations outstrips that of boys ' but equally and sometimes more importantly their presence 'normally conveys positive impressions to parents about ethos and discipline' (Ball and Gewirtz 1996, p. 11). There are other (hetero) sexist reasons, too!

> More women are on the prospectus than there are males. I think it is true that we do tend to be female dominated. They take a very nice picture. A college that looks as if it has lots of females and treats them well will get lots of women and that will always attract the males anyway. (Marketing Manager, Burbley College)

However, the research into gender inequalities in the distribution of vocational qualifications in the UK demonstrates that:

Women persistently lose out in attaining high level vocational qualification. Moreover, closer inspection reveals that vocational qualifications are more sharply gendered than academic ones. (Felstead 1996,
p. 40)

While the evidence of stratification may be less clear here – there are no
women-only further education (FE) providers or institutions (although
there are girl-only sixth form providers) and few institutions claim to be
female dominated – closer interrogation of those on particular gendered
routes (Care courses, NNEB (Nursery Nursing) etc.) give some indication of internal stratification and hierarchies.

What of special educational needs in the post-compulsory market?
Again, this is a complex area not least because of problems of definition.
However, 'special needs' (like class or 'race' or gender) can also work to
stratify and contain the aspirations and expectations of students. There
is again a form of niche marketing developing. In general terms Riddell
believes that much of what occurs in the FE setting continues 'to operate
as an instrument of social control offering few benefits to young people
with special needs' (Riddell 1993, p. 453). Her point is that further
education generally prepares these young people for a life of under-
employment, unemployment and dependence on others. However, this
area of course provision is complex and diverse in design as well as in
conceptualisation. Some courses are certainly limited to addressing
educational learning difficulties or social disadvantage as a form of
pathology or deficit, others are part of a medicalised provision for
special needs, while a few attempt to be 'inclusive' and 'empowering' in
philosophy and purpose. Each type of course offers potential for niche
marketing and offers students different kinds of 'opportunities'.

An example of inclusive provision came from one provider which
takes its responsibilities for 'special needs' students very seriously and
has dedicated substantial resources to this area of its work. If this is
niche marketing, it is not done on the cheap. It also commands respect
within the wider setting of the institution and has gained national
recognition for its quality of provision:

We have got a very strong provision for students with learning difficulties which is organised in a thing called the School of Supported
Learning, but the plan is, the strategy is what we call inclusiveness.
Now in that we have students who have severe learning difficulties,
cerebral palsy, Down's syndrome and what we are funded to do is

teach them or provide them with independent living skills. But we actually try and push them into the vocational so the students with severe learning difficulties, the progression route here is through to a course which is actually run as a business. They buy and sell flowers and they run a business themselves. For real. They go up to Covent Garden, I think it is at 6 o'clock in the morning, and buy flowers, so if you came here on Valentine's Day they would be selling you red roses and, you know, they have a huge internal business within the college. (Vice-Principal, Mainwaring College)

In other cases, it is clear that higher-status institutions are checking out and into this new, and potentially remunerative, market area. One such provider indicated that it is useful to be seen to be 'doing good to less fortunate people' and noted that, 'it is quite exciting and good for our (normal) students' who benefit from working with students with special needs. 'It is quite good to have on your CV' (Vice-Principal, St Faith's Sixth Form College). At the same time, there are no moves to enrol 'emotionally and behaviourally disturbed' students, who are carefully 'cooled out' in the admissions procedures. For all post-16 institutions this is one of several points of tension and sources of ethical dilemmas within which income maximisation, cost of provision and principled decision-making have to be weighed against one another.

It is in the non-course-related 'training' context, outside mainstream school/college segments of post-16 provision of educational and training, that it is possible to see the lowest stratum of a hierarchised provision, and an almost behaviourist approach to the vocational needs of some young people:

They know what they want to do but they have a low level of skills and particularly a low level of those basic skills which are about being able to communicate and go into a work place and take a simple message. So what we do now is we give those young people who are identified as having a low level of basic skills, we give them intensive basic skills training to get them up to a minimum standard. You know, before they go to an employer we make sure they can turn the computer on. (Training and Young People Adviser, Rushworth TEC)

For the students in our study such 'training' programmes were very much a last resort.[3]

STRATIFICATION AND HIERARCHY – BOUNDARIES AND
BLURS

Having tried to sketch out some of the structure and dynamics which
characterise one particular post-16 market, it is important to insert some
caveats. For the students themselves, there are many powerful social and
political reasons for being with 'people like me' (Hemsley-Brown 1994).
While the most desirable high-fliers, who are predominantly middle-
class students, will move to colleges with strong traditional academic
reputations in a linear manner (a form of progression and continuity),
students who are doing a combination of GNVQs and A-levels, as well
as some resits, may well stay at school or move to a local college with a
sound and solid reputation in these areas. Students who are keen to
follow vocational routes are likely to move from school to one of a
variety of local colleges. Hence the boundaries between these 'median'
students are less clearly defined. For special needs students a degree of
niche marketing obtains. But for students who are least desirable – the
'problem' school students, 'slow learners' and 'disaffected' – their location at the bottom of the hierarchy is explicit and emphatically marked.
They are on training courses. What this suggests is that exclusion and
exclusivity are in operation at either end of the hierarchy. In between
these polarised positions there are overlaps, fuzzy boundaries and
degrees of transition. But within all this, 'quality and reputation are
related in good part to the clientele themselves, not solely to the service'
(Ball 1993, p. 8).[4]

Fundamentally the post-16 market is stratified and hierarchical, as it
has always been. However the post-16 sector now caters for many more
people, including some who are making new kinds of demands on the
methods, structures and costs of providers. Some parts of the FE sector
now have to provide new courses to meet the needs of a broader, more
diverse clientele. Intakes have increased but there has been a price to pay
for this additional business:

> The 'new further education' is in the main a response to rising rates of
> unemployment, but the courses offered to trainees do little to create
> new jobs. There are therefore understandable reactions from staff to
> their colleges being used as temporary warehouses for the short-term
> storage of the unemployed. (Furlong 1992, p. 179)

The post-16 market is highly competitive, complex, and not a little
confusing, for all those involved. The extension of post-compulsory

education has occurred in a context where jobs for school-leavers have all but vanished and at a time when the competition between institutional providers has been accelerated and ratcheted up through various funding mechanisms. One consequence has been the emergence of a form of 'guerrilla warfare' between institutional providers (and between the examination boards and trade certificate awarding bodies). Another development has been an intensification of polarisation in the post-16 sector which signals the increasing division between the well-behaved middle class who proceed through a high-status route and the 'disaffected' or 'less able' working-class students who are steered firmly toward the vocational or work-based tracks. All these outcomes would appear to be examples of what Cockett (1996, p. 139) calls 'culpable chaos' which arises from an inability or unwillingness to address the structural anomalies about which something could be done. It is certainly difficult to see that the market in post-16 provision is in any general sense 'empowering' consumers or bringing about a significant shift from course-led to more student-centred planning (Gleeson 1996, p. 13), for in many ways the current extension of post-compulsory education and training simply 'masks social antagonism, oppression and social exploitation' (Avis 1993, p. 11).

NOTES

1 This is an ESRC-funded study no. L123251006, part of the Learning Society Initiative.
2 Another aspect of our project is focused upon this process.
3 We will have more to say about this type of provision elsewhere in reporting our research.
4 Clearly there is another group of students who 'escape' entirely from the provision of post-16 education and training: the missing 20 per cent who 'make out' in permanent unemployment, the grey economy or crime.

REFERENCES

Acker, S. (1994) *Gendered Education*. Buckingham and Philadelphia: Open University Press.
Avis, J. (1993) 'Post-Fordism, curriculum modernisers and radical practice: the case of vocational education and training in England', *Journal of Vocational Education and Training: The Vocational Aspect of Education*, 45 (1), pp.3–11.
Ball, S.J. (1993) 'Education markets, choice and social class: the market as a class

strategy in the UK and the USA' *British Journal of Sociology of Education*, 14 (1), pp. 3–21.

Ball, S. J . and Gewirtz, S. (1996) 'Girls in the education market: choice: competition and complexity', *Gender and Education* (in press).

Banks, M., Bates, I., Breakwell, G., Bynner, J., Emler, N., Jamieson, L. and Roberts, K. (1992) *Career Identities*. Milton Keynes: Open University Press.

Cockett, M. (1996). 'Chaos or coherence, progression and continuity' in R. Halshall and M. Cockett M. (eds), *Education and Training 14–19: Chaos on Coherence?* London: David Fulton.

Cross, M. and Smith. D.I. (eds) (1987) *Black Youth Futures – Ethnic Minorities and the Youth Training Scheme*. Leicester: National Youth Bureau.

Cross, M. and Wrench, J. (1990) 'Racial inequality on YTS: careers service or disservice', *British Journal of Education and Work*, 4 (3), pp. 5–23.

Department for Education (1994) *Participation in Education by 16–18 Year Olds in England: 1983/84*, Statistical Bulletin, 10/94.

Felstead, Alan (1996) 'Identifying gender inequalities in the distribution of vocational qualification in the UK', *Gender, Work and Organisation*, 3 (1), January, pp. 38–50.

Foskett, N. H. and Hesketh, A. (1995) 'Interpreting 15 and 16 year olds' demand for further education: a market ideology', paper presented at BERA Conference, University of Bath, September 1995.

Furlong, A. (1992) *Growing up in a Classless Society? School to Work Transitions*. Edinburgh: Edinburgh University Press.

Gleeson, D. (1996) 'Continuity and change in post compulsory education and training reform', in R. Halshall and M. Cockett (eds), *Education and Training 14–19: Chaos or Coherence?* London: David Fulton.

Hemsley-Brown, J. (1994) 'Marketing the school's sixth form', *Inside Education Marketing*, 1 (1), pp. 2–3.

Hutton, W (1996) *The State We're In*. London: Vintage.

Lewis, M. G. (1993) *Without a word. Teaching Beyond Women's Silence*. New York and London: Routledge.

Mirza, H (1995) 'The myth of underachievement' in L. Dawtrey, J. Holland and M. Hammer M. with S. Sheldon (eds) *Equality and Inequality in Education Policy*. Clevedon, Avon: Multilingual Matters in association with the Open University, pp. 182–203.

Raffe, David (1994) 'Compulsory education and what then? Signals, choices pathways' in OECD, *Vocational Education and Training for Youth: Towards Coherent Policy and Practice*. Paris: Organisation for Economic Co-operation and Development.

Riddell, Sheila (1993) 'The politics of disability: post school experience', *British Journal of Education and Work*, 14 (4), pp. 445–55.

Safia-Mirza, H (1992) *Young, Female and Black*. London: Routledge.

Sullivan, Sheila (1989) *Differentiation and Stratification in the Post-16 Vocational and Pre-Vocational Curriculum*, unpublished MA Dissertation, Institute of Education, University of London.

7

The 14–19 Curriculum in Private Schools

Geoffrey Walford

INTRODUCTION

Problems of unemployment and a growing need and desire for young people to increase their qualifications has acted as a catalyst for the restructuring of state-maintained schooling for 14–19-year-olds. As greater numbers of students have found themselves in full- or part-time study beyond school-leaving age, the rhetoric and reality of 14–19 as requiring a coherent policy has grown. As a result, 14–19 is increasingly seen as a distinct and progressive stage in education and training.

But, while this conception is a relatively new one for the state system, within the private (or independent) school sector, especially for boys, 14–19 (or more usually 13–19) has long been viewed as a logically distinct and progressive stage of education. For most such students it simply bridges the space between preparatory school and higher education. The expectation and reality within the major schools is that only a very few students will leave school after General Certificate of Secondary Education (GCSE) at 16, and that the vast majority will stay for the full five-year course to A-level. Schools and teachers can thus plan their task within a five-year horizon.

The private sector in England and Wales is highly diverse (Walford 1991). The most prominent private schools are undoubtedly those such as Eton, Harrow and Winchester which have long histories and serve an elite sector of boys. Such schools are the most visible part of the 236 schools with heads in membership of the Headmasters' Conference (HMC – since January 1996 called the Headmasters' and Head-mistresses' Conference). Membership is only granted if the school is fully independent and has a large and academically successful sixth form. While many of the boys' schools have ancient origins, similar schools for girls developed only in the nineteenth century. The Girls' Schools Association (GSA) now has a comparable standing to the HMC and includes such schools as Cheltenham Ladies' College, Roedean and Benenden. The six schools so far named are all boarding schools, but in practice the importance of boarding has decreased dramatically over the last decade. By 1995 only 25 per cent of students in HMC schools were boarders and only 15 per cent of students in GSA schools boarded. In both the HMC and GSA there are now more day-only schools in membership than schools that have any boarding at all. The decline in the number of boarding-only schools parallels a rapid decline in the number of schools catering for boys only. Less than a third of HMC schools now accept only boys. About a third have girls in the sixth forms, and the rest are fully co-educational. Several GSA schools now accept boys, but they have been generally far less successful than the HMC schools in moving to co-education. Beyond the schools in these two groups there is a range of private schools where parents pay fees – some highly respectable and others less so. But most of these do not have such high retention rates after 16 and thus are not able to view 13–19 as their target.

Even within the HMC and GSA schools, there are considerable differences in terms of the extent to which 13–19 can be seen as a distinct and continuous stage of schooling. Within the HMC there are two broad groups of school – the day schools that have their main entry at 11 and the schools with boarding that have their main intake at 13. Statistics from the Independent Schools Information Service (1995) show that there are relatively few boarders in the HMC schools before the age of 13, and the intake of day students sharply increases at 13 as well as the main rise at 11 due to the day schools. The numbers of students boarding actually rises at 16 and 17, partially counteracting the decrease in day students. In contrast, the numbers of students in GSA schools is relatively flat from 11 to 15, then declines at 16 (some girls transferring to HMC schools). The vast majority of GSA schools have their main intake at 11 and only a minority of the most prestigious boarding schools have their intake at 13. Boarding is less important for GSA schools. The numbers rise gently to a peak at 15, then decline only slightly.

Although the data are actually a 'snapshot' at one particular time rather than longitudinal, and there may be some changeover between boarding and day in individual cases, they suggest that very few boarders in HMC schools leave after GCSE, but continue on a full five-year course to A-level. For day students, however, most of whom are in the day schools, the three years from 13 to 15 show relatively stable numbers, but there is a distinct jump downwards at 16 and 17. The idea that 13–19 is a coherent stage of schooling appears to be less firmly held for HMC day students than for the boarders. In the GSA schools, an even larger proportion of day girls leave after GCSE, while the fall for boarders is smaller.

It would appear that it is within the major HMC and GSA boarding schools that the idea of a continuous period of education between 13 and 19 has taken root, and it is this group of schools that will be considered in detail in this chapter. It will be shown that these major schools are now increasingly seeing their function as being that of ensuring that students eventually find employment at as high a level as possible. For most students this involves providing examination certification and access to university. The schools seek to provide a direct route into employment for only a small proportion of their students.

EXAMINATION PRESSURE

Private schools in England educated about 7 per cent of the child population in 1994. Yet, in that same year, they provided for about 22 per cent of 17-year-olds still in schools full-time, and for 10 per cent of all 17-year-old full-time students. Sixteen per cent of 17-year-old students studying A or A/S levels were in private schools. In recent years the increase in the proportion of young people continuing with their education and training beyond the compulsory school-leaving age has led to a slight decline in the private schools' share of A-level students, but the success of these schools in enabling their students to gain high A-level qualifications and entry to higher education has actually increased. In 1990, 76 per cent of HMC and 75 per cent of GSA post-A-level leavers went on to higher education. By 1995 this had risen to 89 per cent for both groups (Independent Schools Information Service, 1990, 1995). This increase is indicative of the schools' responses to growing competition for places in high-quality universities and the demands for greater certification for all jobs. These pressures have led to a dramatic increase in the examination orientation of the schools and a rethinking of the nature of the occupational training task of the schools.

For many years now the curriculum of the schools with membership of the HMC and GSA has been geared to the requirements of the universities and the professions, which has meant a strong focus on GCSE and A-level. However, this emphasis on academic work has traditionally been moderated by an additional emphasis on cultural and sporting pursuits, as was thought fit for members of the future ruling class. This was possible and thought highly desirable within boarding school communities, and was seen as a central part of the training for elite status that these schools offered. As the importance of boarding has decreased and the demands for academic certification grown, so the emphasis on examination success has increased.

That these schools have gradually become more and more fiercely examination-orientated is open to little doubt. In an earlier ethnographic study of two of the major HMC schools, I documented the way in which this was occurring in the 1980s (Walford 1986). Even in the early 1980s Fox's (1984, 1985) interview study of parents using HMC schools found that examination results and successful entry to higher education were a major part of the information given to parents of prospective students and the ability of the schools to produce better results was one of the two most frequently mentioned reasons for parents sending their children to HMC schools. Fox (1984) summarised this as:

> Academic results are essentially about examination performance, doing well at GCE O-levels and A-levels and above all gaining entrance to the universities and the professions. It is in this sense that the 'academic revolution' referred to by Rae (1981) is fuelled by parents who can no longer turn to the grammar schools to ensure that such results are achieved. Marsden may well have been correct when he concluded at the beginning of the sixties that whilst academic results were important to the parents using the day schools they were not the exclusive or the main reason for their use, but by the eighties the situation has changed dramatically. (p. 57)

If the change was dramatic in the 1980s, it was even more significant by the 1990s. The 1988 Education Act for England and Wales brought the state sector into direct competition with the private schools. No longer are parents forced either to use the local catchment area school or go private; instead they have the right to express a preference for any state-maintained school. Moreover, at least in theory, there is now greater diversity of type of school within the state-funded system. There are now: grant-maintained schools, City Technology Colleges, schools offering specialisms in dance, music, technology or languages, and various voluntary schools, as well as the local education authority schools. The extent of the diversity in terms of the nature of what is offered may be more of an illusion than a reality (Walford 1996), but the competition is real enough. State schools have increasingly entered the world of marketing – producing glossy prospectuses, videos and ample local media coverage. The private schools have been forced to sharpen their own images and to ensure that their major selling point – high A-levels – is maintained. This selling point is, for the first time, open to clear public scrutiny, for the legislation enforcing the publication of the examination results of all schools applies to the private sector as well as state schools. Winchester finds itself listed in league tables alongside Sunnyside Comprehensive. While this comparison is of little concern to Winchester, some of the less prestigious private schools find the clarity with which parents can compare outcomes more embarrassing. As a result, the last few years have seen many closures of small, less well known schools, particularly those for girls.

Many of the school teachers and others may well mourn the change, and the wisdom of such an overwhelming emphasis on examinations is in question (Walford 1995), but the shift is undeniable: these major schools are now geared to ensuring that students obtain sufficient qualifications to enter the universities of their choice and their chosen careers.

NEW CURRICULUM DEVELOPMENTS

For most HMC schools the ideal curriculum for 13–19 is undoubtedly GCSE followed by A-level, and it is worth remembering that, when O and A-level examinations were first introduced, schools were encouraged *not* to enter students for the O-level if the same subject was to be taken at A-level. The O-level was seen as an unnecessary interruption to the full course of study to A-level. The dominance of the traditional O-level/ GCSE and A-level route remains firm. In 1995 there were 70,828 students in the fifth and sixth forms of HMC schools. Of these, 24,657 were in the fifth form: 23,779 were in the first year of A-level, Higher Grade or Certificate of Sixth Year Studies (CSYS); and 22,144 were in the second or third year of A-level, Higher Grade or CSYS (Independent Schools Information Service, 1995). A mere 90 (0.4 per cent of first-year sixth) were in the sixth form retaking GCSE or Standard Grade, and only 158 (0.7 per cent of first-year sixth) were in the sixth form taking other courses. Figures for GSA schools show similarly low percentages studying anything other than A-level. It is clear that the HMC and GSA schools have not been at the forefront of developments in new educational and vocational qualifications.

However, the views of the HMC are not as conservative on this issue as might be expected. The official position is that, while the HMC wishes A-levels to be retained, it strongly supports a unified but differentiated system of qualifications post-16 (Headmasters' Conference, 1994). It believes that the current division between 'academic' and 'vocational' is misleading and damaging, and wishes to see a single umbrella qualification at 18 controlled by a single authority. This umbrella qualification would embrace A, A/S, Intermediate, International Baccalaureate, General National Vocational Qualifications (GNVQ) and National Vocational Qualifications (NVQ) routes, and a system of tariffs would be attached to each course giving a numerical value that could be aggregated to a total in the award of a final qualification. Moreover, while the HMC wishes to retain the possibility of traditional end-of-two-year examinations for A-level, it also advocates the development of alternative modular approaches to A-level to encourage motivation and flexibility. Further the HMC welcomes the GNVQ in principle, but believes that the assessment and grading of advanced GNVQ must contain a sufficient element of externally validated assessment to command as much credibility as A-levels. These views were supported by the Joint Six private sector associations (Joint Six, 1995) and in submissions from the HMC to the Dearing review (Headmasters' Conference, 1995).

This perceived lack of credibility of GNVQs and the reluctance of some universities to accept alternative qualifications to A-level means that the standard academic GCSE and A-level route still dominates HMC and GSA schools. Only a few schools have been innovative. One area of innovation is the International Baccalaureate (IB) qualification which was developed within the private sector and is highly regarded internationally. It was established to provide an international pre-university curriculum and an international university entry qualification. Students choose six subjects – normally three at higher and three at subsidiary level – within groups such that every student studies a combination of the social sciences and languages together with the natural sciences and mathematics. Every Diploma student also writes an extended essay based on a piece of personal research work, follows a course in Theory of Knowledge; and must spend the equivalent of one half-day per week on some form of Creative, Action and Service activity. The main aims of the IB Organisation are to promote international understanding and promote student mobility, and, in principle, the IB would seem to be a very appropriate qualification for many students within the HMC schools.

Over the past few years private schools have experienced a considerable decline in the demand for boarding. The total number of students within ISIS schools rose between 1989 and 1995 by about 1 per cent, but the percentage of boarders fell from 23 per cent of the total to 18 per cent. The fall for HMC schools in the same period was from 30 per cent to 25 per cent boarders. This change in demand has meant that some schools have now closed their boarding accommodation, while others have looked for new markets. In 1989 there were 1,394 new entrants to HMC schools who were foreign nationals, plus 626 expatriates. In 1995 the figures were 2,391 and 611. This 72 per cent increase in foreign nationals is important for the survival of boarding, for practically all of them will be boarders. In spite of this, the number of new boarders fell by 12 per cent in the same period. This includes the effect of an additional eight schools coming into membership of the HMC (Independent Schools Information Service, 1995 and other dates). The IB would appear to be an ideal qualification for some of these overseas students to aim at, as well as the possibility that it will provide a 'portable' qualification for the sort of students who might well apply to universities in USA, Canada and Europe where IB is well recognised.

In 1995 there were only 30 schools and colleges in the UK that were registered with the International Baccalaureate Organisation as centres for the examinations. Many of these are International Schools or American schools serving particular clientele. Only three HMC schools offer IB – Sevenoaks, Cheltenham and Malvern. Sevenoaks has for many years emphasised its international flavour. It has about 10 per cent of parents living overseas, about a third of sixth-formers taking IB, and offers courses in French, German, Spanish, Dutch and Italian. It has two International Houses. Both Cheltenham and Malvern wish to maintain their boarding nature and have made considerable efforts to attract overseas students.

Amongst the 30 schools and colleges offering IB is Kingshurst City Technology College. Although the City Technology Colleges receive the bulk of their funding from the state, they are officially independent schools. When they were first suggested the idea was that sponsors would pay the bulk of capital costs and a considerable proportion of the current expenditure. In practice, companies were unprepared to take on what they saw as the state's responsibility, and the government had to pay heavily to keep the idea afloat. But the way that they were established, as independent charitable trusts, means that they are a small, but interesting part of the private sector. Significantly in the context of this chapter, one of the criteria by which students are selected is that the parents and children have to state that they wish the child to continue with full-time education until 19. The CTCs had 14–19 as a priority. The CTC Kingshurst was the first CTC to be established, and bravely offers IB and vocational qualifications rather than A-levels. This decision was only possible because of the private status of the college (Walford and Miller 1991). The rest of the 15 CTCs have been less adventurous. They offer a more traditional fare of A-levels, with the addition of GNVQ qualifications.

The other main possibility for a more diversified curriculum post-16 would be for schools to offer GNVQs. Again the list of private schools doing so is small. Excluding the CTCs, just 23 independently funded private schools were known by NCVQ to be approved to offer GNVQ in 1994–95. Four of these were in membership of the HMC – Arnold, Lancashire; Millfield, Somerset; Taunton, Somerset; and St Edmund's, Hertfordshire. All four only offered courses in Business Studies, with the exception of St Edmund's which also offered a course in Art and Design. In contrast, the City Technology Colleges have been in the forefront of such developments.

THE WIDER CURRICULUM

The discussion so far has been in terms of the formal subject-based curriculum. In spite of the major schools' official support for a more diverse curriculum, it has been argued that the academic subject curriculum has been given greater prominence as a result of various pressures on the schools. However, the formal curriculum has traditionally been only a part of what the HMC and GSA boarding schools have to offer students. Many of the schools make elaborate claims to be educating the 'whole person' and not just to be narrowly concerned with academic success. The prospectuses of schools make it clear that a whole range of what Lambert (1975) has catalogued as 'expressive goals' are to be seen as an essential part of the school process. With regard to parents, Fox (1984, 1985) has shown that the reasons they chose HMC schools for their boys centre on two general features that the schools are perceived to be able to offer – the ability to produce better academic results and to develop the character by instilling discipline. The second of these may be seen to be related to educating the 'whole person' and thus to the wider curriculum of these schools.

I have discussed this element of the HMC boarding schools' provision elsewhere in terms of the formal extra-curriculum and formal social life (Walford 1995). I argued that in boarding schools the term 'curriculum' had to be widened to include a much broader range of student activities, for much that would elsewhere be regarded as private, and outside the province of the school is a necessary part of school life. In day schools, extra-curricular activities are, by definition, ultimately optional, but in boarding schools these very same activities become part of the formal expectations. Involvement in various sports, and in cultural and artistic activities such as music or drama, is expected for all students.

In boarding schools the school curriculum must be seen to be far wider than merely timetabled lessons and even these formal 'extra-curricular' activities, for the influence of the school extends deep into areas which elsewhere would be in the private domain and no business of the school. Day students live only part of their lives in schools and, for many students, school-based judgements play only a small part in their own self-conceptions or in the evaluations made of them by others. The influence of parents in the home, and certainly friends, may well have a greater impact than that of the school. For the boarding school student, however, life is lived completely within the school's influence for most of the term. Official regulations thus extend to cover all activities of students, from the time a student must be out of bed and into breakfast until the time that lights must be out in the dormitories. But, although the rules may be many, this part of the total school curriculum is essentially open to negotiation between masters and students, as it is simply not possible to lay down rules for every eventuality. Schools rely on a general fundamental rule such as 'You are expected to show common sense, good discipline and good manners at all times' with all its possible ambiguity and space for different interpretations.

Thus, while the increased emphasis on the formal curriculum may be seen as a direct result of the increasingly competitive pressures on all schools, the major boarding schools, through the formal extra-curriculum and the formalisation of social life, have been able to offer a total school curriculum which supports the development of the 'whole person' as well. The key to understanding this is that, in boarding schools, 'work' and 'play' become intertwined, while for day students work and play are essentially separate domains. For the boarding school student the work and responsibilities of school are ever present. Lives are lived in the expectation that all aspects of 'work' and 'play', be these academic, cultural, behavioural or attitudinal, are open to being evaluated at any time.

Students in the major boarding schools essentially live under the invisible pedagogy (Bernstein 1973), where criteria for evaluation are multiple and diffuse. Their activities are constantly open to evaluation (in the formal curriculum of subject teaching, the extra-curriculum of sport and cultural activities and in the social activities in Houses). The expectation is that the best students will not only be successful academically, but that they will also flourish at sport, art and other cultural pursuits as well. Just as important, students are expected to acquire a whole set of behaviour patterns, morals, tastes and attitudes which are the essence of appropriate character training for their anticipated future positions in society. Here the emphasis is on the 'whole person' who is taught and evaluated through the invisible pedagogy, where there is much reduced emphasis on the mere transmission and acquisition of specific skills and knowledges as in the visible pedagogy.

Having recognised the several elements of the curriculum available in HMC and GSA boarding schools, it can be seen that there is a high degree of continuity between school and the high status professional work that these students desire. The ruling-class and professional level occupations that are sought by parents and students at these schools demand a broad range of abilities, interests and attitudes. The golf and yachting club provide not only a forum at which business people may meet, but also an informal social setting at which others may be evaluated as being worthy of doing business with. Individuals will be evaluated on a whole range of diffuse criteria, and judgements will be made about whether or not he or she is the 'right sort' of person. Professionals are always 'on call', work spills over from timetabled limitations into personal life, the boundaries between 'work' and 'play' are low, the pacing, organisation and timing of activities in both spheres are largely controlled by the professional. In terms of the formal curriculum of these boarding schools there is a clear discontinuity here between school and work but, as has just been shown, the extension of the school's evaluation and scrutiny into the 'formal extra-curriculum' and 'formal' social life is such that students are well prepared for the needs of professional and ruling-class occupations.

CONCLUSION

The HMC and GSA boarding schools have traditionally managed to find a way of organising the entire curriculum such that the visible pedagogy of subject teaching enables the attainment of high qualifications and entry into higher education, yet, at the same time, students experience elements of the invisible pedagogy which enable them to be prepared for their future preferred occupations. But it has already been shown that there have been many recent changes within these schools. In particular, boarding has declined in importance, and certification has been given extreme prominence. The schools have become narrowly academic with little chance for any students to become involved in any newer forms of vocational education. However, while there has been an increase in the importance of academic certification, there has been a corresponding decrease in other activities. Sporting activities no longer hold a great power over most students. Older students are now less inclined to play major parts in the organisation of the younger boys in the Houses, and the claims of work are more frequently heard to be in conflict with prefectural duties or playing sport for the House or the school.

As the emphasis on academic success continues, the distinctiveness of what the HMC and GSA schools can offer declines. As boarding has become less popular, so the ability of the schools to offer those distinctive aspects of the wider curriculum has declined. There are now hardly any HMC schools which only cater for boarding students, and the vast majority have expanded their total rolls by taking in high numbers of day students. The school's ability to offer both the visible and invisible pedagogy is under threat for, as the proportion of day students increases, the 'ethos' of the school changes and the formal curriculum dominates.

It seems likely that the HMC and GSA schools will still be well placed to ensure advantaged entry of their students to higher education, but after that stage, on entry into work, these ex-students will no longer have an advantage in having prior experience of the invisible pedagogy. There will be a resulting contradiction between the experiences of school and work. If this is so, we should expect that, in the future, once university entry has been gained, the advantages of a private school education will have a smaller part to play in ensuring success in professional ruling-class occupations.

REFERENCES

Bernstein, B. (1973) *Class and Pedagogies: Visible and Invisible.* Paris: OECD, CER, reprinted as chapter 6 of B. Bernstein (1975) *Class, Codes and Control, Volume 3.* London, Routledge and Kegan Paul.

Department for Education and Employment (1995) *Education Statistics for the United Kingdom, News 284/95.* London: DFEE.

Fox, I. (1984) 'The demand for a public school education: a crisis of confidence in comprehensive schooling', in G. Walford (ed.), *British Public Schools: Policy and Practice.* Lewes: Falmer.

Fox, I. (1985) *Private Schools and Public Issues.* London: Macmillan.

Headmasters' Conference (1994) *Education 14–19.* Leicester: HMC.

Headmasters' Conference (1995) *Submission to the Dearing Review, Stage Two.* Leicester: HMC.

Independent Schools Information Service (1990) *Annual Census 1990.* London: ISIS.

Independent Schools Information Service (1995) *Annual Census 1995.* London: ISIS.

Joint Six (1995) *Post Compulsory Education and Training.* London: Joint Six.

Lambert, R. (1975) *The Chance of a Lifetime: A Study of Boarding Education.* London: Weidenfeld and Nicolson.

Rae, J. (1981) *The Public Schools Revolution.* London: Faber.

Walford, G. (1986) *Life in Public Schools.* London: Methuen.

Walford, G. (1991) (ed.) *Private Schooling: Tradition, Change and Diversity.* London: Paul Chapman.

Walford, G. (1995) 'Classification and framing in English public boarding schools', in Paul Atkinson, Brian Davies and Sara Delamont (eds) *Discourse and Reproduction: Essays in Honor of Basil Bernstein.* New Jersey: Hampton.

Walford, G. (1996) 'Diversity and choice in school education: an alternative view', *Oxford Review of Education,* 22 (2).

Walford, G. and Miller, H. (1991) *City Technology College.* Buckingham: Open University Press.

PART II

Examples: 14–19 Policy and Practice

8

Race and Ethnicity in Education 14–19
David Gillborn

There is a clear line of division at the age of 14. I have become more persuaded that this is the natural age for transfer, for by that age the pupils, with guidance from their teachers, will select for themselves the type of education which is most appropriate for them . . . let us recognise that 14 is the watershed, not 11 or 16. Even if we cannot at this time contemplate the physical changes in the schools to reflect that, we should be looking to create a different approach post-14. . . . By the age of 14 pupils, as well as their teachers, know whether they want to follow a more academic course – which would involve studying in greater depth science and arts subjects . . . then they can move towards a GCSE and A-levels in those subjects and on to university admission. They might wish to pursue, however, studies with a more practical, technological, technical and vocational aspect. These studies are not of a lower order – they are *different*. (Kenneth Baker, architect of the Education Reform Act 1988, on the possible shape of education reforms to come (Baker 1996))

Education policy debate is increasingly coming to emphasise the importance of the 14–19 phase. It is not only Conservatives, such as Kenneth Baker (above) who have argued for reforms to further institutionalise this 'watershed': Sir Peter Newsam, former chair of the Commission for Racial Equality, for example, has argued that a solution to London's educational needs may be 'gradually to convert the present vertically-organised system from the age of 11 into one arranged horizontally, with a break at 14' (Newsam 1996, p. 16). Perhaps most influential of all, Ron Dearing, through a succession of government-sponsored reviews, has argued for the development of discrete educational 'pathways' that cater for the different needs and aspirations of students (see Dearing 1994; 1996). Amid all of this, Dearing's talk of separating the 'academic' from the 'occupational' and 'vocational' strongly echoes the kinds of assumption that underlay the 1943 Norwood Committee's view that there were different 'types' of student: the academically gifted, the more technically minded and those who 'deal more easily with concrete things than ideas' (Cox 1979, p. 119). Norwood's ideas came to shape the system of selective education that operated at 11-plus in the post-war years: it is possible that Dearing's recommendations might see a return to selection, this time at the age of 14, albeit in a more varied form, using selection *within*, as well as *between*, schools.

As the impetus grows for more explicit and far reaching differentiation at the age of 14, this chapter examines the issues from the standpoint of research on ethnic and 'racial' inequalities in educational experience and achievement. In particular, I examine data on the position of students of black/African Caribbean and South Asian ethnic backgrounds.[1] The chapter begins with a review of the current situation and then moves to explore the possible ramifications of increased selection and differentiation at 14-plus.

MAPPING INEQUALITIES: THE CURRENT SITUATION.

This section reviews the current state of knowledge concerning the position of ethnic minority students in 14–19 education. The first part focuses on differences in experience and achievement up to the end of compulsory education at age 16. Subsequently, the section looks at ethnic minority young people's representation in post-compulsory education.

ACHIEVEMENT INEQUALITIES IN COMPULSORY SCHOOLING

Attainment in examinations at the end of compulsory schooling can be crucial to a young person's future educational and job market opportunities. For many years a concern with levels of achievement at 16 dominated debates about the education of young people of ethnic minority background. The tone was set by a Committee of Inquiry established, in 1979, to report on the education of children from ethnic minority groups. In an interim report concerned specifically with 'West Indian' children, the committee concluded that black young people '*as a group* are underachieving in our education system' (Rampton 1981, p. 10, original emphasis): a conclusion echoed in the committee's full report (Swann 1985, p. 63). Over time the notion of 'underachievement' has been widely misinterpreted; in many ways it has become a stereotype, seeming to denote all black young people as somehow destined to fail

(Troyna 1984). For this reason I will use the phrase *achievement inequalities* as a means of drawing attention to important differences in average attainment whilst retaining some measure of uncertainty and critique regarding the source(s) and scale of the inequalities (see Gillborn and Gipps 1996, section 2; Wright 1987, p. 126)

Race, gender and social class
In a review of previous studies in this field, between 1972 and 1985, David Drew and John Gray identify a 'relatively stable picture' of significant and consistent inequalities of achievement between black students and their white peers (Drew and Gray 1991, p. 163). Only one of the studies they examine (their own) was based on a nationally representative sample. Their research also stands out as offering the most rigorous examination to date of the cross-cutting dynamics of race, class and gender. Before considering changes in achievement following the national reforms of the late 1980s and early 1990s, therefore, it is useful to examine Drew and Gray's findings as a means of understanding the situation in the mid-1980s and exploring the intersections of race, class and gender.

Figure 8.1 shows a clear association between differences in average achievement and students' social class and ethnic group background. *Social class is directly associated with differences in average examination*

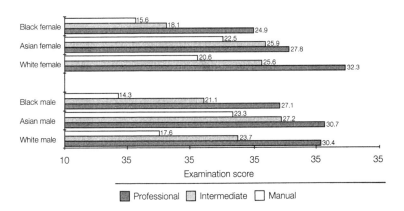

Figure 8.1   Average exam scores by ethnic origin, gender and social class, England and Wales (1985). Source: *Adapted from D. Drew and J. Gray 'The fifth-year examination achievements of Black young people in England and Wales'*, Educational Research, *32 (3), 1990, p. 114.*

scores regardless of gender and ethnic origin: within each ethnic group (and for both sexes) the higher the social class, the higher the average score. Figure 8.1 also illustrates the salience of ethnicity as a factor. Regardless of gender, in the mid-1980s black students were not achieving as highly as their white and South Asian (Indian, Pakistani, Bangladeshi) counterparts of the same sex and social class.[2]

Drew and Gray's data raise some interesting questions in relation to gender. It is now widely known that at 16 (but not 18) girls tend to achieve somewhat better average results than boys (see Elwood 1995). Although the white scores are in the predicted direction (with girls averaging higher than boys of the same social class background) this is only true for black girls from working-class (manual) backgrounds. For South Asian students the pattern is reversed throughout. These data suggest, therefore, that national statistics on the achievement of girls at 16 may give a somewhat misleading picture, generalising erroneously from a pattern that may only be true for white students. More recent data collected from a range of local education authorities (LEAs) (Gillborn and Gipps 1996) highlight the difficulty of constructing general conclusions based on material from widely differing regions. Additionally, local education authorities (LEAs) collect social class data so rarely that it is not possible to say whether the relatively higher performance typical of black young women over their male counterparts (Mirza 1992) is achieved regardless of social class. It may be that the overall averages are skewed by the fact that disproportionate numbers of black students are from working-class backgrounds.

It is clear, therefore, that social class, gender and ethnic origin are each important variables, which can interconnect and cross-cut in unpredictable but significant ways (see Gillborn 1995; Rattansi 1992; Rizvi 1993; Weis 1988; Young and Dickerson 1994). Although these factors cannot always be explored simultaneously, it is necessary to retain a sense of their complexity when considering the more up-to-date material.

Changes in attainment since the late 1980s
Much has changed since the mid-1980s when Drew and Gray's material was gathered. The education system has experienced a period of top-down reform unprecedented in the post-war period. In terms of examination achievements this period has also seen significant changes: see Figure 8.2.

Since the late 1980s there has been a year-on-year improvement in the proportion of students attaining five or more higher grade passes. The

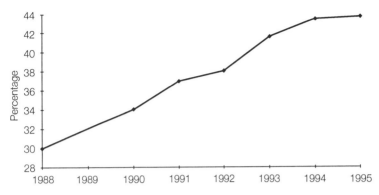

Figure 8.2   15–16-year-olds gaining five or more GCSE higher grade passes, England (1988–95). Source: *Adapted from DfE/DfEE performance tables and J. Payne,* Routes Beyond Compulsory Schooling: England and Wales Youth Cohort Study Report no. 31. *Sheffield: Employment Department, 1995, p. 6.*

proportion of school-leavers attaining this high degree of success has risen by almost half as much again since 1988, now including 43 per cent of young people finishing their compulsory schooling.

Unfortunately, there are few reliable statistics on national perform-ance levels before 1988. It is not possible, therefore, to say with certainty how far these changes represent a wholly new pattern, let alone to decide what proportion of the improvement can be traced to processes associ-ated with the specific reforms initiated as part of the Conservative res-torationist project. It has been argued, for example, that by including a significant role for continual assessment (where students' work is graded throughout a two-year period) the GCSE examination itself has allowed young people to demonstrate their abilities more fairly than previous examination systems, which relied more heavily on terminal examin-ations by unseen written papers (see Gipps and Murphy 1994). Add-itionally, it is clear that the rate of improvement has slowed, with only a modest change (from 43.3 per cent to 43.5 per cent) in the most recent statistics. There are no clear explanations for this; some claim that a subsequent reduction in coursework is now depressing performance. It has also been argued that having initially been forced to raise their expectations of students' abilities, teachers may now have reached a stage where further significant improvements are simply not possible within existing budgetary constraints.

Despite this degree of uncertainty, it is clear that the reforms have forced schools and LEAs to pay much greater attention to levels of academic attainment. In particular, the proportion of students reaching the 'benchmark' level of *five or more higher grade passes* has become extremely important: this is the most often quoted statistic in the annually published school performance tables and the first place many commentators look when seeking to describe/judge a school. In a survey of current school improvement projects, for example, the *Times Educational Supplement* revealed that the most frequently adopted strategy among respondents was explicitly to focus greater attention on 'pupils at the five-A-to-C margins' (Doe 1995).

Whatever the processes that lie behind the statistics, it is clear that *more young people than ever before now leave compulsory schooling having achieved relatively high levels of academic success.* However, the Department for Education and Employment (DfEE)'s statistics do not tell us about possible differences in achievement between ethnic groups: for this we must turn to new data gathered as part of a review of recent research on the achievements of ethnic minority young people (Gillborn and Gipps 1996). In all 34 LEAs were approached for statistical data relating to recent trends in educational experience and achievement. The sample was selected in order to cover a wide range of authorities, including inner London, outer London, metropolitan districts and shire counties: the authorities serve more than half the total ethnic minority population of Britain. Additionally the sample includes the ten most populous LEAs for each of the principal ethnic minority groups. A response rate of 50 per cent included examples of each type of LEA, produced a great deal of information and provided a good basis for analysis. Many LEAs were able to provide statistics for several years and some produced new (more detailed) breakdowns after further consultations.

African Caribbean students
The data supplied by LEAs reveal a great deal of variation across geographical regions; this is likely to reflect several factors, not least social class. In London, for example, it is known that the white population is relatively skewed towards a lower social class profile than would be representative of the white population of Britain as a whole (Nuttall *et al.* 1989). Consequently white students in the capital frequently achieve at lower levels than certain ethnic minority groups. Even here, however, it is rare to find black students achieving higher average results than their white peers. The London Borough of Brent serves as an interesting

example. Of all English LEAs, Brent has a student population with the greatest *proportion* of ethnic minority students: whites account for less than 40 per cent of 5–15-year-olds in the borough. Between 1990 and 1994 Brent students achieved an increase in average exam score[3] of more than a third in four years (from 24.8 to 33.5), equivalent to an additional pass at the highest possible grade. When the data are broken down by ethnicity it emerges that young people in each major ethnic group enjoyed increased success – *but not equally so.* The biggest increase was achieved by the group that already achieved greatest success: Asian students improved by an average of 8 points; in contrast the lowest achieving group (African Caribbeans) improved by 6.5 points – meaning that *the gap grew between highest and lowest achievers in the borough.* A similar picture emerges when considering the proportion of each group achieving five or more higher grade passes (see Figure 8.3).

In most LEAs, and especially outside London, the highest achieving group are white students. The position of African Caribbean students as the lowest achieving group, however, remains relatively stable wherever data are gathered. This is true, for example, in Birmingham which has the largest minority population of all LEAs in terms of *absolute size*: more than 200,000 people of minority ethnic origin live in Birmingham – almost 7 per cent of the entire minority population of Britain (Runnymede Trust 1994, p. 14–15). Additionally, the LEA has the largest population of black students in the country.

Figure 8.4 compares the average achievements of the major ethnic

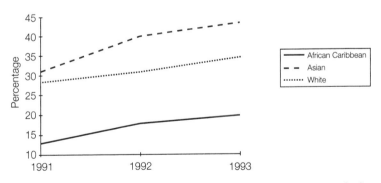

Figure 8.3   15–16-year-olds of both sexes gaining five or more GCSE higher grade passes, by ethnic origin, London Borough of Brent, (1991–93). Source: Brent, Report summarising the analysis of the 1993 GCSE results. *London Borough of Brent.*

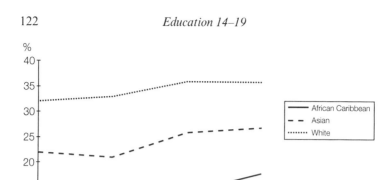

Figure 8.4   15–16-year-olds of both sexes gaining five or more GCSE higher grade passes, by ethnic origin, Birmingham (1992–95). Source: *Birmingham Education Department.*

groups in Birmingham and combines the statistics for both sexes: *the data reveal a consistently significant gap between the average achievements of black and white young people.* The Birmingham data are especially noteworthy; in addition to the city's importance as a major centre for minority residence, the LEA has made available detailed statistical breakdowns covering a four-year period – this is a major advance in a field where most previous analyses rely on data from a single year.

When we consider gender and the performance of African Caribbean students, the Birmingham data confirm that on average black girls achieve at a higher level than their male counterparts: a greater proportion of black young women have achieved five or more higher grade passes in each of the last four years. However, the levels of achievement have not followed any simple pattern: in 1993 black boys improved considerably, only to fall back the following year. In contrast, black girls in Birmingham suffered a slight fall in achievement in 1993 but had significantly greater success in 1995.

That African Caribbean young women tend to achieve more highly than their male counterparts is not news (Fuller 1980; Mirza 1992; Tomlinson 1983). Recently this fact has received a good deal of attention in the media, including the black press. *It is a mistake, however, to assume that black/white achievement inequalities are a male-only issue.* Once again the Birmingham data provide a good empirical basis for examining this issue. Figure 8.5 illustrates the scale of the inequalities of

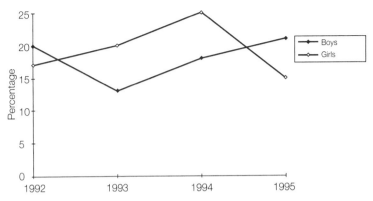

Figure 8.5   Black/white inqualities of achievement, by gender: five or more GCSE higher grade passes, Birmingham (1992–95). Source: *Birmingham Education Department.*

achievement between black and white boys and girls. The data compare separately the black/white gap for boys and girls over a four-year period, depicting the performance of black young people relative to their white counterparts of the same sex. In 1992, for example, 20 per cent *more* white young men achieved this level of success compared with black males. Once again, the black/white gap fluctuates. For males the gap fell in 1993 (when black young men performed relatively well) but has since risen steadily. For young women the black/white gap grew each year until 1995 when it declined sharply (reflecting both an improvement by black young women and a small decline on the part of white females). Throughout the four-year period, however, *African Caribbean students of both sexes experienced significant inequalities of achievement in comparison with their white counterparts. Indeed, in two of the four years, the black/white inequalities were most pronounced for African Caribbean young women.* This is an important finding in view of the gendered nature of the educational and labour markets facing young people.

No other LEA data allow comparison over such a long period as the Birmingham material. Where statistics are available for more than a single year, however, *there are cases where black populations have suffered both a relative and an absolute decline in their achievements.* Between 1993 and 1994 in the Borough of Camden (in inner London), for example, while the average examination score in the LEA rose by almost 3 points, the average for black students fell by 1.7 points: taken together, this represents an increase in the gap between black students and the rest of their cohort of almost 5 points: equivalent to an additional higher grade pass (at grade C) (Camden 1995).

The lack of nationally representative statistics make it difficult to draw definitive conclusions about the size and nature of black inequalities in educational achievement. However, based on locally produced data, spanning up to a four-year period, some conclusions can be drawn with a degree of certainty:

- Black inequalities in educational achievement are persisting at a significant level despite the general increase in attainment.
- Inequality of educational achievement is not restricted to African Caribbean young men: in relation to their white counterparts, black young women are also experiencing significant levels of inequality of achievement.
- In some local areas there is evidence that ethnic groups are not sharing equally in the improvements: here black/white inequalities are not simply persisting, they are growing.

South Asian students

As noted earlier, research during the 1980s tended to show 'Asian' students achieving average levels of attainment close to (sometimes in excess of) their white peers. These studies, however, rarely distinguished between different South Asian populations and often focused on urban areas, such as London, which may have presented a depressed picture of white attainments because of social class factors. The practice of aggregating Indian, Pakistani and Bangladeshi young people into a single category has increasingly been criticised; these groups differ considerably in their religious, political and economic compositions. According to the 1991 census, for example, of all major ethnic groups, the Indian group had the largest proportion of people in non-manual occupations (58.4 per cent): in contrast the Bangladeshi group had the largest proportion in manual occupations (58.7 per cent) (Runnymede Trust 1994, p. 26). Additionally, Bangladeshi communities have a less well established presence in many areas and are known to suffer additional levels of disadvantage because of poverty and generally lower levels of English language fluency (Tomlinson 1992). Given these facts it is not surprising that the most recent review of this field pointed to important differences in attainment between different South Asian groups.

On average Indian young people appear to finish compulsory schooling with a relatively good profile of examination results. They tend to be the highest qualified of the main South Asian groups and, in many areas, they achieve average results that are superior to their white peers. In contrast, Bangladeshi and Pakistani students have tended to suffer significant inequalities of achievement. Data from Birmingham, for 1995, demonstrate the size of the average differences in educational attainment between students of different ethnic origins: in comparison with their white and Indian peers (and like their African Caribbean counterparts) Bangladeshi and Pakistani young people emerged from compulsory schooling less likely to have obtained five or more higher grade passes, but more likely to have achieved no graded results: see Figure 8.6.

ETHNIC ORIGIN AND POST-COMPULSORY EDUCATION
It has been known for some time that, in comparison with their white peers, ethnic minority young people are more likely to remain in full-time education beyond the minimum. Indeed, drawing on questionnaire research with a sample of more than 28,000 16-year-olds (in 1985 and 1986) David Drew states that:

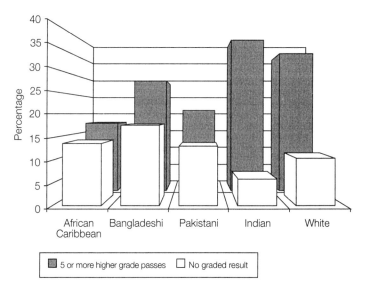

Figure 8.6   Ethnic origin and GCSE attainment for both sexes, Birmingham (1995). Source: Birmingham Education Department.

once attainment was taken into account, ethnic origin was the single
most important variable in determining the chances of staying on . . .
other things being equal, the odds of Afro-Caribbeans staying on
were three times higher than for whites; and for Asians they were ten
times higher than for whites (Drew 1995, p. 101).

The higher rates of minority participation are maintained throughout
the three years following the end of compulsory schooling. Again, the
participation of South Asian young people is especially striking; *a
majority of Asian young people are still in full-time education three years
after leaving school* (Drew 1995). Data drawn from the 1991 census provide a more detailed picture of differences between minority groups and
allow comparison between different social class backgrounds. The data
indicate that *in almost every case ethnic minority young people stay in full-
time education more often than whites of the same social class*. Indeed,
despite the fact that students from middle-class backgrounds usually
stay on more often, the census material demonstrate that in some cases
young people from less affluent minority backgrounds are more likely to
stay on than whites from higher social class backgrounds (see Figure
8.7). There appear to be several reasons why ethnic minority young
people are more highly motivated to stay in education beyond the

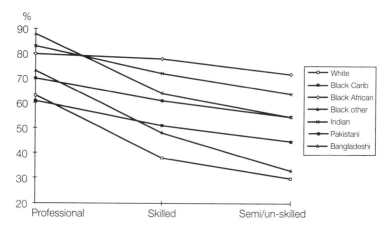

*Figure 8.7   Participation rates of 16–19-year-olds in full-time education by
social class and ethnic origin (1991). Source: D. Drew, J. Gray and D.
Sporton, 'Ethnic differences in the educational participation of 16–19 year
olds', unpublished paper presented to the OPCS/ESRC Cencus Analysis
Group Conference, University of Leeds, September 1994, table 2.2.*

compulsory phase. Children from minority backgrounds report greater parental support for staying on, even where family poverty might be assumed to push them into the labour market (Drew 1995, p. 95). Additionally, young people from minority backgrounds tend to experience significantly worse levels of youth unemployment: in these circumstances post-compulsory education not only postpones entry into the labour market, it also offers the chance of improving certification and, possibly, offsetting the influence of racism in recruitment processes that demand increasingly high levels of qualifications (Drew 1995; Hagell and Shaw 1996).

The greater rates of minority participation, however, are not the whole story. In addition to recognising *how many stay on*, we should also focus on *what they are doing* while in post-compulsory education. Once again significant differences emerge between the major ethnic groups. White and Asian young people are more likely to follow a traditional 'academic' route of two or more A-levels, while African Caribbean young people are more likely to follow vocational courses. Among South Asian students there is a particular emphasis upon improving/gaining additional GCSE qualifications in the first post-compulsory year, and then transferring onto A-level courses. Consequently, by the age of 18 Asian young people are the most highly qualified group. African Caribbeans, on the other hand, emerge as the group with the highest profile of vocational qualifications – a mark of their determination to succeed in education, but not generally viewed as equivalent in status or market value in terms of entry to higher education (see Drew *et al.* 1992; Gillborn and Gipps 1996).

PATHWAYS, FAST-TRACKS AND DEADENDS: RACE AND 14–19 EDUCATION POST-DEARING

It is too early to say with certainty how students of ethnic minority background might be influenced by reforms of 14–19 education. However, it is possible to hypothesise about future developments, given an awareness of the current situation (outlined above) and by examining existing research on areas of policy and practice that seem destined to shape future patterns of experience and achievement between 14 and 19. In particular, this section focuses on two areas of concern: first, the use of selection within secondary schools (via banding, setting and tracking); second, processes of curricular differentiation at 14 (previously structured through subject 'options' systems). In both cases, research suggests that increased differentiation at 14 may further disadvantage ethnic minority students.

RACE, EXPECTATIONS AND SELECTION: BANDING, STREAMING, TRACKING
AND SETTING

Selection has emerged as one of the central issues in contemporary educational debates. In 1996 Gillian Shepherd (Conservative Secretary of State for Education and Employment) signalled the government's intention to remove existing restrictions on schools' ability to select students such that 'No type of school is excluded, no form of selection is ruled out, and no limit is put on the number of selected pupils' (*Times Educational Supplement*, 5 April 1996, p. 5). In fact, the subsequent White Paper proposed different limits for different types of school, reflecting the government's belief that selection would prove to be an incentive for more schools to 'opt out' of LEA control: grant-maintained schools would be able to select up to 50 per cent of their intake; LEA Technology and Language Colleges up to 30 per cent; and LEA schools up to 20 per cent (DfEE 1996). Additionally, it was proposed that all school governing bodies should annually consider whether to introduce selection for part of their intake.

   Whilst the Labour Party criticised moves to extend selection at the point of entry to secondary schools, it took a different view of selection *within* schools. At the 1995 party conference, Labour leader Tony Blair promised 'No return to selection, academic or social' but, in the same speech, committed his party to 'assessment for all five year olds', more specialist interests for particular schools and 'Tougher inspection. Higher targets' (Blair 1995). These are exactly the kind of measures that have pressed many schools into adopting earlier and more extensive selection *within* their student populations – through streaming, banding or setting by ability. In fact, by 1996, Blair was committing his party to this form of internal selection: criticising mixed ability teaching as an 'ideology' and stating that a Labour Government would 'start from a general presumption in favour of grouping by ability and attainment' (Blair 1996). *Although the major political parties differ about the kinds of selection they favour, therefore, they are agreed on the need to differentiate between different groups of students. This is not new, but threatens to escalate the already clear trend towards greater academic selection that has arisen as a result of the education reforms to date.*

   In fact selection has never totally left the English educational system:

even within state-maintained comprehensive schools certain subjects (notably mathematics, science and modern foreign languages) have fought hard to retain the use of hierarchically organised teaching groups that are 'set' by ability. The use of setting tends to become more common in the latter years of compulsory schooling, as students embark on examination courses. In the late 1970s, for example, Her Majesty's Inspectorate (HMI) reported just 2 per cent of comprehensives retaining mixed-ability teaching throughout the timetable (HMI 1978). Although mixed-ability teaching has enjoyed widespread support in the past, many practitioners now feel that their schools are compelled to maximise academic attainment at the expense of less easily quantified aspects of the education they provide. The concern with measurable 'standards' and performance tables is especially acute at the school level, where the proportion of students achieving high grade passes is now routinely used as a basis for comparison: listing the best/worst schools on a national and local level. *The result has been to lead schools to concentrate as never before on rates of performance in public examinations*:

> To be a successful school [in the performance tables] you need to be full of academically bright children – they are the priority (Classroom teacher quoted by Gillborn 1995, p. 190).

> Results are the be-all-and-end-all (Director of Studies in a northern school quoted in the *Times Educational Supplement*, 8 March 1996, p. 11).

Where raw examination results become the single most important measure of a school's performance, calls for increased use of academic selection can gain considerable force. In particular, the use of setting appears to be increasing (National Curriculum Council 1991). Even in schools with strong track records on equal opportunities and anti-racism, some teachers feel an inexorable push towards a return to more selective and hierarchical structures:

> I think setting is going to become more paramount, simply because of the implementation of the National Curriculum and SATs and league tables and all the other things. I am afraid we are going back. I think it is against our [school] policies and our philosophy, but we are being *forced* into this because of Government legislation (. . .) I think we are in a dilemma because I think it is anti everything that we stand for.

And yet we are being forced into it. (Head of Department, quoted by Gillborn 1995, p. 191)

As setting by ability becomes more widespread, previous research suggests that among the first to suffer will be students of ethnic minority and/or working-class background: groups that frequently have to contend with stereotypes of low ability and poor motivation (see, for example, Bates and Riseborough 1993; Eggleston *et al.* 1986; Gillborn 1990; Hallam and Toutounji 1996; Mac an Ghaill 1988). The findings of previous studies suggest that African Caribbean students are especially likely to suffer increased inequalities of opportunity and achievement through a return to more frequent and extensive selection. Cecile Wright and Peter Foster, for example, have taken opposite views on the collection, interpretation and presentation of research on the school experiences of black young people (Foster 1990a; Wright 1990); and yet both demonstrate that black secondary students were less likely to achieve a place in high-status teaching groups in the schools they researched (Foster 1990b; Wright 1986). Although Foster denies any wrong-doing on the part of teachers, he echoes Wright's finding that black students could find themselves in low sets *despite* relatively good test performances: in both studies, judgements about disciplinary issues led to some black students being placed in lower sets than would be predicted on the basis of their 'ability' as indicated in written tests:

> [In the English department] a number of students who were defined as 'bright enough' were ruled out because of their record of past behaviour. Interestingly these students were nearly all Afro/Caribbean boys (Foster 1990b, p. 143).

> The Science teachers then created their male class of 'difficult' students, the majority of whom ... were Afro/Caribbean, and the Humanities department selected a 'remedial' group of 'those who need most help'. Again the majority were Afro/Caribbean boys. (Foster 1990b, p. 144)

Foster defends the distribution of black students to low-status groups arguing that teachers' decisions were based on legitimate judgements about 'which students are likely to make best use of a place in a high status group' (Foster 1990b, p. 145). In contrast, others have argued that the level of conflict between white teachers and black students (in primary and secondary schools) may owe more to the beliefs and expectations of teachers than the actions of their students (Gillborn and Gipps 1996, section 4). In an ethnographic study of an inner city comprehensive, for example, I noted that teachers acted more quickly to discipline black students, controlled them when peers of other ethnic groups escaped punishment, and associated individual incidents with a supposed threat that black students were thought to present to teachers' authority and personal safety (Gillborn 1990; see also Wright 1992). If such processes are reproduced more widely, it would lead to a significant disadvantaging of black students wherever internal selection took account of behavioural issues. It is perhaps worth noting that recently published statistics indicate that black students may suffer exceptionally large inequalities of achievement in science and mathematics (see Figure 8.8): two subjects that have historically fought for and retained relatively early and extensive use of setting in many secondary schools (Hallam and Toutounji 1996, p. 19).

South Asian students also seem likely to experience increased inequalities of opportunity through any extension in the use of selection within schools. Here, however, it is teachers' interpretation of linguistic abilities

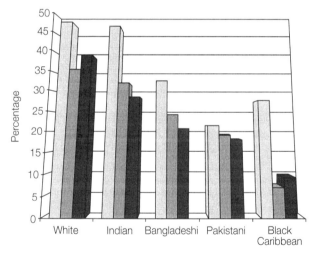

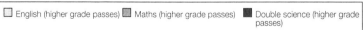

Figure 8.8   Ethnic origin and achievement in the core subjects for both sexes in one LEA (1994). Source: *African Caribbean Network for Science and Technology.*

that provides one of the major causes for concern. Specifically, it has been argued that Asian students might be placed in lower groups than they could cope with through teachers' misreading of *language* difficulties as deeper-seated *learning* problems (Troyna 1991; Troyna and Siraj-Blatchford 1993). The use of hierarchically organised teaching sets can add to the problem by institutionalising early judgements about the ability of Asian students:

> Sets were rarely changed, and, given that they played a large part in determining whether pupils could take GCSE courses in their fourth and fifth years – that is, the higher sets were the GCSE sets – for some pupils the final outcome was largely predetermined in their very first year. For the significant number of Asian pupils who were incorrectly set for Maths and English when they started at [secondary school], the chances of subsequently taking these subjects for GCSE examinations were low. (Commission for Racial Equality 1992, pp. 40–1)

Similar findings have emerged from international research on the social consequences of grouping students by ability. In the United States, in particular, research has exposed the racialised character of such selection (Oakes 1985; 1990); there are increasing calls for a movement away from 'tracking' (broadly equivalent to streaming and banding in the United Kingdom) so as to equalize the chances that are substantively available to young people regardless of ethnic origin. James Banks, one of the leading American scholars in this field, summarises the situation as follows:

> The tracking system, which is widespread within U.S. schools, perpetuates social-class and ethnic inequality and teaches students to be content with their social-class status. The genetic paradigm is used to support and justify the tracking system. It perpetuates dominant ethnic group hegemony, inequality, and class and ethnic stratification. (Banks 1994, p. 114)

SUBJECT OPTIONS AT 14

> Option-allocation is a point at which school careers become firmly differentiated and at which the informal differences between pupils in terms of social reputation and their experiences of the curriculum lower down the school are formalized into separate curricular routes and examination destinations. (Ball 1981, p. 152)

As we have seen, many schools retain some form of internal selection, if

only for a minority of subjects at the later stages of compulsory education. In the same way that policy-makers are now encouraging greater
use of grouping by ability, so it seems likely that *another* source of
internal selection seems ready to make a comeback: the subjects options
process.

Prior to the introduction of the National Curriculum, in the Education Reform Act (ERA) 1988, most secondary schools operated some
form of subject options system whereby students followed a common
curriculum for the first three years of secondary education, but then
faced a 'choice' as to the kinds of subject they would study for the
remaining two years, possibly towards external examination. The ERA
signalled a move away from such a reliance on options systems: the
National Curriculum dominated teaching time in secondary schools,
leaving much less scope for curricular choice and specialisation. Nevertheless, many schools seem to have retained a modified version (see, for
example, Harris *et al.* 1996). However, in view of the reduced statutory
component of the National Curriculum, following Dearing's 1994
report, there now seems scope for a return to options – particularly in
view of his recommendations that learning and examinations should
identify separate pathways beginning at 14 and moving through to the
age of 18 or 19. It is too soon to report on new research into the contemporary situation. However, it may be useful to examine the lessons of
previous research that analysed the role of subject options processes
prior to the ERA.

Most published research on subject options processes indicates that,
despite the rhetoric of 'choice' that commonly features in schools' pre-
sentations (to students and their parents), the systems actually represent
a point of significant academic selection. In particular, students identified as 'able' are encouraged to choose high status options, with a good
record of achievement and a wider reputation as 'academic' subjects;
alternatively, many students are 'cooled out' (Ball 1981, after Goffman
1952), that is, encouraged to lower their sights, be more 'realistic' and
choose 'appropriate' subjects – of lesser academic standing (Abraham
1995; Ball 1981; Hurman 1978; Woods 1976; 1977; 1979). Where schools
operate some form of internal selection during the first three years of
secondary education (streaming, banding and/or setting) this has been
seen to exert a particularly strong influence. Iain Smith and Dave
Woodhouse, for example, used standardised tests, questionnaires and
interviews to examine options processes in four 11–18 mixed comprehensives; they concluded that band and set positions can act as 'the

dominant cues whereby teachers make judgements about pupils and whereby pupils make judgements about themselves' (Smith and Woodhouse 1982, p. 47). In this way, early selection within comprehensives can bestow relatively fixed labels on students which crystallise in the options process to produce a form of curricular stratification that echoes earlier divisions between grammar and secondary modern schools:

> Despite the notions of equality of opportunity that have been attached to the reorganization of comprehensive education, the internal organization of the schools may still allow the maintenance of a system of early selection and separate provision of curriculum, that is essentially similar to that of tripartitism and sponsorship. (Ball 1981, p. 152)

Where early selection was less pronounced (for example, through the use of mixed-ability teaching for most subjects in the lower school) studies produced contrasting findings. Stephen Ball argues that in 'Beachside Comprehensive', following the introduction of mixed-ability teaching, staff intervened less often to warm up/cool out students (Ball 1981). In contrast, during a two-year ethnography (of City Road Comprehensive), I found that the majority of students were involved in some form of further negotiation with staff following their initial choice of subjects: of the three mixed-ability tutor groups I followed through the options process only seven students (10 per cent) eventually gained access to all their chosen courses without further negotiation (Gillborn 1987, p. 93). More than half the students (56 per cent) had a formal meeting (involving a parent/guardian and members of staff); the remainder (34 per cent) had some form of informal negotiation with a member of staff. Regardless of the nature of the negotiation (formal or informal) in both cases more than two out of every three students emerged from the meetings with one or more changes to their original choices. Despite the rhetoric of choice that surrounded the process in City Road, therefore, students experienced a good deal of staff intervention. Furthermore, the intervention often resulted in significant changes to the academic status of the 'chosen' subjects: 21 per cent of changes moved a student from a subject with low academic status to one of high status (warming up); 33 per cent of changes shifted students from an 'academic' to non-academic subject (cooling out)[4] (Gillborn 1987, pp. 165–7).

As I have already noted, of course, teachers' assessments of 'ability' and aptitude have frequently been examined for signs of bias against

particular groups of students. Ball's analysis of banding and options decisions ascribes an especially important role to issues of social class, where:

> The experiential differences between the band 1 (predominantly middle-class) forms, and the band 2 and band 3 (predominantly working-class) forms include curricular differences, syllabus differences, pedagogical differences, and relational differences. (Ball 1981, p. 281)

The role of student gender has also been examined and reveals the subject options process to be a point of differentiation where the gendered expectations of both teachers and students frequently lead to a closing down of opportunities for female students, even when their 'ability' is thought to be high (see, for example, Delamont 1990; Gillborn 1990; Measor and Sikes 1992; Pratt *et al*. 1984; Riddell 1992).

Relatively little work has focused on the role of race and ethnicity in subject options processes. A major survey of 18 multi-ethnic comprehensives included questionnaires to students about their views of the process and observations of meetings between students, parents and teachers. Although little space was devoted to this aspect of the research in the main report (Smith and Tomlinson 1989), more detail is available in a separate paper and an unpublished report (Tomlinson 1987; Tomlinson and Tomes 1986). The study highlights the wide variation in option procedures between schools and concludes that 'Curriculum option choice at 13+ ... can be regarded as a structural inequality' (Tomlinson 1987, p. 106). The main report attempts to disentangle the influences of prior attainment, social class, ethnic origin and gender. It notes that ethnic minority students were over-represented in 'lower course levels', but indicates that this may be explained in terms of differences in prior attainments and social class (Smith and Tomlinson 1989, p. 216). The more detailed accounts of the options research make greater use of qualitative material and note that, in practice, issues related to ethnic origin might inter-relate with judgements about ability and behaviour in complex, sometimes hidden, ways:

> Although ability is supposedly the major criterion for placement in subject and examination levels, ability is an ambiguous concept and school conceptions of ability can be affected by perceptions that pupils are members of particular social or ethnic groups and by the behaviour of individual pupils. (Tomlinson 1987, p. 106)

When the experiences of ethnic minority students are examined in detail, a number of inequalities emerge from the data. Sally Tomlinson and Hilary Tomes' report to the Department of Education and Science, for example, demonstrates that students for whom English is a second language 'were likely to have a more restricted curriculum and be guided to non-exam options' (1986, p. 202): a finding supported by the Commision for Racial Equality (CRE)'s later research on the placement of Asian students in set groups (see above). Black students 'felt they had less choice, as did pupils of manual working-class, non-working and single parents . . . The 'white middle-class male from the two-parent family' was most satisfied at option time' (Tomlinson and Tomes 1986, p. 205). By coincidence, my own ethnographic research in City Road Comprehensive overlapped with Tomlinson and Tomes' work: not only was the school part of both projects, but students in the same year group were the focus of attention. Because my work involved a more detailed study of only one school, the research offers an interesting complement to the more broadly based survey. Of particular significance is the way that African Caribbean students were more likely to experience apparently spontaneous challenges to their option choices. Typically a student would be passing a teacher in the corridor, or leaving a lesson, when the teacher would ask them what subjects they had chosen. The enquiry would frequently turn into a challenge, with the student asked to defend his or her choice in opposition to some other alternative, often a subject of less academic standing, such as one of the 'applied' (non-examination) courses offered in the school. The following extract, for example, is based on field notes reporting a teacher's attempt to have an African Caribbean young man reconsider his options:

TEACHER: There's a lot of science there. Physics – a lot of maths, which you don't get on with do you? You can tell me to *[he blows a raspberry]* but I'm wondering if you should do 'applied science' . . . *[After recapping on the mathematics involved in physics]* They might not explain it properly, just quickly mention it, then expect you to know it. And there's nothing worse than not knowing what's going off. If I were you I'd avoid physics like the plague. (quoted in Gillborn 1990, p. 139)

In the case of white and Asian students even the slightest challenge from teachers was usually sufficient to bring about a change; this was not the case with African Caribbean students who often resisted such pressure, even when it became as insistent as the 'advice' above. In this way, black students in City Road were able to retain many of their choices – exploiting the rhetoric of choice in the system. Nevertheless, their greater receipt of such 'spontaneous' enquiries meant that they had to fight harder than peers to retain their chosen subjects. Furthermore, it is unlikely that the black students could have achieved the same results if the system were to have adopted a more authoritarian character, by abandoning its claim to give students a choice.

CONCLUSIONS: WATCH THESE SPACES

This chapter has sought to identify the importance of ethnic origin as a factor in young people's experience and achievement in education 14–19: to date research reveals, first, that many young people of ethnic minority background face additional hurdles to success in the current system; and, second, it suggests that the future may subject the same students to increasing disadvantage. Issues of race and ethnicity no longer feature prominently in the mainstream of educational debate: indeed, the majority of contemporary social policy is presented in a deracialised fashion such that matters of racial and ethnic inequality are removed from the agenda (Gillborn 1995; Troyna 1993). This provides a context where existing inequalities may be sustained, and even extended, without critique.

In many ways Ron Dearing's review of qualifications for 16–19-year-olds (Dearing 1996) exemplifies the characteristics of recent policy-making in education: race and ethnicity are given little serious attention and, when they are addressed, the issues are viewed in terms of the limitations of students, rather than structural constraints working on and through the education system itself. For example, the report assigns just three paragraphs specifically to 'Ethnic issues' (Dearing 1996, paras 14.22–14.24, pp. 130–1) and refers to a single piece of research (by the Further Education Development Agency (FEDA)). The paragraphs show no awareness of research on racism (operating in the classroom via teachers' expectations or institutionally through selection): all we have are statements about young people for whom English is a second language, the need for learning (and language) support and the problems that can arise if examinations clash with 'religious festivals'. In short, it is a simplistic and patronizing picture of the ways ethnic origin might relate to achievement and experience – one that singularly fails to see racism (in any form) as an issue.

Under the heading 'Countering stereotypes' another two paragraphs build on the FEDA study, noting that 'the qualifications framework alone will not redress patterns of under-achievement. The quality of student–teacher relationships and of the learning experience, and the way in which expectations are shaped by stereotypes, are influential factors' (Dearing 1996, para 14.31, p. 132). This could have offered an opportunity to address the kinds of inequality of experience highlighted earlier in this chapter; unfortunately, the concern with 'under-achievement', 'student–teacher relationships' and 'stereotypes' does not find translation into race issues nor the consequences of selection/stereotyping by teachers. On the contrary, the subsequent paragraph presents stereotyping as a problem resting in the mind of young people (rather than their teachers) and although the Equal Opportunities Commission is mentioned, no parallel role is envisaged for the Commission for Racial Equality:

> Young people often have in their minds stereotypes of suitable and realistic ways forward, whether in education or work. Such stereotypes may help to sustain patterns of under-achievement by race, class, gender and disability. . . . Those from less favoured backgrounds may have stereotyped concepts of what may be feasible options for them, based on family experience and expectations. These are issues which those giving careers education and guidance need to have in mind. The Equal Opportunities Commission has agreed the specification for training of Careers Service staff so that the advice they provide to young people, and to employers about placements, is non discriminatory and does not reinforce stereotyped occupational choices. (Dearing 1996, para. 14.32: p. 132)

The Dearing review, therefore, follows dominant trends in contemporary policy discourse: race and ethnicity are marginalised while racism disappears from view altogether. In this context there is an urgent need for practitioners and researchers to keep these issues in sight and, where possible, to work against the inequalities. Current patterns of post-compulsory participation highlight the great value placed on education by many ethnic minority young people, their parents and communities. These communities have shown themselves to be immensely resourceful, strong and resilient: given current trends in 14–19 education there is reason to believe that those qualities will be needed as much in the future as ever they were in the past.

ACKNOWLEDGEMENT

I would like to thank all the teachers and students who have given their time to participate in my research. Thanks also to Deborah Youdell for her perceptive comments on an earlier draft.

NOTES

1 Around 5.5 per cent of the British population was identified as of ethnic minority background in the 1991 census. The largest groups are of African Caribbean and South Asian (Indian, Pakistani and Bangladeshi) origin: accounting for 78.6 per cent of the minority population (Runnymede Trust 1994, p. 12).

2 In Figure 8.1 South Asian students appear to achieve relatively well; sometimes attaining higher averages than white students of the same sex and social class. However, the use of the combined category (South Asian) has been criticised: more detailed breakdowns reveal considerable differences between different South Asian groups – discussed in detail later in this chapter.

3 A student's 'examination score' is calculated by assigning a number value to each GCSE grade awarded: 8 for an A* 7 for an A; 6 for a B; 5 for a C; and so on until 1 point for a G and no points for a U (unclassified). The sum of each student's grades gives their examination score.

4 For the purposes of these calculations the academic character of each subject was determined in relation to the availability and status of equivalent A-level subjects in applications for university entry. This distinction echoed internal status differences within City Road (see Gillborn 1987, pp. 143–56).

REFERENCES

Abraham, J. (1995) *Divide and School: Gender and Class Dynamics in Comprehensive Education*. London: Falmer.

Baker, K. (1996) 'The last ten years: the next ten years', a public lecture at the University of London, Institute of Education, 3 June 1996.

Ball, S.J. (1981) *Beachside Comprehensive: A Case Study of Secondary Schooling*. Cambridge: Cambridge University Press.

Banks, J.A. (1994) *Multiethnic Education: Theory and Practice*, 3rd edn. Boston: Allyn and Bacon.

Bates, I. and Riseborough, G. (eds)(1993) *Youth and Inequality*. Buckingham: Open University Press.

Blair, T. (1995) 'Speech to the Labour Party Conference', *News from Labour*. London: Labour Party.

Blair, T. (1996) Transcript from a speech as broadcast on BBC TV *Newsnight*, 7 June.

Brent (1994) *Report Summarising the Analysis of the 1993 GCSE Results*. London Borough of Brent.

Camden (1995) *Analysis of 1994 London Reading Test and GCSE Results by Ethnic Group: Report of the Director of Education to the Education (Strategy) Sub-Committee*. London Borough of Camden.

Commission for Racial Equality (1992) *Set to Fail? Setting and Banding in Secondary Schools*. London: Commission for Racial Equality.

Cox, R.E. (1979) 'Education', in David C. Marsh (ed.), *Introducing Social Policy*. London: Routledge and Kegan Paul.

Dearing, R. (1994) *The National Curriculum and its Assessment: Final Report*. London: School Curriculum and Assessment Authority.

Dearing, R. (1996) *Review of Qualifications for 16–19 Year Olds: Full Report*, Ref. COM/96/460. London: School Curriculum and Assessment Authority.

Delamont, S. (1990) *Sex Roles in the School*, 2nd edn. London: Routledge.

DfEE (Department for Education and Employment) (1996) *Self-Government for Schools*, Cm 3315. London: HMSO.

Doe, B. (1995) 'They also can achieve who live in the lower ranks', *Times Educational Supplement*, 27 October, TES 2, p. 6.

Drew, D. (1995) *'Race', Education and Work: The Statistics of Inequality*. Aldershot: Avebury.

Drew, D. and Gray, J. (1990) 'The fifth year examination achievements of black young people in England and Wales', *Educational Research*, 32 (3), pp. 107–17.

Drew, D. and Gray, J. (1991) 'The Black–White gap in examination results: a statistical critique of a decade's research', *New Community*, 17 (2), pp. 159–72.

Drew, D., Gray, J. and Sime, N. (1992) *Against the Odds: The Education and Labour Market Experiences of Black Young People. England and Wales Youth Cohort Study*, Report R&D no. 68. Sheffield: Employment Department.

Drew, D., Gray, J. and Sporton, D. (1994) 'Ethnic differences in the educational participation of 16–19 year olds', unpublished paper presented at the OPCS/ESRC Census Analysis Group Conference, University of Leeds, September.

Eggleston, S.J., Dunn, D.K. and Anjali, M. (1986) *Education for Some: The Educational and Vocational Experiences of 15–18 Year Old Members of Minority Ethnic Groups*. Stoke-on-Trent: Trentham.

Elwood, J. (1995) 'Gender, equity and the Gold Standard: examination and coursework performance in the UK at 18', paper presented at the special session 'Equity issues in education', Annual Meeting of the American Educational Research Association, San Francisco.

Foster, P. (1990a) 'Cases not proven: an evaluation of two studies of teacher racism', *British Educational Research Journal*, 16 (4), pp. 335–49.

Foster, P. (1990b) *Policy and Practice in Multicultural and Anti-Racist Education*. London: Routledge.

Fuller, M. (1980) 'Black girls in a London comprehensive school', in M.

Hammersley and P. Woods (eds) (1984) *Life in School: The Sociology of Pupil Culture*. Milton Keynes: Open University Press, pp. 77–88.

Gillborn, D. (1987) 'The negotiation of educational opportunity: the final years of compulsory schooling in a multi-ethnic inner city comprehensive', Unpublished PhD thesis, University of Nottingham.

Gillborn, D. (1990) *'Race', Ethnicity and Education: Teaching and Learning in Multi-Ethnic Schools*. London: Unwin-Hyman/Routledge.

Gillborn, D. (1995) *Racism and Antiracism in Real Schools: Theory, Policy, Practice*. Buckingham: Open University Press.

Gillborn, D. and Gipps, C. (1996) *Recent Research on the Achievements of Ethnic Minority* Pupils. London: HMSO.

Gipps, C. and Murphy, P. (1994) *A Fair Test? Assessment, Achievement and Equity*. Buckingham: Open University Press.

Goffman, E. (1952) 'On cooling the mark out', *Psychiatry*, 25, pp. 451–63.

Hagell, A. and Shaw, C. (1996) *Opportunity and Disadvantage at Age 16*. London: Policy Studies Institute.

Hallam, S. and Toutounji, I. (1996) *What Do We Know About the Grouping of Pupils by Ability? A Research Review*. London: University of London Institute of Education.

Harris, S., Rudduck, J. and Wallace, G. (1996) 'Political contexts and school careers', in M. Hughes (ed.), *Teaching and Learning in Changing Times*. Oxford: Basil Blackwell.

HMI (Her Majesty's Inspectorate) (1978) *Mixed Ability Work in Comprehensive Schools*. London: HMSO.

Hurman, A. (1978) *A Charter for Choice: A Study of Options Schemes*. Windsor: NFER.

Mac an Ghaill, M. (1988) *Young, Gifted and Black: Student–Teacher Relations in the Schooling of Black Youth*. Milton Keynes: Open University Press.

Measor, L. and Sikes, P. (1992) *Gender and Schools*. London: Cassell.

Mirza, H.S. (1992) *Young, Female and Black*. London: Routledge.

National Curriculum Council (1991) *Report on Monitoring the Implementation of the National Curriculum Core Subjects: 1989–1990*. York: National Curriculum Council.

Newsam, P. (1996) 'Capital idea', *Times Educational Supplement*, 7 June, p. 16.

Nuttall, D.L., Goldstein, H., Prosser, R. and Rasbash, J. (1989) 'Differential school effectiveness', *International Journal of Educational Research*, 13, pp. 769–76.

Oakes, J. (1985) *Keeping Track: How Schools Structure Inequality*. New Haven: Yale University Press.

Oakes, J. (1990) *Multiplying Inequalities: The Effects of Race, Social Class, and Tracking on Opportunities to Learn Mathematics and Science*. Santa Monica, CA: Rand Corporation.

Payne, J. (1995) *Routes Beyond Compulsory Schooling. England and Wales Youth Cohort*, Study Report no. 31. Sheffield: Employment Department.

Pratt, J., Bloomfield, J. and Seale, C. (1984) *Option Choice: A Question of Equal Opportunity*. Windsor: NFER.

Rampton, A. (1981) *West Indian Children in Our Schools*, Cmnd 8273. London: HMSO.

Rattansi, A. (1992) 'Changing the subject? Racism, culture and education', in J. Donald and A. Rattansi (eds), *'Race', Culture and Difference*. London: Sage.

Riddell, S. (1992) *Gender and the Politics of the Curriculum*. London: Routledge.

Rizvi, F. (1993) 'Race, gender and the cultural assumptions of schooling', in C. Marshall (ed.), *The New Politics of Race and Gender*. London: Falmer.

Runnymede Trust (1994) *Multi-Ethnic Britain: Facts and Trends*. London: Runnymede Trust.

Smith, D.J. and Tomlinson, S. (1989) *The School Effect: A Study of Multi-Racial Comprehensives*. London: Policy Studies Institute.

Smith, I. and Woodhouse, D. (1982) 'Sorting Them Out', unpublished interim report to the Social Science Research Council.

Swann, Lord (1985) *Education for All: Final Report of the Committee of Inquiry into the Education of Children from Ethnic Minority Groups*, Cmnd 9453. London: HMSO.

Tomlinson, S. (1983) *Ethnic Minorities in British Schools: A Review of the Literature, 1960–1982*. London: Heinemann Educational with the Policy Studies Institute.

Tomlinson, S. (1987) 'Curriculum option choices in multi-ethnic schools', in B. Troyna (ed.), *Racial Inequality in Education*. London: Tavistock.

Tomlinson, S. (1992) 'Disadvantaging the disadvantaged: Bangladeshis and education in Tower Hamlets', *British Journal of Sociology of Education*, 13 (4), pp. 437–46.

Tomlinson, S. and Tomes, H. (1986) 'Curriculum Option Choice in Multi-Ethnic Schools', unpublished project report to the Department of Education and Science.

Troyna, B. (1984) 'Fact or artefact? The "educational underachievement" of black pupils', *British Journal of Sociology of Education*, 5(2), pp. 153–66.

Troyna, B. (1991) 'Underachievers or underrated? The experiences of pupils of South Asian origin in a secondary school', *British Educational Research Journal*, 17(4), pp. 361–76.

Troyna, B. (1993) *Racism and Education: Research Perspectives*. Buckingham: Open University Press.

Troyna, B. and Siraj-Blatchford, I. (1993) 'Providing support or denying access? The experiences of students designated as 'ESL' and 'SN' in a multi-ethnic secondary school', *Educational Review*, 45(1), pp. 3–11.

Weis, L. (ed.) (1988) *Class, Race and Gender in American Education*. Albany: State University of New York Press.

Woods, P. (1976) 'The myth of subject choice', *British Journal of Sociology*, 27 (2), pp. 130–49.

Woods, P. (1977) 'How teachers decide pupils' subject choices', *Cambridge Journal of Education*, vol. 7, pp. 21–32.

Woods, P. (1979) *The Divided School*. London: Routledge and Kegan Paul.

Wright, C. (1986) 'School processes – an ethnographic study', in J. Eggleston,

D. Dunn and M. Anjali (eds), *Education for Some: The Educational and Vocational Experiences of 15–18 year old Members of Minority Ethnic Groups.* Stoke-on-Trent: Trentham.

Wright, C. (1987) 'Black students – white teachers', in B. Troyna (ed.), *Racial Inequality in Education.* London: Tavistock.

Wright, C. (1990) 'Comments in reply to the article by P. Foster, 'Cases not proven: an evaluation of two studies of teacher racism'', *British Educational Research Journal,* 16 (4), pp. 351–5.

Wright, C. (1992) *Race Relations in the Primary School.* London: David Fulton.

Young, G. and Dickerson, B.J. (1994) *Color, Class and Country: Experiences of Gender.* London: Zed.

9

Girls in the Sixth Form
Tamsyn Imison

This chapter presents two students' perspectives on completing their studies in an inner city school sixth form, elicited during conversations with the headteacher in June 1996. The two girls are friends. One has come through a very unsettled and disturbed family disintegration and had to grow up before her time. The other comes from a very supportive family background where her family chose to send her to the local mixed comprehensive school. The borough has 23 more forms of entry for girls than boys as there are four girls' schools, three of which operate some selection, one small boys' school and five mixed schools. This results in a serious imbalance in the mixed sector, although this school had managed, by targeting and supporting girls, to retain almost equal numbers.

The school is a large mixed county comprehensive with nearly 1,300 students and with about 250 in the sixth form. About 55 per cent of students are bilingual learners and between them speak over 80 different home languages. There are over 150 asylum seekers in school – 50 arriving in this country as unaccompanied minors. The OFSTED inspection in June 1996 described the school as good because of the quality of its teaching, with over 60 per cent of lessons observed rating good to outstanding. The number staying on post-16 in 1984 was 30 per cent of the fifth-year roll. Since 1990 this number has been over 90 per cent. The expectation from all staff is for every student to stay on, and all careers education and guidance in the school is geared accordingly.

There is a large core taught at Key Stage 4 to all students – English language and literature, mathematics, double integrated science, technology, one of the modern languages, humanities and creative arts. This has ensured all girls take science, mathematics and technology, and equal numbers of girls and boys go on to A-level courses in those areas. If it were possible the school would like to complete Key Stage 3 in two years and then teach Key Stage 4 for three years to ensure a better spread of languages, humanities and creative arts. At present additional subjects are only offered in twilight sessions. At Key Stage 5 the school offers A-levels and General National Vocational Qualifications (GNVQs) at foundation, intermediate and advanced level.

Students' perspectives are both important and valid and are considered carefully before shaping and developing policy. The issues the young women were asked about were those currently of concern to the senior executive team: what makes students leave and/or stay on; supporting girls in mixed comprehensives; the new issue – raising boys' achievement; sixth-form induction; supporting the leap from General Certificate of Secondary Education (GCSE) to A-level; bridging the academic–vocational divide; the use and value of work experience; retaining a liberal humanist tradition where education is valued for its own sake; supporting students in making realistic and flexible career plans; ensuring maximum progression; financial support for those post-16 and beyond; political agendas for education; and, most important, teachers' effectiveness in making a difference to the students' understanding, enjoyment and achievements.

Issues that were significant to the school in listening and reflecting on sixth-form students' perceptions included:

- the real warmth shown by students towards each other and towards teachers;
- the confidence of girls;
- the mature understanding of students to both inside and outside agendas, particularly those of government;
- the value students place on being given conceptual frameworks and time frames for their studies;
- students' appreciation of the zest and energy, the professional commitment and the scholarship of teachers;
- students' awareness that schools need to improve further.

The students' awareness of issues may have been influenced by the 'School Statement of Intent' which declares that:
At Hampstead School everyone will strive to:

- enjoy the challenges and achievements of learning
- develop individual strengths
- experience academic, social and personal success
- manage setbacks
- develop consideration and co-operation

within a stimulating and supportive environment and with the support of family and the wider community.

CONVERSATION WITH SIXTH FORM GIRLS, JUNE 1996

DEBBIE: My name is Debbie Shaw, eighteen, been coming to school since year seven, started 1989. Still here.

'Enjoyed it?'

DEBBIE: I've had a good time here. This school has definitely done a lot for me. I nearly dropped out a few years back but I came back of course because it's a good school. No , I have very much enjoyed my stay here. I have seen a lot of teachers come and go and a lot of changes, good changes I might add. I feel, I am sorry to leave actually, I am quite sad about leaving because I feel part of the school.

HARRIET: My name is Harriet Carter. I am eighteen years old. I have also been here since year seven. I nearly left to go to sixth form college but I didn't; and I stayed.

Do you think that was a good decision?

HARRIET: Yes I do. Yeah.

What made you stay?

HARRIET: The same reason I was thinking of going – people know you . They know your capabilities. They know your bad tendencies and they tend to pick you up on it. There is a supportive atmosphere. I felt I wanted to go out and strike out on my own, but I decided that that support might come in handy during A-levels so I stayed and I am happy I did. On the whole, I am happy here. It is a very good school and I know if I had my time over again I would come here. I would choose to come here every time [*Debbie echoes this*] which is not a set thing for me, being middle class, I could have gone to a posh school with a uniform but I wasn't having any.

So what about a mixed school, the pair of you, because a lot of people say that girls' schools are much better for girls.

HARRIET: Rubbish!

DEBBIE: I don't agree at all, because, I think that the idea of school is to prepare you for life outside of school, and whether you be male or female, going to a single sex school is not going to sufficiently prepare you for life outside of school, because you are never going to be in a single sex environment. Obviously, there may be jobs dominated by females or males, but on the whole, you are never going to be in a single sex environment.

Well, you haven't felt daunted by the boys?

HARRIET: Quite the opposite. I think the boys have been daunted by us. The old argument used to be that, academically speaking, girls did better in a single sex environment, and increasingly that isn't the case. Where it was it could be attributed to privilege, and it's just not like that anymore. Any argument for it has gone out of the window, quite frankly, and being female has never been an issue. I mean, if anything, it is the girls that dominate the boys!

You don't think it is bad for the boys having the girls in there?

DEBBIE: No! No!

HARRIET: No! No, not at all! But I think, increasingly, boys need encouragement. And now we have the emphasis on the girls, and girls do feel supported, certainly up to GCSE level. 'Boys, some of them, are falling by the wayside and obviously that's got to do with things outside of education itself, but I can see it becoming a bit of a problem. I feel sorry for them, not threatened by them, actually.

Do you see any difference in the way the school is organised pre-sixteen and post-sixteen? and what are the pluses and minuses of this?

DEBBIE: It is definitely very different.

Has that helped you stay, do you think?

DEBBIE: Well yes, the reason that I stayed is pretty much the same as Harriet. I felt that I was part of it. Then, all the teachers knew me and so on and I wanted to kind of use that support. It is definitely very different. The reason I wanted to leave was because I thought it was going to be another two years of the same, and obviously, having been here for five years, you start to feel a little bit fed up. But it was nice to start the sixth form because the atmosphere is a lot more relaxed, more informal. I think you have a better relationship with your teachers.

HARRIET: Oh yes! I get on better with my teachers than some of my year.

DEBBIE: Yes. I get on better with the teachers than the students in some cases.

Did the Induction help you? [2]

HARRIET: It was wonderful!

DEBBIE: I thought that was great! The History of Ideas was brilliant! I know there were some that didn't appreciate it, but I can only pity them. I really enjoyed that. It was a revelation in fact.

HARRIET: It was the most brilliant induction course, because it set you up for A-levels.

So what did you get out of it?

DEBBIE: I learnt a lot in just two weeks. Its not about learning specific facts. Its more of getting a kind of 'concept' of – everything.

HARRIET: It's the sense of chronology. Our A-levels are so intensive, and by their very nature they have to be very narrow. The whole thing can pass you by sometimes; and yet, the History of Ideas puts things into a context. For instance, doing lyrical ballads, you are able to look at that, in the period of romanticism, as a reaction against the age that went before it, whereas you might not have done that. It encourages you to go away and to do it for yourself – knowledge for knowledge's sake – so it was a good idea, especially in this day and age.

DEBBIE: Some of the lecturers were wonderful! Obviously there was the odd one that was not too good but – I loved the Leonardo da Vinci guy!

HARRIET: Everyone loved him!

DEBBIE: Some of the lectures were really really good and I was sorry when they ended. I really did enjoy the History of Ideas. It put a lot of ideas into context. A lot of A-levels are different subjects – economics, sociology, psychology – all these different A-levels, but they all have a basis in similar things. I am doing Sociology and I know what Sociology is about and that's it, but having done the History of Ideas I have an idea of where all these A-levels are coming from and what they are trying to teach. I think it was very beneficial to me.

Did you think there was anything special in that for girls or did you think it would be equally good for boys?

DEBBIE: There was the Emmeline Pankhurst in the balloon debate! and James's helpful comment about women drivers that went down really well!

HARRIET: It's always James, isn't it! Apart from that I can't see it really made any difference what gender you were. It was an experience, and if you were open to it, it was good, and if not you missed out!

Do you think it was good that the A-levels and GNVQ Induction was separate in your year?[3]

HARRIET: I thought that was sad. In a way I think it could have been even more valuable for the GNVQ group to do it, because the qualifications they are working for are far more vocational, aren't they? Because of that, it would have been nice to have given them more variety. They joined us occasionally and that was great, but there is a very firm division between A-levels and GNVQs. It is very easy to kind of think you are a little better or a bit superior because you are a bit more on the intellectual side and I don't think that is an idea to be encouraged, really, and it is especially easy to do when you do have these divisions on things like that.

DEBBIE: There definitely is a clear division between GNVQ students and A-level students.

HARRIET: Very much so.

DEBBIE: And I wasnt too happy with that. I would probably be even less happy with it if I was a GNVQ student.

Have you any ideas for changing it?

HARRIET: Bring them in!

DEBBIE: I can understand why. Perhaps some GNVQ students might not be interested in the History of Ideas because they may feel it is not necessary for them and their qualifications.

How would you sell it to them?

HARRIET: Well, it's useful on a number of grounds, apart from the knowledge they are having accessed. It introduces you to your year. It sets you up and it introduces you to new ideas which are valuable in themselves, rather than for what you are doing. That's the idea that should be encouraged, really. Aside from setting you up for your A-levels and seeing things in context, it is interesting. It is good to know it for itself, really. Go to a museum. Listen to someone speaking. You might not agree with them. You might not find them particularly interesting, but you give them a hearing. I think you have got to approach it from that angle really. Some A-level people weren't interested and some of them were a bit rude, but – tough: you sit through it and you learn to sit through it.

Do you think that your A-level courses should be more vocational?

DEBBIE: No! I don't, because vocational courses are very good and they are very well recognised by employers. I dont think that A levels can be taken on their own. I don't think it is wise to stop there. A-levels are there to prepare you for more, for higher education, and I think vocational A-levels wouldn't work. That is the idea behind it isn't it? What I think is wrong, fundamentally, is the idea that education is simply to prepare you for the world of work, to set you up for a job. I don't think that that is what it should be about. I don't even think that the emphasis should be wholly on the academic. You know the nice thing about our school is that it turns out nice citizens. It turns out good people. You know, you don't care what colour someone is or where they're from because you have been there, seen it and got the tee shirt and it's not an issue. You know, I think that is the good thing about this school and I think that should be encouraged.

Had you both thought about a career when you first came?

DEBBIE: At Year Seven? Not really, but yes, when I was a kid, obviously I had the kind of dreams every kid has. Mine in particular was writing. I would like to do journalism or go into the media. I'm going to Bristol University to do English Literature.

Did your work experience help you?[4]

HARRIET: Well, the one at GCSE was useful because it taught me exactly what I didn't want to do ever!

Well that is quite useful!

HARRIET: Yes! This is the view I take, even if you have a really miserable time, at least you know what you don't want to do, so it is not a wasted couple of weeks. I managed to break every machine in the place at one stage. I was doing office work. I was at 'NewTec'. They had donated a computer. Some were very nice people. Some of them didn't want to know because I wasn't important. I just went about feeling invisible and inadequate for two weeks; but no, I met some nice people there as well and some surprising people for the kind of work it was. The one I did at A-level, that was good. I worked in chambers for a week and then, the other week, I was with Joy [Refugee Co-ordinator and Head of Year 11] in her office and that was all useful stuff. It was family law I was with. I wouldn't go on to that. I saw some of the ugliest cases. It is the nastiest side of people, but it was really interesting and it was a worthwhile experience in itself.

What are your A-levels?

HARRIET: History, English and Sociology. I want to do a History degree at Leeds.

What do you want to do eventually, then?

HARRIET: This is a problem. I might just go and do another one.

DEBBIE: Yes, that's – I might never stop!

HARRIET: I can see myself riding out for the rest of my life and never doing anything responsible!

DEBBIE: No – do more and more and get degrees.

So how are you going to finance yourselves during this next training phase? Or, in fact, how do you finance yourselves at the moment? It's not easy, is it, in the sixth form, because you don't get funding.

HARRIET: It is more of a problem for Debbie than me, because I have got my mum at the moment. Yea! In the future I will try to get a grant. I will be eligible for something. I will get a job. At the moment, I am trying to set myself up, doing bar work, because once you have done that, once you know how to pull a pint, you can find a job somewhere. I have got friends working there, so it will be quite nice. But, it will be a struggle whatever we do. There is no certainty any more.

DEBBIE: I have always had money problems so I don't expect that, and I know that for a lot of people going to university will be a shock, because they are going to be broke and they won't have experienced that before and they will be kind of destitute. I have been there and done that and I know that it is not going to be much of a change, to be quite honest. Maybe a slight change, but not much. I did have a Saturday job up to February of this year from when I was fifteen but I gave it up because I wanted to concentrate on my exams, and I am now just about to start a job this summer, seeing what I can do, saving up a little bit, and hopefully with the way I am working at the moment when I go to York I may be transferred, it is a large company and I hope to keep the job up there.

Do you both envisage some sort of job to keep you going?

BOTH: Oh yes, yes definitely. We have to these days.

What about the student loan? Will you take advantage of that?

HARRIET: Do we have a choice?! Am I going to be in debt when I am forty?!

DEBBIE: The Government, they are still giving grants but they are due to change that pretty soon. I will get the full government grant, I know that much. Three-quarters or more is going to go on accommodation.

HARRIET: It doesn't stretch, does it?

DEBBIE: The student loan is not an option, it is a necessity.

HARRIET: I am going to delay by one year and then I don't know what the situation will be like.

What are you going to do in your year off?

HARRIET: Work, hopefully – when I get a job in this pub. I could just lounge about but I would rather not do that. For the other half of the time I have a job in Eritraea.[5] I am going to be an assistant teacher. I am raising the money to do that myself and with the help of a trust. So, all being well, I will be doing that. It's a bit daunting, the idea of going off on your own for six months across the other side of the world. But if I do it and I get through it, I can face anything, and being an impoverished student will be welcome relief.

So what do you think the Government's agenda is for what we should be doing in school and how we should be preparing young people for work?

DEBBIE: At the risk of sounding slightly cynical, I'd say, all they really think is that education is very closely related to the economy of this country and that their kind of prime objective in educating young people is to make sure the economy benefits and not necessarily the young people involved. It's sad, actually, because learning, being educated for the economy is not always a good experience for yourself. You are not educated to the extent that you want to be. Some people are not even aware of this – that you are just being educated into the workforce to work, to make this country great, and they are not going to have any satisfaction.

HARRIET: You come to the conclusion that it is going to leave a large proportion of school-leavers disillusioned, having gained nothing, coming out with no qualifications, a bleak future and little hope for tomorrow. I think that is the aim of it. They do a grand job in some areas. Our school is one of the few notable exceptions.

They make it very difficult for schools to provide everybody with equal opportunities. We have limited resources and there are a number of people for whom you cannot provide. That's the way it is. There are lots of kids who gain nothing from school, and school isn't designed to do that at present. It is not there to give everyone the same chance and the same opportunity. There aren't the jobs. Society is not structured that way.

So you think the Government is behind this? To provide education at different levels?

HARRIET: Yes, to preserve the elite. There will be a few who filter through.

DEBBIE: And even those that do get through, those that do get qualifications, because I place a lot of value on knowledge and I personally kind of seek it wherever I go. That is why I am furthering my education. I am not necessarily furthering my education because I want this qualification and because I want this kind of job, although that is a factor, of course. But I am doing this for my own personal satisfaction, and I think that that attitude needs to be encouraged in all young people. I don't think the Government are doing that at all. I think that what the Government are saying is, 'We will teach you this if you prove to us that you have learnt it. We will give you a certificate and that means you can get a job.' Not, learn – have knowledge, not learn it because you want to learn it. I think with a value of knowledge in everybody, everybody would be better off...

HARRIET: Because the job market is as insecure as it is, an increasing emphasis is placed on qualifications, and so if you don't have them you are in an even worse situation than you might have been a few years ago.

*Do you think that the Government is right in feeling that educationalists
have failed, in that we are not producing students who know how to spell
and know the basic skills?*

HARRIET: I would be rather wary of that, of all this rubbishing of the
education system. A lot of schools do quite well, despite the lack of
support. I think that it is used as a justification for reintroducing
selection, not that it ever went away, but they are upping the amount
of selective schools and I don't agree with it. I don't like it. I went to a
school that I consider to be very good and that is a comprehensive. I
am very proud to be here and I didn't have to make that choice. You
have these OFSTED reports where they kind of fiddle about with the
figures and say you have got 90 per cent wonderful teaching and they
say you have 10 per cent bad. They say it supports for the education
system but it does the opposite. And that is what it is designed to do. It
is unhelpful.[6]

DEBBIE: Lots of statistics in newspapers, they would rather say that 15
per cent of children today aren't making the grade than say 85 per
cent of these children are doing really well in school. And it really
misleads people and people say 'Oh, our education system is disgrace-
ful.' Yes, Ok, there are a lot of schools where the students aren't
making the grade but there are a hell of a lot where they are. Our
school being one of them.

HARRIET: You don't build something up by knocking it down and you
don't instil faith in it and get people behind it and you don't get
society at large to support the system by saying it's rubbish.

DEBBIE: I think it is disgusting that schools have to do fund-raising. But
if we believed in our education system, if the Government and newspapers presented the picture – our schools are doing really well but we
want them to do better still, people would give their support, 'Ah, our
schools are doing really great! Let's help them out.' But people saying
our schools are 'Crap' basically and the teachers are terrible and no
one is learning anything. Who is going to want to contribute to that? I
don't think anybody.

HARRIET: Of course there is vast room for improvement. I am not suggesting otherwise. It's not constructive and it is not designed to be. I
have got no time for it. As with this latest thing that mixed-ability
teaching is awful and it should be outlawed. I had mixed-ability teaching all the way up the school to the third year. It did me no harm.
Quite the opposite. And I don't think there is much solid evidence to
suggest otherwise, really. I mean, you know, it doesn't hold you back.

It brings everyone forward and together you support each other and that's what the learning experience should be about, surely? I have no time for this.

DEBBIE: I really think the Government has got it wrong in where they place the emphasis because they just feed these young people. Although I am not blaming everybody, there are also a lot of teachers who really place the emphasis on just getting the certificate at the end of the year. I just think it is the wrong emphasis. And I don't think it produces the kind of people that there should be.

What sort of people should there be?

HARRIET: People who value knowledge for knowledge's sake, which is not a view that is widely held now because you cannot afford to hold it.

DEBBIE: Yea. Yea. But if you value knowledge for knowledge's sake then you will get the qualifications and you will have the knowledge to go into these really well paid jobs, which is of course everybody's aim.

What skills do you think you are going to be taking away with you from being at school?

HARRIET: I am highly socialised in a way I might not have been had I gone to another school, which is of great value. Because I could have bypassed this whole thing altogether. Not so much now that I live in a different street and what have you. But once upon a time I could have gone to a uniformed girls' school and not thought anything of it, As it is I didn't, I didn't go, and of course I wouldn't now. Even if there was a 99.9 per cent chance of my child coming out with mediocre qualifications I would send my child to the comprehensive. I don't care! But I could have gone through life blissfully happy and unaware. I have had a very valuable experience – you know you can't put a price on that. That is what it should all be about.

DEBBIE: And I could have gone the other way. I could have gone to a school which is not so successful as this one because, despite the fact that this is a comprehensive school, there are lots of middle-class people in this school and not being middle class myself I could have gone to a totally working-class comprehensive school and gone completely the opposite way from Harriet and never known about, I don't know how to term it, high society, culture .

HARRIET: That's not right. . . . The middle class is not superior, and here you've got a mix, and the different influences, and you have the room, and if they are in your class people chat about resources and you can bring them in. You are not in a position to do that in the working

classes because no one wants to know and that's the difference. . . . This school has been good for both of us for very different reasons.
What, then, is special about this school?
DEBBIE: It is advantageous to both middle class and working class because it has the full range. It is a proper comprehensive. It's not full of middle class, certainly not.
Is there anything about the school's agenda?
HARRIET: I think one good thing about our school – although it is very easy for me to say this because mine is the dominant culture, but where it might be more evident in other schools – there isn't the attempt to ram a specific set of ideas or way of life down peoples throats. I think the absence of morning prayers – I don't know how common things like that are, but I think it is really important because huge chunks of people would be completely alienated by that because it is not their experience. I mean I would be alienated even though even I am an atheist, but I would understand the language, but I think that's good and I think encouraging people to embrace other cultures and what have you. I think that is a very good idea. I certainly remember that being a big part of life in the lower school and I think that is very positive. It is very difficult for any one group to be that dominant because there are so many different cultures.
DEBBIE: For the most part, obviously, it's not always that people get on, because within the school, between the pupils, I don't think that there are prejudices as regards colour or culture or whatever. There could be a lot of these pupils whose parents do have prejudices but on entering the school you leave it behind and you are in your own world where I, being white, come into contact with black and more Asian people and people of many different cultures and, you know, I don't care. I get on well with all of them, that is a very good part of the school because that prepares you for life outside. Obviously I am not going to go somewhere, an environment where it is going to be one culture, one colour, one set of people. I am going to meet a lot of different people and I need to know how to cope with them.
Do you think you have met here those sort of teachers that people say 'There is one teacher or a couple of teachers who changed my life or have made a difference to me'?
HARRIET: Yes, great.
DEBBIE: The majority of them actually. The thing about teachers here as a whole is that they genuinely care about you and about what happens to you in the future. They don't kind of say, 'OK, I am going to teach

you this, you will get an A and that will make me look good.' I mean, quite frankly they just care about how well you do and its effect on you and not how it reflects upon them, and that really really matters. They like to spend time with you, and always I have found teachers have gone out of their way to help me, which is so valuable. It is so disheartening if you go to a teacher and say 'Oh excuse me, Sir or Miss, I would like to see you after class,' and they said 'No I don't have enough time, go away.' It would be disheartening and you wouldn't go another time. But they say 'OK, I have got the time for you and I will see you whenever you need me,' and it is very valuable and I have found it has been very beneficial to me.

You have both got a zest for learning. How have you got that?

DEBBIE: I think because this school is an exception to the majority of comprehensive schools in that the teachers here give you a kind of confidence and a positive outlook. I don't know, they are always positive over everything. It rubs off on you. They say 'You can do this. I know you can. I know you know it. You have got what it takes.'

Do you think expectations make a difference?

BOTH: Yes.

HARRIET: Enthusiasm is infectious – for their subject.

DEBBIE: I think we both have a certain person in mind! Teachers are so enthusiastic and when teachers are enthusiastic and they show you how much they kind of love their subject you think, well maybe this subject has something to offer me, and you want to continue.

CONCLUSION

This chapter has recorded the views and perspectives of two young women who had just completed their schooling in an 11–18 multiracial comprehensive school. Both girls had been offered university places, both valued the work experience they had been able to undertake and both planned a year out between school and university. Both valued the support the school had offered in helping them make flexible career plans. The girls described themselves respectively as middle class and working class, and were very much aware of the social class, racial and gender dimensions of schooling. They took the view that a school with dedicated teachers could help students overcome socio-economic and racial disadvantage and persuade all students of the advantages education can offer. Both were aware that while girls were improving their school achievements and gaining confidence it was boys who were now likely to 'fall by the wayside'.

Education, to these two students, was more than simply academic preparations for examinations. They were able to articulate the importance of a liberal education that valued lifelong learning as more than a means to the end of employment. They noted and regretted the academic–vocational divide which separated A-level from GNVQ students and the inevitable sense of superiority which was felt by A-level students. As one noted, 'it's very easy to think you are a little better or superior' – and they regarded joint courses, such as the 'History of Ideas' they experienced, as one way to overcome the divide.

The girls were fortunate to have attended a school with an academic, social and racial mix that aimed to maximise the life chances, employment possibilities and commitment to lifelong learning of all students, despite constraining national policies.

NOTES

1 The school has made a very strong commitment to supporting girls because in the past girls felt very marginalised. A strong equal opportunities thrust from all staff has significantly changed the culture of the school. It is now working equally hard to raise boys' – particularly the 5 per cent Afro-Caribbean boys' – achievement and self image.

2 The school runs an ambitious ten-day induction course for the new Year 12 starting A-levels, which aims to provide amongst other things a framework, a brief history of Western thought, background on how ideas and discoveries have developed and changed through time as well as helping students to understand the jump from GCSE to A-level and appropriate study methods. It is unusual in being a joint exploration with teachers who are also prioritising their own learning. It covers 'The Classical Age: Order and Harmony' to 'Post-Modernism and the Technological Age' (see Appendix 1).

3 The school is concerned about the academic-vocational divide. Previously all A-level students were required to take two modules from the Diploma of Vocational Education. This is no longer practical with the GNVQ. Some advanced GNVQs are being introduced. There is still a long way to go, starting low down in the school.

4 All students have two weeks' work experience in Year 10 and in Year 13, which aims to match up to students' initial career plan areas.

5 The school has over 150 refugees or asylum seekers who are supported by a charity set up by staff and students. Sixth-formers give up two afternoons' twilight sessions to help these students. As part of the school programme to support refugees, strong links have been estblished with a school in Eritraea.

Several of the students are Eritraean in origin. A significant number of sixth-formers use their year between school and higher education to do voluntary work of this kind.

6 The school had its OFSTED Inspection in June 1996 with the main finding that the school was a good school because of the quality of its teaching. No mention was made about the behaviour of the students other than that they were confident and that school relationships were very good.

APPENDIX 1   WHY THE HISTORY OF IDEAS?

STUDY PROGRAMME AIMS

Welcome to A-level study! You are about to embark on a challenging adventure into the world of new ideas and knowledge. You will be studying in greater depth a smaller number of subjects than you have done before, but you will find that the demands on your time will increase. We really want to make sure that you have a positive start to A-levels and that is the reason we have organised this induction programme.

PURPOSES OF THE INDUCTION PROGRAMME

- To give you an exciting and inspiring start to A-level study.
- To give some background knowledge about how ideas and discoveries have developed and changed through time.
- To introduce you to some ideas which might be new to you but which will be important for the understanding of your A-level courses.
- To illustrate that, even though you maybe specialising in either arts or sciences, ideas in these two areas have always been connected and still are.
- To help you make the jump from GCSE to A-level, because you will be surprised how different these two examination courses are.
- To help you gain some of the study methods and new ways of working which will be necessary for A-level, such as small group discussion, essay writing, research methods, presentation skills and using different types of resources.
- To make you realise the importance of working steadily and meeting work deadlines.
- To show you how London is full of exciting opportunities for enriching your studies, in terms of people, organisations and places.

- To join your teachers in an exploration of ideas and knowledge and the joy of learning.
- To help your first steps in gaining good A-level grades for your future success in life.

AREAS OF STUDY

During the programme we are going to explore how some ideas have developed in philosophy, politics, sociology, scientific discovery and thought, and artistic movements, and have shaped the world we live and study in today. We are going to cover the following historical periods:

The Classical Age: Order and Harmony
The Medieval World and the Impact of Christianity
The Renaissance: Questioning and Exploring
The Age of Reason
The Age of Unreason: Romantics and Revolutionaries
Realism and Materialism: The Victorians
The Age of Doubt: Modernism
Post-Modernism and the Technological Age

10

Transition to What? Young People with Special Educational Needs

Jenny Corbett

INTRODUCTION

This chapter explores four key elements of the 14–19 age experiences of young people with disabilities and learning difficulties. The first of these is the process of transition from school to further education, training, work or community living. The second is the specialised curriculum which has evolved in special schools and colleges and which both prepares these young people for life in the community and distinguishes their needs from those of their peers. The third is the concept of employability commonly used by trainers of young people whose degree of learning difficulty or behavioural problems are seen to preclude the possibility of gaining or sustaining paid employment. The fourth is the issue of integration or inclusion in the mainstream of the school, college, training, workplace or social community, which has become of increasing concern in relation to civil rights and individual entitlement.

The young people who are the subject of discussion are made up of many diverse and contrasting individuals, each with distinctive needs'. The concept of 'special educational needs', embodied in the Warnock Report (DES 1978), was designed to overcome the former stigma attached to labelling of certain disabilities, like 'educationally subnormal' and 'maladjusted'. Whilst it has achieved this, to some extent, there is now a rather nebulous notion of what constitutes a special need. The demand to clarify special educational needs in order to gain resource support has ensured that distinctive categories remain and new labels emerge. Within the special school sector, more pupils now have severe, complex and multiple disabilities, requiring medical and therapeutic services. Pupils who used to attend special schools in the recent past are now being integrated into mainstream provision. They tend to have physical or sensory disabilities, without additional learning difficulties, or to have Down's Syndrome, without additional challenging behaviours. Those left behind in the special school sector for their 14–19 secondary school experience are usually students who, for whatever reason, have been deemed unmanageable in mainstream schools and colleges. Alongside these learners with special educational needs are those who label themselves as having specific learning difficulties (dyslexia), who now constitute a rapidly expanding clientele for colleges. In addition, there are the substantial 'bottom 40 per cent' of those with poor levels of literacy and numeracy who continue to concern government and to threaten Britain's qualifications and training status in Europe.

Thus, there are two distinct areas of concern: the small group of statemented young people, whose special requirements have been stipulated by law; and the large group of non-statemented but high-risk young people who tend to slip through the net of qualifications. This chapter will deal firstly with the former group, in exploring the concept of transition and the nature of the special curriculum. It will then examine the experiences of the latter group, in relation to employability and the qualifications dilemma. Finally, the overall issues relating to inclusion will link related experiences in both groups.

TRANSITION

Within the 1994 Code of Practice on the Identification and Assessment of Special Educational Needs, there is a recommendation that a Transition Plan is introduced at the first annual review following a young person's fourteenth birthday as a way of bringing together relevant participants to form a coherent plan. The rationale behind this procedure is that there are often so many different agencies involved in the support of a young person who may have a wide range of special needs that it can only benefit both the young person and those who contribute to their overall development to meet and plan together. Those involved include headteachers, college special needs co-ordinators, educational psychologists, parents, the young person, possibly social workers and therapists and careers advisers.

Recent research (Wilenius 1996) has raised the following major points relating to the transition planning process under the Code of Practice:

- The needs of the young people concerned will vary considerably and some will require a much longer period of planning than others.

- The role of the LEA is still confused and requires more uniformity of practice.
- The additional resources which are essential if transition plans are to be followed through are not yet being addressed, nor is there sufficient knowledge of special needs among mainstream staff, who may be unable to meet complex demands.

In addition, views of what qualifications are appropriate are often unrealistic; there is a need for an agreed age at which a young person moves from the responsibility of child to adult services if a smooth transition into post-19 provision is to be achieved, and the young person him/herself should be present where possible and encouraged to participate in decision-making in issues which relate to future placement and opportunities.

It is important not to imply that the Code of Practice is the instigator of any interest or concern in the process by which young people are supported in their move from child to adult status. For many years now, there has been a move towards supporting young people with disabilities and learning difficulties towards a more autonomous, assertive and empowered level of decision-making in issues relating to their everyday lives (e.g. Fenton and Hughes 1989; Craft 1994). Such a degree of independence of mind does not imply a forced self-reliance, in which being responsible for looking after oneself can become an intolerable and unreasonable burden (Corbett 1989).

There are evident reasons why the period of adolescence can present considerable obstacles to young people whose physical and/or learning disabilities are complex or severe. They may have needed to rely upon the support of their parents or carers for the most intimate aspects of daily living. This makes it difficult for them to demonstrate the ordinary stages of adolescent rebellion and exploration which facilitate the process of emotional maturation. How can you walk out of the house in a rage, if you have to ask your parents to push your wheelchair out for you? For many young people with significant learning difficulties, their capacity to meet with their peers in social settings beyond home, school, college or community provision has been reliant upon the support and approval of parents or carers. That easy and *ad hoc* process of exploring possibilities in relationships, interests and adventures, which is the hallmark of adolescent learning, can be denied to this group of young people who are often perceived as being unable to look after themselves and in need of protection. There is a real dilemma in seeking skills of decision-making among this vulnerable group of young people, in order that they participate fully in the Transition Planning under the Code of Practice, whilst acknowledging that acquiring such skills presents a considerable challenge for them and their teachers.

DELIVERING THE EMPOWERING CURRICULUM

The term 'empowerment' is much in use within education and social service provision for learners with disabilities and difficulties. An increased awareness of the vulnerability of this group to exploitation and abuse and an effort to include their views in discussions and decision-making has led to the notion of an empowering curriculum. In this programme, students are encouraged to develop skills of self-advocacy. When they might have very real problems in articulating their needs and opinions by use of speech or alternative methods of communication, they are helped to learn those skills of assertiveness and expression which will enable them to participate and no longer be ignored.

Like many apparently simple ideologies, the concept of empowerment is fraught with complexity and confusion. It is a value-laden minefield. What may be decidedly empowering for one person may be thoroughly frightening for another. In recent years, there have been several national conferences at which empowered people with learning disabilities were invited to display the fruits of their labours. Witnessing several of these performances, I was troubled by the degree of pressure that was some-times placed upon nervous individuals. It is not easy for any of us to show a group of strangers how we can express our personal views and assert our individual rights. It might be said that those who are most truly empowered, such as key members of political parties, make certain that they carefully prepare any publically aired views and conceal any vestige of personal vulnerability. To witness a frightened individual with learning disabilities feeling obligated to advocate their needs in order to get approval can become a travesty of what really empowers. Surely, if they are to be helped towards a real feeling of self-ownership, it involves having the right to say, 'No'. For a group of young people who have become conditioned to trying to please parents, carers and teachers, advocacy can become just one more form of obligation and duty. I shall never forget the uncomfortable spectacle of a young woman with learn-ing disabilities sobbing that she had learnt to advocate for herself and had a nervous breakdown in the process.

Two fundamental values need to underpin the delivery of an empowerment curriculum. The first is a recognition that encouraging self-advocacy means accepting the possibly conflicting views which may be expressed. The second is a realistic presentation of the limitations of power and choices for all of us. In recent literature (e.g. Mosley 1994; Sandow and Garner 1995) there has been a timely warning of the delicate nature of self-advocacy and the complexity of seeking to empower others. As the rhetoric stipulates, none of us can empower others. We can only empower ourselves. This is where the challenge lies for this most vulnerable group of learners. They have usually had minimal experience of taking responsibility for their own lives. Ensuring that they have the practice they need, whilst not endangering their wellbeing, can become a precarious balancing act for anxious staff.

It is not uncommon for the advocacy and empowerment curriculum for senior pupils in special schools and students on special college courses to include elements of the following: travel training on buses, underground and trains; domestic training in household skills; budgeting for meals by using local shops; running small-scale enterprise initiatives like cafés; drama role-playing of possible conflicts and how to approach them; sex education and discussions on assertiveness and harrassment. Recognising that most 14–19-year-olds with disabilities and learning difficulties will still be living with their parents and may be more closely supervised by them than is usual for their age, there are areas of potential stress. What happens if students, sent out without a member of staff in order to gain independence skills, get lost on the Underground? What if the assertiveness training leads to conflict between parents and student relating to going out at night or entering relationships? How should staff respond when the self-advocacy leads to what they perceive as inappropriate behaviour? Just how far should the notion of empowerment be encouraged before it runs the risk of being regarded as lacking responsibility?

Whilst these dilemmas make this a difficult area, it is undeniable that the attitudes towards this group of learners have changed significantly, and this is reflected in the special 14–19 curriculum. Gone are the days when those young people who experienced severe and complex disabilities were always seen as perpetual children. There is now a recognition within the curriculum that they need preparation for adulthood. Part of this preparation is an evaluation of exactly what they are going to require in order to sustain a reasonable quality of life in the community. The concept of 'significant living without work' was embodied in the early special college programmes (e.g. Hutchinson and Tennyson 1986). It accepts that some young people are unlikely to go into any form of employment but are most likely to transfer from school or college courses into day centre provision. This is a social service operated service, designed to provide daily activities for people with a range of special needs who may be living with parents or in community homes. The range of choices available will depend upon local college courses, the initiative of centre staff to stimulate a wide use of community recreational services and the interests and level of confidence of individual members.

Whilst Johnstone (1995) recognises that the current impetus within training and accreditation rhetoric is to prepare all learners for employment, this is not a possibility in relation to some young people. The move towards National Vocational Qualifications (NVQs) to ensure a cohesive, qualifications-led assessment procedure for all learners has been one which has left the least academically able behind. Their need for non-NVQ assessments is only just being addressed and presents an uncomfortable challenge in a skills-based framework.Part of the special school and college curriculum is to confront this reality, acknowledging that employment opportunities are not available for all, instead making the links into a full and active participation in community life as richly varied as resources and the immediate environment will allow. In this, as in other aspects of post-school provision for vulnerable young people, there are broad inequalities relating to demographic differences.

TRAINING FOR EMPLOYABILITY

The Mode B Youth Training Schemes of the 1980s used to take the form of sheltered, workshop-based provision designed to simulate work placements for those trainees perceived to lack the most basic skills which would grant them ease of access to real work environments. Whilst they were presented as a preparation for specific vocational areas, such schemes rarely offered opportunities to acquire either the qualifications or the knowledge of the market which could lead to real jobs in a competitive and shrinking field (Wilkinson 1990; Macfarlane 1993). With the heightened current awareness of youth unemployment, encapsulated in the moral panic about the crisis of young, job-less males, the challenge of how to train the untrainable has become even more of a political, economic and social issue which relates only peripherally to pedagogy. In order to explore the complexities and dilemmas which confront the training agencies, it is useful to draw upon two recent sources of debate. The first is a research survey which examined vulnerable young people in the North East of England and their experiences of being in training programmes (Wilkinson 1995). The second is a review of the current framework of 16–19 qualifications, with a detailed evaluation of the implications of that section which relates to the specific needs of low achievers and learners with special educational needs (Dearing 1996).

In his analysis, Wilkinson (1995) reflects that there are some young people whose experiences of social exclusion are such that they already have what he terms 'an outside view' in their teens. This perspective dislocates them from the usual structures, setting them beyond other people's frame of reference. The notion of acquiring a work ethic through what they perceive as 'slave labour' is, understandably, anathema to them. They may well be living in a culture which has long forgotten the concept of work. As one trainee suggested,

> I think people in Sunderland are very disheartened and have become apathetic because they have had such a hard time trying to find jobs. and if their parents and grandparents have not had jobs it does not give them a positive influence about the job scene. (p. 87)

Among the training agencies, there are to be found the familiar complicities and struggles against an unpalatable reality which I recorded in my earlier research of special needs training provision (Corbett 1990). In my research, I found that trainees were aspiring to become caterers, graphic designers or carpenters, attached to specific vocational areas, whilst their instructors in these specialisms perceived that they lacked the skills to get beyond the most menial tasks in that area of work. The Sunderland City TEC (Training and Enterprise Council) recognises that, even though there is always going to be a group of young people who are unlikely to be able to slot into the current opportunities in the labour market, it is important to support the status quo by assuming that they are trainable for the openings which are there. That this duplicity does neither them nor the training bodies any favours in the long term is overlooked in the urgent impetus to maintain a fragile credibility.

Trainers are all too aware of the pecking-order on the employability ladder. Those young people who have the basic skills necessary to do routine, non-skilled jobs are now being overtaken by more able young people who are naturally taken on by employers in the current, competitive employment market. Employers get the same financial support on Youth Training schemes, whatever the skills of the young person, so it is not surprising that they tend to opt for the more able and easily assimilated. This pattern ensures that those 16-year-olds leaving school with few conventional achievements and qualifications are more likely to be marginalised and to drop out from schemes which include others who have more to offer employers. Where special training schemes are recognising the need for non-NVQ work, there is a disincentive for them to pursue this under financial pressure for resources and a perception from training providers that this area is being squeezed out within the dominant NVQ ideology. As a direct result of this mismatch of needs to services, there is a high drop-out rate from youth training and a high failure rate within the narrowly competence-based NVQ criteria.

In his analysis of youth training Dearing (1996) expresses concern at both the low completion rate of 46 per cent and the lack of general education within the NVQ framework. Section 12 of his report recognises the diversity of need among the 16–19 age group and focuses particularly on those at the lower end of the average ability range as well as those with major learning difficulties who are likely to be statemented. There are three elements of this report which require closer discussion in order to assess their long-term implications. These are:

1 The context of learning being in colleges as well as schools, from 14 years;
2 The need for pre-NVQ qualifications and broader general educational aims;
3 Special needs courses, such as 'Skills for Life', being accredited in national frameworks.

Dearing makes particular reference to notions of social integration and community inclusion which reach beyond the narrowly educational into wider ethical and moral dimensions.

SECOND CHANCE LEARNING: THE PERENNIAL ROLE OF THE FURTHER EDUCATION COLLEGE

The Dearing Report endorses the concept of second chance learning which has long been seen as one of the qualities of further education colleges. For disaffected students in schools, the report suggests that college may be far more acceptable as a learning environment, with its more vocationally focused activities. The value of GNVQs and NVQs is seen as being both the acquisition of relevant qualifications and the process of short-term goal setting in the unit structure. A range of extra-curricular activities, like the Youth Award Scheme and the Duke of Edinburgh's Award, are presented as steps towards building self-esteem and confidence. The use of information technology is also suggested as a confidence enhancer, which allows for a degree of autonomy. Dearing concludes this section on low achievers by saying that, 'the central objective should reflect concern to serve students well in ways that are meaningful to them, whilst maintaining the entitlement to the statutory curriculum' (Dearing 1996, p.116, para. 12.39). To a considerable extent it may be observed that such recommendations are a return to the philosophy embedded in the school-leavers' curriculum of the 1970s, with an earlier school-leaving age and a clearer delineation of academic from vocational learners. The main difference between then and now may be seen to be the influence of National Curriculum requirements and the deteriorating youth employment prospects. Of particular significance in this respect is the reflection in the report that 'under-achievers who cannot find or keep jobs may become disaffected citizens' (p.114, para. 12.25). The potential for urban riot, increased crime and an expanding prison population which might result from a disaffected group in the school context can be seen as a social as well as an educational crisis. Fourteen-year-olds from Pupil Referral Units catering for those with difficult behaviour which has proved unmanageable in schools have been attending college courses for some time. Dearing legitimates this prevelant pattern by recognising its value for a group who need a change of context in which to learn. The impact on further education colleges of a possible expansion of this younger and particularly challenging clientele might be to make them more like an extension of the special education sector, with an imbalanced student body composed of a high proportion of both low achievers from mainstream schools and those coming in from special schools. This could radically alter the culture of colleges, especially in areas with a high density of post-14 drop-outs.

BROADER THAN EXISTING NVQS: A MORE FLEXIBLE FRAMEWORK

Despite the considerable effort to date to create more cohesive systems of qualifications, including the General Certificate of Secondary Education (GCSE), GNVQ and NVQ, this report considered that it is 'undesirable and impractical to introduce a single qualification for this group, with its diverse needs' (p.111, para. 12.13). The report encourages an emphasis upon communication, numeracy and information technology, using as sources for appropriate standards the National Curriculum level descriptions, National Council for Vocational Qualifications (NCVQ) units at foundation level and the expertise within the Basic Skills Agency. The recommendations are for a clear focus on learning outcomes, evident opportunities for progression, quality assurance mechanisms from the awarding bodies and a commitment to equality of access. The acknowledgement that some students are being overlooked in the current awards framework is to be welcomed. Whether the level of flexibility and time which individually focused assessment requires will really be forthcoming in a climate of increased staff cuts and pressures is yet to be seen. It may be that this remains theoretically accessible and progressive but practically unworkable.

THE RECOGNITION OF 'SKILLS FOR LIFE' COURSES

Just as the report's conclusions on what is useful for low achievers from mainstream schools is redolent of earlier research findings, so the suggestions for students with severe learning difficulties is reflective of the aims and strategies of earlier reports. The Dearing emphasis upon punctuality, teamwork and general employment skills, relationship skills, daily living skills and an understanding of local transport and services is to be found in an expanded form in the DES (1985) staff development manual *From Coping to Confidence* and in Dee (1988) *New Directions*. Where the Dearing Report offers a next step is in the suggestion of a recognition of progress, linked to individually tailored units of work which can gain formal accreditation. The report cites National Records of Achievement as being particularly appropriate. The recommendations conclude that 'the regulatory bodies should devise simple quality assurance measures for schemes to accredit small, worthwhile steps of progress by those with severe learning difficulties' (p.118, para. 12.51).

This suggestion is again to be welcomed as a form of integration within the qualifications framework. For the students concerned, progression to employment or NVQs may be quite inappropriate, but that they are seen as part of the overall learning community and, as such, entitled to recognition in the gaining of a suitable award, is important. It is a step towards acknowledging their humanity and their basic rights as citizens.

The influence of the Further Education Funding Council (FEFC) upon provision for students with disabilities and learning difficulties has been significant. It has allocated specific funding to individual students based upon perceived need, similar in many respects to the statementing procedures in schools. This process places obligations on colleges and ensures that students who require a high level of support have an entitlement. However, just as the school statementing procedure led to resource allocation being constrained by LEA budgets and priorities, college principals vary in their degree of commitment to supporting students who are likely to prove expensive and who may not meet their targeted outcomes. Another key influence upon provision and practice has been the inspection process, in which colleges are graded by FEFC inspectors, on a scale of one to five. Each separate section of the college is given a grade, thus enhancing a competitive and potentially divisive institutional climate. Most colleges have now moved from a special needs section, composed often of ex-special school staff and operating special, segregated courses, into a cross-college learning support system, which focuses upon study skills at a range of levels. The impact of these inspections and the subsequent reports and re-inspections has been to alert staff to the expectations of a validating body which assesses quality in a way which may challenge old ideologies and assumptions.

A new concept of inclusive provision has emerged, with an emphasis upon the learning process rather than the individual need. For several years, special needs sections in colleges had often reinforced the segregated special curriculum culture, isolating both staff and students from the main body of the institution. It has not always been easy for staff to adapt to new ways of working. In many instances, staff in positions of power have been demoted or surplanted when new staff with different skills and attitudes have been appointed to operate the Learning Support Resource. This has, naturally, led to some bitterness and resentment. Supported by an approach within the FEFC inspection team which rates quality assurance and student entitlement as fundamental benchmarks of achievement, some college principals have adopted a market mentality in radically altering the staffing to suit changing times. This has even included getting rid of the special needs teams with their out-dated approaches and replacing them with staff who have no legacy of specialism but an emphasis upon learning strategies and efficiency of delivery. It is an exclusion of the old; an inclusion of the new. The special needs co-ordinators of the early 1980s were essentially seen as caring for students with vulnerabilities. They themselves are now no longer valued: caring is replaced by quality measures and cost-effectiveness.

INCLUSION AND A MARKET ECONOMY

'Inclusion' has become something of a buzz word in special education. It has replaced the word 'integration' in radical circles, as it is perceived as more powerful,assertive and strong. 'Integration' as a term is redolent of the Warnock (DES 1978) definitions of three sequential stages – locational, social and functional – the last being a full participation in the curriculum of the school or college. 'Inclusion' is not just about what happens in schools and colleges. It is much more holistic. It is about fundamental value systems, reflecting how we as a society accord status, purpose and worth to individuals with unequal talents. It is a particularly vulnerable concept at a stage of social and economic history in which goals of competition and competency are promoted within a fiercely combative culture.

The tensions within the inclusive ideology are evident. At one level, concepts of 'entitlement for all' and quality assurance measures suggest that the most vulnerable young people are no longer to be offered a second-rate education and training diet but are to be assessed and guided in a way that equates with the treatment given to their peers. At another level, they are no longer seen as 'special' or in need of additional protective care, which can open up opportunities for real progression into mainstream developments but can also mean that they become casualties of a market culture in which the weakest go to the wall. If they are included, this means inclusion into a harsh and uncaring economy where there are no favours given, only deals bargained for. As Warnock noted, in her reflection on how naively she and her colleagues approached their 1978 report, integration or inclusive policies in the 1990s have to recognise that the advocates for those with special educational needs either become hard-edged or sink; there is no more room for soft care (Warnock 1991). I see these current tensions as one of the major challenges for special educational provision in the twenty-first century. If inclusion means to treat equally, it can mean to treat equally harshly and to remove all safety nets. It can also mean to stop the caring ideology, which many see as patronising, and to acknowledge that all people, whatever their needs, have to make the transition into an adult, and therefore hazardous, life in a precarious social world.

The issue of inclusion has to be linked to my title, 'Transition to What?' for it to have any contextual meaning. As Dearing speculated, where young people perceive themselves as school failures and opt out of the system altogether, their tranference can be to become potential adult law-breakers and members of the long-term unemployed underclass. This presents an unacceptable form of social transition, to be resisted through efforts to maintain their interest in learning and training. In relation to young people with severe and complex disabilities, Dearing indicates that their training needs to equip them for a fuller life in the community than that which they historically pursued within institutional care.

When Wilkinson (1995) refers to disaffected young people having already acquired 'an outside view' of the society of school, training schemes, workplace and community, he is raising the issue of coercion and compliance on which notions of good citizenship depend. Dearing's suggestion about appropriate training for young people with severe learning difficulties also relates to this concept of what it means to be an active citizen: learning the basic skills to run a home, cope as independently as possible and manage on a limited budget, making maximum use of restricted, low-cost recreational provision. To a significant degree, the transition for low-achieving young people from mainstream schools, and young people with complex needs from the special sector, is one which takes them from school to college to training and to long-term unemployment, with possible interludes of short-term jobs. Dearing is confronting this reality when he shows such concern for maintaining the 'good citizen' status of low-achieving and disaffected young people by relocating them in colleges and adapting vocational training to provide qualifications which will induce them to stay in some form of education.

The fragile status of mainstream society, as viewed by marginalised young people, is vividly reflected in recent films like *Trainspotting*. In this, the audience is taken into the sub-culture of young drug addicts whose transition has been from an unfulfilling mainstream social role to a precarious but thrilling life on the edge. This way of life can be seen as the very antithesis of what educators and trainers would wish to encourage: a dangerous dependency, a life of petty crime and a disregard for traditional human values and social mores.

Yet it is an uncomfortable reminder that young people can often see beyond the rhetoric. They may reject what they see as unacceptable forms of training and job preparation. If they are not indoctrinated into a work ethic, they are unlikely to perceive the dole as demeaning. Above all, they are not easily seduced into the merits of being good citizens. The degree of compromise this entails is not worth the dubious honour of becoming a member of a community they disregard and even despise.

There has been an influence on young people with severe disabilities which has been brought about through the politics of the disability movement, a civil rights campaigning body composed of different factions yet working together to improve opportunities. The conceptual frameworks proposed by disabled academics (e.g. Abberley 1995; Barnes and Oliver 1995) outline a social model of disability which challenges medically defined and individually focused perceptions. This political and social critique is reflected in the day care provision of the 1990s. For many adolescents with complex disabilities, their transition is from special school to college to day centre provision. Whereas in the early 1980s day care tended to offer in-house recreational activities, often geared to the needs of their middle-aged clients and dependent upon the skills and imagination of their managers and staff, they now tend to be more receptive to ideas from members. Day centre users will sometimes opt for local college classes, use local community facilities and establish user-run committees which include issues of advocacy, women's rights and understanding the benefits system. The concept of 'independence' is being interpreted more sensitively than in the past. Whilst many users may need intensive physical help from staff, they can set their own personal agenda of how they manage their daily lives and decide their own priorities. The notion of 'quality of life', often debated in relation to people with severe disabilities, is inextricably bound up with individual perceptions of citizenship. Disabled young people, in their transition to a life in the community which may involve their gradual move away from parental care, can be supported by sensitive staff in finding their own roles as citizens and in forming their own judgements about where their allegiancies rest. For some disabled young people, the support they receive from their disabled peers is of critical importance. Campaigning groups, political networks and advocacy systems are all potential sources of real empowerment. If they are run by disabled people for disabled people, their power to provide positive role models and to nurture a process of maturation into active citizenship is tremendous. Within an inclusive ideology, there needs to be room for a transition which can take disabled young people into a wider social community as well as into an exclusive community of disabled allies who can foster a quality of life which gives solidarity and support.

CONCLUSION: TRANSITION TO WHAT?

In the school process of transition planning, young people with statemented special needs are ostensibly presented with potential options for their future adult life. These may realistically include an eventual transition to community placement and attendance at a day centre. One of the most valuable contacts that they should be making at that transition planning stage is one which leads them into the political and campaigning disability community where a deep awareness of dilemmas, rights and potential conflicts will form their education as disabled citizens. Better, perhaps, that they become politically educated as early as possible, rather than that they have false expectations which can possibly transform into depression and apathy.

Dearing's emphasis on the key areas of numeracy, literacy and information technology as basic skills for low-achieving young people may assist their transition into low-skilled jobs but could simply serve to make life on benefits more interesting. Enhancing the range of recreational options is an evident aspect of quality of adult life. If all young people are to become computer literate, the public libraries need to be intensely funded to improve their computer facilities rather than being starved of funds as has been the recent trend. Currently, good citizenship is still equated in the public imagination with having a job, a home and social status. This effectively dismisses a whole section of young people who have left school under-qualified, who may have left home with nowhere to live and have acquired no sense of fitting in to something called 'the community'. The rhetoric of 'skills training' is dishonest in its application to all school-leavers, whatever their individual aptitudes. Unless this is confronted and a realistic attitude to actual work choices addressed, young people will continue to be blamed as deficient, weak individuals when they are being influenced by economic forces beyond their control.

The hard-edged approach to students with special educational needs in further education can lead to the most vulnerable being re-excluded as non-productive and non-cost-effective (Dee and Corbett 1994). Disabled students may wish to be included as of right but also to participate in some exclusive group provision as a source of peer support and solidarity (Maudsley and Dee 1995). What is happening in colleges of further education reflects broader dilemmas in society at large.

REFERENCES

Abberley, P. (1995) 'Disabling ideology in health and welfare – the case of occupational therapy', *Disability and Society*, 10 (2), pp. 221–32.

Barnes, C. and Oliver, M. (1995) 'Disability rights: rhetoric and reality in the UK', *Disability and Society*, 10 (1), pp.111–16.

Corbett, J. (1989) 'The quality of life in the "independence" curriculum', *Disability, Handicap and Society*, 4 (2), pp. 145–63.

Corbett, J. (1990) 'It's almost like work: a study of a YTS workshop', in J. Corbett, (ed.), *Uneasy Transitions.* Basingstoke: Falmer.

Craft, A. (ed.) (1994) *Practice Issues in Sexuality and Learning Disabilities.* London: Routledge.

Dearing, R. (1996) *Review of Qualifications for 16–19 Year Olds: Full Report.* Hayes, Middlesex: SCAA.

Dee, L. (1988) *New Directions.* London: Further Education Unit.

Dee, L. and Corbett, J. (1994) 'Individual rights in further education: lost, stolen or strayed?' *British Educational Research Journal*, 20 (3), pp. 319–25.

DES (Department of Education and Science) (1978) *Special Educational Needs: Report of the Committee of Enquiry into the Education of Handicapped Children and Young People*, (Warnock Report). London: HMSO.

DES (1985) *From Coping to Confidence.* London: DES and FEU.

Fenton, M. and Hughes, P. (1989) *Passivity to Empowerment.* London: RADA.

Hutchinson, D. and Tennyson, C. (1986) *Transition to Adulthood.* London: FEU.

Johnstone, D. (1995) *Further Opportunities: Learning Difficulties and Disabilities in Further Education.* London: Cassell.

Macfarlane, E. (1993) *Education 16–19.* London: Routledge.

Maudsley, E. and Dee, L. (1995) 'Beyond the "inclusionist" debate', in E. Maudsley, and Dee, L. (eds.), *Redefining the Future: Perspectives on Students with Learning Difficulties and Disabilities in Further Education.* London: Institute of Education.

Mosley, J. (1994) *You Choose.* Wisbech: Learning Development Association.

Sandow, S. and Garner, P. (eds.) (1995) *Advocacy, Self-Advocacy and Special Needs.* London: David Fulton.

Warnock, M. (1991) 'Equality fifteen years on', *Oxford Review of Education*, (2), pp. 145–54.

Wilenius, F. (1996) *The Practice and Experience of Transition*, report of the London Post-16 Network. London: University of East London.

Wilkinson, A. (1990) 'Complicated lives: students with special needs in the inner city', in J. Corbett, (ed.), *Uneasy Transitions.* Basingstoke: Falmer.

Wilkinson, C. (1995) *The Drop Out Society: Young People on the Margins.* Leicester: Youth Work.

11

Disruptive Behaviour and the Educational Wasteland

Roger Slee

LAMBS TO THE SLAUGHTER

A particularly regrettable series of incidents occurred in the middle of 1995 involving secondary school students, their teachers, politicians and the media. I raise it because it demonstrates the complex matrix of issues which are often reduced to a problem of student behaviour. In a set of events that might well have been penned by William Golding, a group of senior students who were attending a school camp on a small island off the coast of Queensland, Australia, entered into a 'frenzied' slaughter of a colony of nesting sea birds. To be sure, the students' behaviour was an offence against nature. Equally, the responses provoked by this act represent an irrational political frenzy.

The reportage was widespread and intense. The focus spread from the original incident to general speculation about the atrophy of standards of behaviour in 'youth' and encouraged the mourning for the death of authority in families in general and schools in particular. Perhaps the most serious miscalculation on the students' part, though the incident was an act of combustion rather than premeditation, was their mistiming. The incident occurred in the run up to a State election. Thenceforth, law and order was resurrected by the conservative opposition for particular electoral scrutiny. These students, representing the student body in general, were 'out of control'.

Official reprisals were swift and severe. The students entered into a feast of public shaming far beyond criminologist John Braithwaite's (1989) recommendations for humiliation and atonement. Media reportage at the time televised the school Principal disowning the students, alongside interviews with similarly horrified students in lower years at the same school. The offending students were brought before a tribunal convened to adjudicate their offences against the provisions of the

Wildlife Act. Found guilty, they were ordered to undertake supervised community service work. This legally constituted body provided a forum for natural justice where rights to representation were guaranteed. Due process, however, soon became a casualty to the politics of trouble in schools. Public debate continued about whether or not the students had been dealt with severely enough, about whether or not they had learnt their lesson. The opposition used the issue as an integral component of their election campaign. Then Minister for Education, David Hamill, waded in, ordering that the students also be dealt with according to the Education Department's disciplinary regulations. Some of the students involved were brought before an official departmental inquiry and were excluded from school, despite their preparation for final year examinations, and were given the option of attending an adult night school some distance from where they lived. In a departure from legal precedent, the students were effectively tried twice, discounting the media trials, and incurred additional punishments.

This event and the reaction to it is useful to the analysis of disruption in schools for a number of reasons. It reveals the complexity of the issues involved, and it demonstrates the futility of traditional approaches to the problem of indiscipline. Moreover, it clearly establishes that disruptive behaviour is better understood as a problem of the complex interactions of political economy, differing approaches to teaching and learning, school cultures, identities of class, gender, ethnicity intersecting with youth cultures, changing patterns of authority and individual teachers and students, than as a problem of deviant or impaired individual student pathologies.

Let us consider what happened to the students involved. First, they clearly had exceeded the limits of acceptable behaviour and were responsible for an ecological crime, much the same as those ignored when the aristocracy goes hunting. They were punished. Did the punishment assist the students in receiving the environmental education that they were in need of? The issues summoned by the slaughter of the birds remain an educational problem that schools are well situated to deal with. Second, their dismissal from school had devastating implications for their academic progress at a critical juncture and would intensify their growing hostility towards schools and society. I would speculate that the summary treatment of young people such as this will be paid for by the state (through the welfare, health or criminal justice systems) at a later date in their lives.

The incident was not without collateral damage. The Education

Department was at that time engaged in re-writing its discipline strategy to ensure that it gave the right message to the community:

• Schools were not going to tolerate disruptive students;
• Suspensions would be more frequently applied and the duration of suspensions prior to official enquiry would be extended;
• Teachers would be instructed in behaviour management skills;
• More counsellors would be provided to help disruptive students; and
• Additional behaviour units would be supplied for the removal of these students from the educational mainstream.

The electorate had to be reassured that teachers were in charge. The government and opposition entered into a machismo auction where the bidding escalated from *'three strikes and they're out'* to *'one strike and they're out'*.

Readers will identify global resonance in this narrative. British readers will recognise a forerunner to Mandelson and Liddle's (1996) recent blueprint for 'New Labour' in *The Blair Revolution*, wherein they advocate Friday night and Saturday detentions for disruptive students, the withdrawal of students' rights to watch football(!), more frequent application of exclusion and referral [*sic*] to special centres (Pupil Referral Units) for disruptive students (pp. 135–9). The Secretary of State for Education, Gillian Shephard, tried to put 'blue water' between the Conservatives and Labour in part by strengthening schools' disciplinary arsenal (*The Guardian*, 7 June, p. 6) and promoting instruction in classroom discipline within a National Curriculum for Teacher Training (*TES*, 20 September 1996). American readers may be horrified by mention of *three strikes legislation* when their experience has been a forfeiture of judicial flexibility resulting sometimes in the issuing of serious penalties for minor infractions.

This introduction remains at the level of popular debate. It lacks an analytical treatment. In this chapter, I will attempt that analysis by paying particular attention to student behaviour in the 14–19 years of schooling, examining the discourses of discipline and control manifest in traditional responses to disruption, and by proposing alternative approaches which draw on the educational role of teaching in preference to increasing surveillance and legal controls in schools.

DISCOURSES OF DISCIPLINE AS A PRACTICAL CONCERN IN EDUCATIONAL REFORM

There is considerable conceptual slippage when it comes to the problem of school discipline. In its most frequent usage, discipline is applied as a synonym for control and or punishment. It proceeds from a conceptual framework theoretically tied to the quasi-science of behaviourism (Skinner 1972). Accordingly discipline refers to the successful management and conditioning of students into a state of compliance.

When disruption occurs, the problem is individualized and described, diagnosed and treated in terms of the 'problem student'. These individual problems are commonly attributed to pathological defects within the student's physiological, cognitive or emotional composition, or to defective familial pathology where parenting skills are lacking.

Such functionalist discourses of discipline are convenient to the bureaucratic imperative of schooling and the professional interest of teachers, for they remove both from the diagnostic gaze. The causes of disruption are located within individual pupils. As C. Wright Mills (1959) observed, the dismissal of fundamental 'social issues' as 'personal troubles', safeguards the status quo. The contribution of the structural and cultural pathology of schools as mediated through curriculum, pedagogy, organisational structure and procedure, is not accounted for in the preceding analyses of disruption (Coulby and Harper 1985). Sociological explanations for disruption in schools (Furlong 1985) ought not to be dismissed as irrelevant, impractical or academic, for they actually provide for an expanding scope for intervention and hence a greater repertoire for amelioration of disruption in schools (Slee 1995).

Behaviour management narrows the possibilities for change to what can be done with the individual. Called in are the programmes and packages which, in lock-step fashion, guide teachers through a sequence of exchanges that will, we are assured, result in student compliance. The focus is narrowed to the behavioural exchanges between teacher and pupil. Bearing titles such as *Assertive Discipline* (Canter and Canter 1976), *Decisive Discipline* (Rogers 1990), *Reality Therapy* and *Control Theory for the Classroom* (Glasser 1965 and 1986) they mask varying degrees of authoritarianism. The authoritarian predisposition is often in conflict with the educational aims stated by schools and with the broader social aim of providing a democratic apprenticeship for young citizens (Knight 1988).

Crittenden contends that studies in school discipline demonstrate a 'preoccupation with the details of effective practice' (Crittenden 1991, p. 67) and calls for a more philosophical approach to classroom discipline.

A philosophical approach to classroom discipline, in its turn, cannot be indifferent to specific tactics and how effectively they work. However, its attention is focused primarily on underlying values that practices of classroom discipline explicitly or implicitly reflect. In this context, the major philosophical questions to be asked about styles of discipline are how they relate to educational values (and the distinctive educational role of the school) (Crittenden 1991, p. 67).

The question is put: are the disciplinary procedures employed by the school consistent, or in tension, with the educational aims and pedagogical preferences within the school? Dewey expounds further upon this epistemological tension between discipline and control.

A person who is trained to consider his actions, to undertake them deliberately, is in so far forth disciplined. Add to this ability a power to endure in an intelligently chosen course in face of distraction, confusion, and difficulty, and you have the essence of discipline. Discipline means power at command; mastery of the resources available for carrying through the action undertaken. To know what one is to do and to move to do it promptly and by use of the requisite means is to be disciplined, whether we are thinking of an army or a mind. Discipline is positive. To cow the spirit, to subdue inclination, to compel obedience, to mortify the flesh, to make a subordinate perform an uncongenial task – these things are not disciplinary according to the development of the power to recognise what one is about and of persistence in accomplishment. (Dewey 1916, p. 129)

In other words, in an educational context, the disciplinary framework adopted by a school ought to exhibit consistency with the educational aims and the pedagogies employed to that end. Connection between the learners, what they are doing and where it is leading them is fundamental to the construction of an educational orderliness (Slee 1995, p. 28). For educators working in schools this is an immensely practical way of thinking, for discipline and student behaviour become a challenge for establishing social attachment, curriculum relevance and a democratic apprenticeship.

A range of discourses of discipline are detected within policy statements emanating from education bureaucracies. Herein lies a linguistic minefield. Responding to disruptive behaviour collapses into a melange of punitive, pastoral and democratic discourses. The constant movement between these competing discourses represents the historical problem of the governance of children and youth. The past two decades have witnessed the movement from the 'spectacle and liturgy of punishment' (Foucault 1979) with the abolition of corporal punishment in the 1980s in Australia and England, through discourses of students' rights and democratic participation and citizenship, pastoral care and behavioural counselling and back, more recently, to punitive frameworks which call for the exclusion of increasing numbers of aberrant or defective individuals (de Gruchy 1996, p. 1). It may well be argued that each came from similar imperatives of regulation and surveillance (Rose 1989). The newest arrival in the disciplinary arsenal of schooling is the pathologising of disruption within a medical discourse of Attention Deficit Hyperactivity Disorder (ADHD).

Each way of 'knowing' the problem of disruption establishes frameworks for policy interpretation and intervention. Behaviourism assumes the need to generate more behaviour management programmes, which traverses the well-trod territory of monitoring and managing teacher student exchanges and generating graded schedules of sanctions to be applied after the fact of disruption (Brophy 1996). Punitive discourses tie educators to sanctions such as exclusion, suspension and detention. It is worth reconsidering research into suspension and exclusion to derive lessons for alternative ways of responding to disruption in the middle years.

THINKING TOUGH OR TOUGHER THINKING?

The global shift in education policy to more draconian discourses and measures is manifest in the press for increasing the application of suspension and exclusion. The identification and exclusion of problem students, it is argued, will deliver schools from disruption. This cleansing of schools could be achieved by greater levels of exclusion and the provision of Pupil Referral Units. The logic is irresistible in its apparent strength of purpose and simplicity. If the bad students were no longer in the classroom, then the task of teaching would be rendered possible and the achievements of the remaining students would improve in the absence of persistent interruptions. This would also act as a deterrent to students contemplating a career of trouble in schools. A clear tough message would be delivered to students and their parents that secondary schools are for serious students. It is worth interrogating this policy direction by reflecting upon the body of research into suspension, exclusion and off-site behaviour units. In doing so, it becomes clear that tough interventions generate further problems.

RESEARCHING SUSPENSION AND EXCLUSION FROM SCHOOL

Findings from international research into suspension, exclusion and off-site behaviour units undermines present policy directions. A number of themes emerge which are useful in reconsidering the problem of educational provision for 14–19-year-olds. In a major review of seriously disruptive behaviour in Western Australian secondary schools Dettman found that while suspension may provide some respite for teachers, it was less than effective as a measure of deterrence or reform.

> If the suspension is being used as a punishment for the purpose of deterring extremely deviant behaviour, then it should be realised that it is relatively ineffective. The students most likely to incur this punishment are those who dislike it least. For these students, suspension may even, inadvertently, become a reward. (Dettman 1972, p. 158)

Dettman concludes that suspension, like corporal punishment, is only effective in its minimal application. Kaeser (1979) supported this view in her US-based study, concluding that frequent suspension simultaneously diminishes its potential for deterrence and school morale, leading to successive disruptive events. The increasing usage of suspension has been charted internationally. The *Times Educational Supplement* (18 March 1983) reported an 80 per cent increase in suspensions over the preceding two years in 1983. Inner London Education Authority (ILEA 1986) data demonstrated the maintenance of this rate of increase over the 1983–85 period. Drawing upon National Union of Teachers data, Pyke (1993, p. 6) points to an 'alarming' increase of 50 per cent in either permanent or temporary exclusions between 1990 and 1992 in England and Wales. These data are replicated in Australia. In Victoria, suspensions between term 2 1983 and term 2 1984 rose by 55.3 per cent (Victorian Education Department statistics cited in Slee 1995) and continued to increase. In 1985 there were 5,044 official suspensions in Victorian state schools rising to 16,228 in 1990 (Edwards 1996).

The data on the growth in suspensions are cause for concern at face value. However, when interrogated further it becomes clear that they shield a number of issues which raise serious questions about schooling and its administration.

• *Due process and appeals*: The forfeiture of 'due process' of the law and the absence of legitimate grievance channels for students have repeatedly been cited as cause for serious concern. This is an area of considerable interest for both researchers and education authorities (OFSTED 1993).

• *Labelling*: The dual issues of labelling and reoffending also undermine arguments about the efficacy of suspension. In his recent investigation of suspensions in a secondary school in an urban centre in Victoria, Australia, Edwards (1996) was able to enlist statewide data to highlight the way in which students were far less likely to complete their secondary education if they had previously been suspended. His study supported earlier findings about the intensification of punitive scrutiny upon students following their first suspension. The Human Rights and Equal Opportunities Commission inquiry into youth homelessness, *Our Homeless Children*, also refers to the spirals of trouble at school, suspension and youth homelessness (HREOC 1989).

• *Race and suspension*: In a recent report on the achievement of ethnic minority students, Gillborn and Gipps (1996) point to the continuing disproportional exclusion of black students: The over-representation of black young people in exclusions is too large and consistent (over time and across regions) to be discounted as a statistical artefact or chance occurrence. (Gillborn and Gipps, 1996, p. 52)

Their observation confirms earlier findings by the Rampton Committee (DES 1981). The disproportionate exclusion of ethnic minority students is not uniquely British. Neilsen (1979) cites Children's Defense Fund data in North America indicating the vulnerability of African-American and Latino students to school suspension. Galloway and Barrett's 1984 New Zealand based research highlights the over-representation of Maori students in suspension and exclusion data. Vickers's (1993) Western Australian study reports the high incidence of suspension for Aboriginal students.

• *Between School Variance*: In my own studies of suspension in Victorian schools I reported, like others elsewhere, on the variability of suspensions between schools. It would seem that some schools are more inclined to exclude than others. Simply put, suspension and exclusion is not always a measure of the deviance of the student cohort, but a reflection of school cultures and administrative ethos (Slee 1995).

• *Year Level and Suspensions*: Perhaps the most significant data for this discussion of the schooling of 14–19-year-olds is the changes in rates and volume of suspensions according to year levels. Statewide data on suspensions in Victoria between the years 1983 and 1986 records that there were 253 suspensions in Year 6 (the last year of primary schooling) rising to 1,861 suspensions in Year 7 (the first year of secondary schooling). The data presses us to investigate differences between the pedagogical, curriculum and organisational characteristics of the educational provision in each sector.

It was also interesting to observe the increasing rates of suspension through the compulsory years of school attendance (up to year 10), dropping in Years 11 and 12. This trend has more recently changed with the steady increase in exclusion and suspension in the post-compulsory years of senior secondary schooling, following the collapse of the unskilled youth labour market. The growth of suspensions at earlier ages has been noted (Edwards 1996). Children are reportedly more pessimistic about the future at a younger age.

The data on suspensions and year level prompt questions about the complex relationships between educational attainment, retention and the future. The relationship between academic failure and trouble in schools has been identified and tracked by a number of researchers (Pink 1982; Knight 1988). The unskilled labour market supported the premature departure of failing and disruptive students. Crisis in the labour market and the promotion of school retention as a part of youth policy and micro-economic reform in Australia makes these students visible in post-compulsory schooling suspension and exclusion data. What we seem to be witnessing is the retention of more students in a largely unreconstructed school system which offers little hope of an independent working adult life for increasing numbers of students. Students' realisation that seemingly pointless curricula and uninspiring teaching are leading nowhere provides a powerful cocktail for disruption and trouble in schools. Put this way, the problem may be more precisely understood as a problem of political economy and historical dislocation, than as the dysfunctional pathologies of individual students.

EXPANDING THE APPARATUS OF CONTROL

Off-site centres
The absence of a substantive reform of secondary schooling underwrites the escalating need for alternatives for problem students. Notwithstanding Her Majesty's Inspectors' reservations about off-site behaviour units published in their report *Behaviour Units* (HMI 1978), the call for off-site centres escalates. The major findings from the research mentioned echoes the discussion of suspension research in respect to the disproportionate referral of ethnic minority and socio- economically disadvantaged students, variable rates of referral between schools and a lack of procedural uniformity in referral decisions. Moreover, while it is relatively easy to send a student to a behaviour unit, the passage back has always been less straightforward (Mongon 1988). Paradoxically, those students who seem to require more extensive educational provision actually receive a narrower curriculum, compounding their disadvantage in the race for credentials.

The existence of off-site centres begets the need for additional centres. Having referred one student, teachers are more inclined to discover additional students for whom the regular classroom is no longer 'suitable'. Moreover, this type of provision takes pressure off schools to examine their own practices which may contribute to disruption. Daines (1981, p. 107) found that over 80 per cent of students referred to units never returned to school and that over 60 per cent of those who did were in trouble within six months of their return.

Attention Deficit Hyperactivity Disorder (ADHD) – from disruptive to defective
Added to the call for more Pupil Referral Units for the containment of disruptive students is the pathologising of disruption as a further displinary technique. Attention Deficit Hyeractivity Disorder (ADHD) has become a global epidemic affecting (or infecting) young, predominantly male, students. The syndrome, it has been suggested, is caused by an imbalance or deficiency of one or more neurotransmitters in the brain. Serfontein describes this *'Hidden Handicap'*:

> these children have difficulty in focusing and sustaining their attention long enough to initiate and complete any set task. They tend to be easily distracted from the task on hand by other stimuli, such as noise or movement. Significant disturbances in concentration may lead to daydreaming and 'switching off'. (Serfontein 1990, p. 19)

Diagnosis is made by a physician or psychologist matching a child's reported or observed behaviour against a checklist from the American Psychiatric Association (1987). The correlation, devoid of contextualisation, is both random and normative as Swan (1995) observes: 'Attention Deficit Disorder is not a disease, it's just part of the spectrum of children's behaviour. The issue is to find the line where abnormality stops and normality begins . . . and the line moves according to who's drawing it.'

Worldwide, there appears to be geographical disproportionality in the prevalence of ADHD which indicates diagnostic predisposition as a causal factor. While 10 students in every 1,000 are being treated in Western Australia and New South Wales for ADHD, not even one per thousand students would be diagnosed in Victoria (Swan, 1995). In the United States there would be up to 80 cases diagnosed in a school of 1,000 students (Barkley 1990). In Sydney the diagnostic tool of neurometrics is employed and subsidised by the national health insurance. However, neurologists remain sceptical about whether ADHD has a patterned abnormality, or even whether computers have the capacity to depict the complex patterning of the brain's electrical impulses.

The two major treatments for ADHD revolve around behavioural therapy and chemical interventions. The central nervous system stimulant methylphenidate (Ritalin) is the most popular treatment. There exists some concern over this intervention as the contraindications of the drug include dizziness, growth supression, drowsiness, nausea, blurred vision, anorexia, and cardio- vascular complications (Govoni and Hayes 1988, pp. 78–9). While the incidence is minimal, chemical intervention remains experimental in the absence of controlled tests with placebos.

ADHD is beguiling. It joins parents and teachers as allies, providing a palatable explanation for the disruptive behaviour of an increasing number of children. For parents it offers respectability. If their child is seen as pathologically defective then it is a better adjudication than having a bad child. Parenting skills are not called into question and the school is also removed from the behavioural equation. Increasing numbers of children are being diagnosed as ADHD children who have special educational needs. Surveillance and control are made complete when we witness the self-regulatory response of parents who are voluntarily submitting their children for diagnosis and treatment. The syndrome has consummate bureaucratic convenience.

EDUCATIONAL RESPONSES TO DISRUPTION IN 14–19-YEAR-OLD SCHOOLING

How else might we confront the reported problem of increasing levels of disruption in secondary schools? While suspension has its place as a measure of last resort to safeguard security in schools, its frequent application is problematic. Skilling teachers in behaviour management techniques is similarly myopic, given its tendency to remove curriculum and pedagogy from the disciplinary frame. Responding to disruption requires lateral and strategic thinking. Previously I have discussed the problem of policy-making for school discipline. The competitive discourse and illusory goals of 'raising standards' and providing 'choice' through the marketization of schooling (Gewirtz, Ball and Bowe 1995) contribute to the problem. Notions of standards are forged through traditional and exclusionary curriculum constructs. The restorationist National Curriculum in England and Wales, for example, has been called the curriculum of the dead (Ball 1994, pp. 28–47), it denies the context of many students and obstructs educational engagement. The drive for testing at key stages in the pupil's schooling proliferates 'scholastic identities' of failure, compounded by the drive to increase selection through the surreptitious return of the Eleven Plus. Add to this the call by Her Majesty's Chief Inspector of Schools to return to whole class teaching on the basis of spurious research into the relationship between pedagogies in Taiwan and their economic progress (Reynolds and Farrell 1996) and we deny a widely recognised body of research which suggests the importance of a range of teaching and learning strategies in meeting the needs of all students (Slavin 1984; Evertson 1996).

Dearing's *Review of Qualifications for 16–19 Year Olds* (Dearing 1996) is long on the rhetoric of 'the imperative of achievement', arguing for the establishment of a three-tiered GNVQ framework of national awards (see pp. 6–12). What is not contained within the Dearing deliberations is an analysis of the processes of schooling which frequently serve to obstruct achievement. Nor does the report take on the problematic issues of labour market structures and how qualifications articulate with work entry. Qualifying, within a hierarchy of achievement, for unemployment may not offer greater attachment to the purposes and processes of schooling for the award holders.

A way of pushing forward might be achieved through a backward glance. I propose to very briefly describe two school reforms in Australia which proved successful in reducing disruptive behaviour and enhancing students' educational and vocational outcomes. Immediately there are difficulties in doing this. Australia, for the moment, does not have a national curriculum for schools which inhibits flexibility, nor is there a drive to tether teacher education to a national curriculum inscribed by populist notions of effective teaching. This does not make the examples redundant, it invites more lateral thinking about educational policy-making and curriculum development.

Elsewhere (Slee 1995) I have described research into a metropolitan technical school in a disadvantaged area in Melbourne which by all accounts was a troubled school. Seriously disruptive behaviour was endemic, as was truancy amongst staff and students alike. Student drop-out and suspension rates were high, and workers' compensation claims and compassionate transfers were frequent and costly. Tougher punitive approaches to the problematic behaviour of students did little to increase students' levels of attachment or commitment to the school and its programmes. It simply drew the line in the sand more deeply. However, a newly appointed Principal shifted the agenda from control to the 'harder questions'. What were the educational goals of the school? What were the needs of the students? Was the school serving these needs? How are students enveloped in a reconstruction of the educational programme?

The development of a new school strategy and programme was pursued on a number of levels involving all those with an interest in the organisation. Of particular interest were the changes to the decision-making processes and fora; the construction of a curriculum which addressed the needs of students as well as teachers; the enlistment of parents and the business community in the school curriculum; the inclusion of La Trobe University in the reform process in order to tie school problem-solving to teachers' formal professional development accreditation and to negotiate direct entry into that institution for students as a bargaining chip to approach other higher education and further education providers with.

Change took time and was stressful, but at the time that our research was being conducted it was clear that the school had lowered all of the indicators of student trouble. More impressively it had also overtaken the local traditional academic schools in student results. More students were getting into higher education, training and employment than recorded by the schools which had excluded many of the students who ended up at the technical school we are considering. Standards were not raised by tougher stands on punishment and exclusion and by drilling people in literacy and numeracy. Improvement was achieved through curriculum reform which started from the assessment of students' needs and the creation of inclusive educational structures and programmes.

The second example is drawn from the state of Queensland where two 'senior colleges' were piloted in an attempt to develop a new post-compulsory curriculum (Warner 1992, pp. 165–92). A school was created which:

- provided a comprehensive academic and vocational curriculum;
- was organised along 'tertiary education' principles that contracted students into programmes comprising core and elective components;
- entitled students to decide how and where they spent their non-contact time;
- established democratic decision-making fora;
- interpreted its care mandate as a question not only of welfare provision, but as a responsibility to demonstrate care in teaching methodology and curriculum development;
- demonstrated that relevance and rigour were not mutually exclusive in the enterprise of 'schooling' young people.

As Warner (1992) argues, the evaluation of such reforms is pursued through measuring the student outcomes. The college has demonstrated its performance in providing transition from secondary schooling to higher education and employment. Like the previous school, its achievement was predominantly with a client base that had drifted from traditional academic provision as the proportion of special educational needs students and/or disruptive students increased.

ON FERTILITY – HARVESTING THE EDUCATIONAL WASTELAND

Quick-fix responses to disruption in schools are myopic and deservedly doomed to failure. For increasing numbers of young people school is a conduit to long-term unemployment. Having nothing to lose, detachment and disruption are irresistible. The free market mantras of competition, choice and standards in the current crop of education policies aggravates this condition pressing schools, particularly through the publication of league tables of exam success. Inevitably some schools are relegated to the lower divisions. Schools in the premiere league tighten the admission procedures for their team.

What have been described as 'failing schools' are in fact symbols of failing conservative educational theories and policies. Drilling for examination success which can be measured and passed off as adding value does not touch structural economic change or move us closer to examining the range of social problems reflected in the microcosm of the schoolyard and classroom. The 14–19 curriculum requires interventions beyond the window-dressing of a review of forms of credentialling, as Dearing provides. Schools will continue to become more difficult places for teachers and students to work in until the more difficult questions about the function and nature of schooling are asked in preference to tinkering with its forms.

REFERENCES

American Psychiatric Association (1987) *Diagnostic and Statistical Manual of Mental Disorders*, 3rd ed. Washington, DC: APA.

Ball, S.J. (1994) *Education Reform: A Critical and Post-Structural Account*. Buckingham: Open University Press.

Barkley, R.A. (1990) *Attention Deficit Hyperactivity Disorder: A Handbook for Diagnosis and Treatment*. New York: Guildford.

Braithwaite, J. (1989) *Crime, Shame and Reintegration*. Cambridge: Cambridge University Press.

Brophy, J. (1996) 'Classroom management as socializing students into clearly articulated roles', paper presented at American Educational Research Association Conference, New York.

Canter, L. and Canter, M. (1976) *Assertive Discipline: A Take Charge Approach for Today's Educator*. Seals, CA: Canter and Associates.

Coulby, D. and Harper, T. (1985) *Preventing Classroom Disruption: Policy, Practice and Evaluation in Urban Schools*. London: Croom Helm.

Crittenden, B. (1991) 'Three approaches to classroom discipline: philosophical perspectives', in M. Lovegrove and R. Lewis (eds), *Classroom Discipline*. Melbourne: Longman Cheshire.

Daines, R. (1981) 'Withdrawal units and the psychology of problem behaviour', in B. Gillham (ed.), *Problem Behaviour in the Secondary School*. London: Croom Helm.

De Gruchy, N. (1996) *The Times*, 28 May, p.1.

Dearing, R. (1996) *Review of Qualifications for 16–19 Year Olds – Summary Report*. London: SCAA Publications/Dearing.

DES (Department of Education and Science) (1981) *West Indian Children in Our Schools (Rampton Report)*. London: Her Majesty's Stationery Office.

Dettman, H.W. (1972) *Discipline in Secondary Schools in Western Australia: Report of the Government Secondary School Discipline Committee*. Perth: Education Department of Western Australia.

Dewey, J. (1916) *Democracy and Education*. New York: Free Press.

Edwards, B. (1996) 'Suspension in Victorian Secondary Schools', unpublished M. Ed. dissertation, La Trobe University, Bundoora.

Evertson, (1996) 'Classroom management and learner centred classrooms: a new call for metaphors', paper presented at the American Educational Research Association Conference, New York.

Foucault, M. (1979) *Discipline and Punish: The Birth of the Prison*. Harmondsworth: Penguin.

Furlong, V.J. (1985) *The Deviant Pupil*. Milton Keynes: Open University Press.

Galloway, D. and Barrett, C. (1984) 'Factors associated with suspension from New Zealand secondary schools', *Educational Review*, 36 (3), pp. 277–85.

Gewirtz, S., Ball, S.J. and Bowe, R. (1995) *Markets, Choice and Equity in Education*. Buckingham: Open University Press.

Gillborn, D. and Gipps, C. (1996) *Recent Research on the Achievements of Ethnic Minority Pupils*. London: OFSTED.

Glasser, W. (1965) *Reality Therapy*. New York: Harper and Row.

Glasser, W. (1986) *Control Theory in the Classroom*. New York: Harper and Row.

Govoni, L.E. and Hayes, J.E. (1988) *Drugs and Nursing Implications*. Englewood Cliffs: Prentice Hall.

HMI (Her Majesty's Inspectors) (1978) *Behaviour Units: A Survey of Special Units for Pupils with Behavioural Problems*. London: Department for Education and Science.

HREOC (Human Rights and Equal Opportunities Commission) (1989) *Our Homeless Children: Report of the National Inquiry into Homeless Children* (Burdekin Report). Sydney: HREOC.

ILEA (Inner London Education Authority) (1986) *Suspension and Expulsion from Schools*, RS1054/80. London: ILEA.

Kaeser, S.C. (1979) 'Suspensions in school discipline', *Education and Urban Society*, 11 (4), pp. 465–84.

Knight, T. (1988) 'Student discipline as a student concern', in R. Slee (ed.) *Discipline and Schools: A Curriculum Perspective*. Melbourne: Macmillan.

Mandelson, P. and Liddle, R. (1996) *The Blair Revolution: Can New Labour Deliver?* London: Faber and Faber.

Mongon, D. (1988) 'Behaviour units, "maladjustment" and student control', in R. Slee (ed.), *Discipline and Schools: A Curriculum Perspective*. Melbourne: Macmillan.

Neilsen, L. (1979) 'Let's suspend suspensions: consequences and alternatives', *Personnel and Guidance Journal*, 57 (9), pp. 442–5.

OFSTED (Office for Standards in Education) (1993) *Education for Disaffected Pupils*. London: DfE, OFSTED.

Pink, W.T. (1982) 'School effects, academic performance and school crime: some inescapable realities of viewing schools from the inside', *Urban Education*, 17 (1), pp. 51–72.

Pyke, N. (1993) 'Banished to the exclusion zone', *The Times Educational Supplement*, 2 April, p. 6.

Reynolds, D. and Farrell, S. (1996) *Worlds Apart? A Review of International Surveys of Educational Achievement involving England*. London: OFSTED.

Rogers, W. (1990) '*You Know the Fair Rule*', *Strategies for Making the Hard Job of Discipline in School Easier*. Hawthorn: Australian Council for Educational Research.

Rose, N (1989) *Governing the Soul: The Shaping of the Private Self*. London: Routledge.

Serfontein, G. (1990) *The Hidden Handicap*. Sydney: Simon and Schuster Australia.

Skinner, B.F. (1972) *Beyond Freedom and Dignity*. London: Jonathan Cape.

Slavin, R.E. (1984) 'Students motivating students to excel: co-operative incentives, co- operative tasks and student achievement', *Elementary School Journal*, 85, pp. 153–63.

Slee, R. (1995) *Changing Theories and Practices of Discipline*. London: Falmer.

Swan, N. (1995) *Speed for Breakfast*, Four Corners Television Documentary. Sydney: Australian Broadcasting Commission.

Vickers, I. (1993) *Exclusion: Procedures and Provisions in Australia with Special Reference to the Role of Distance Education Centre in the Accommodation of Excluded Students*, unpublished M. Ed. dissertation, Edith Cowan University, Perth.

Warner, D. (1992) 'The operation of a postcompulsory college', in T. Seddon and C.E. Deer (eds.), *A Curriculum for the Senior Secondary Years*. Hawthorn: Australian Council for Educational Research.

Wright Mills, C. (1959) *The Sociological Imagination*. New York: Oxford University Press.

12

The Asdan Award Scheme: A celebration of professional practice

Roger Crombie White

INTRODUCTION

The Youth Award Scheme[1] is a remarkable curriculum phenomenon of the 1980s and 1990s. Devised, initiated, implemented and organised entirely by the profession, it now operates in one-third of the secondary schools in England and Wales, with 100,000 young people in the 14–19 age group registered for various levels of the award. It straddles the pre- and post-16 experience of students by offering a progressive series of awards at Bronze, Silver, Gold and Platinum levels. To achieve each level young people are encouraged to complete assignments from a menu of challenges within 'areas of activity' that include International Relations, World of Work, The Community, Economic and Industrial Affairs, Science and Technology, Expressive Arts, Health and Survival, Information Handling, The Environment, Industry and Technology, Home Management, Sport and Leisure. This whole suite of awards provides a 'curriculum enrichment' programme in its own right, as well as a mechanism for assessing and accrediting core-skill competence at NCVQ related levels 1–3.

In 1986 the Youth Award Scheme was running in just one school in one local education authority (LEA); yet ten years later, in 1996, 1800 schools and colleges in 84 LEAs were registered for various levels of the award scheme, with the Universities and Colleges Admissions Service highlighting the significance of the award in its guidance notes to schools and colleges relating to university entrance (UCAS 1996).

Of course there have been a number of other important curriculum initiatives for the 14–19 age group in the last ten years. In addition to the General Certificate of Secondary Education (GCSE) the General National Vocational Qualifications (GNVQ) is perhaps the most well known, with 300,000 students registered for the various levels. Alongside this City and Guilds have developed the Diploma of Vocational

Education (DOVE) and the Technological Baccalaureate, the Royal Society of Arts (RSA) Examination Board accredits a whole range of initial awards in addition to its Information Technology awards, and initiatives like Project Trident, Young Enterprise, Crest Awards, the Diploma of Achievement, and the Liverpool University Enrichment programme have been introduced in a large number of schools, pump-primed in many cases by Technical and Vocational Education Initiative (TVEI) funding (Crombie White, Pring and Brockington 1995, p.18)

However, when the history of curriculum development in the closing decades of the twentieth century is written up at an appropriate point in the future, the Youth Award Scheme is likely to stand apart from all the others, distinguished by certain factors that make it unique. Its uniqueness and its success generate a number of fascinating questions.

For instance, how is it that one teacher's idea for enhancing the extra-curricular experience of students in a south Devon comprehensive in the early 1980s has become transformed into the largest national programme for accreditation of 'core skills' alongside GNVQs? How has this happened without development funds from the large examination boards or from statutory bodies like the School Curriculum and Assessment Authority (SCAA) or the Department of Employment? And how is it that in an era when curriculum development is increasingly becoming centrally directed and controlled, with millions being spent on glossy brochures and advertising, schools and colleges are signing up in their hundreds for an initiative that mostly relies on 'word of mouth' for its publicity?

There have been no 'national launches', no-centre page feature advertisements in the educational press, and no interviews with BBC presenters on 'Today'. Yet each year the take-up of the scheme has continued along an exponential curve. In seeking explanations for this phenomenon and drawing out lessons from a study of this initiative, it seems appropriate to examine first the changing context of curriculum development in England and Wales, alongside the notion of professional autonomy.

CENTRALISED CONTROL AND PROFESSIONAL AUTONOMY

Various writers (such as Lawton 1984, Skilbeck 1984, Whitty 1985, Dale *et al.* 1990, Tomlinson 1992 and Pring 1995) have analysed the shift towards a more centralised control of the curriculum since the Second

World War, which culminated in the 1988 Education Act and the provision of a 'national curriculum' for the 5–16 age group.

There is a strong sense of history repeating itself, as parallels are drawn with what became known as 'payment by results' for state schools in 1862. Although this system was abolished in 1895, central control of the secondary school curriculum was not actually relaxed until the 1944 Education Act. There followed a period of about thirty years during which the responsibility for curriculum issues lay largely with schools and teachers. The public examination system and parental expectations both set some substantial limits on this professional autonomy, but teachers retained (and exercised) considerable control over what they taught in the classroom (Kirk 1985).

During the 1960s and early 1970s, alongside the expanding programme of comprehensivisation, teachers were encouraged to take initiative for curriculum development. The Schools Council, established by the Labour Government in 1964, was an independent organisation charged with the responsibility of promoting, managing and monitoring curriculum development in schools, as well as reforming the examination system (Morrell 1966). Since its management group had a majority of teachers, the profession exercised considerable influence over every aspect of the school curriculum. As well as providing a vehicle for the dissemination of 'good practice' between and amongst schools and colleges, the Schools Council initiated and funded remarkable curriculum development programmes of its own. Some like Lawrence Stenhouse's Humanities Curriculum Project (Stenhouse 1967), The Geography for the Young School Leaver (Walker 1979, Dalton 1988), or The Science 5–13 Project (Harlen 1973), quickly gained a national reputation for excellence.

Around this time the introduction of the Certificate of Secondary Education (CSE), with its Mode 3 regulations, provided an opportunity for teachers to devise and examine their own syllabuses in subject areas of their own choosing.

In 1970 I took up my first post teaching science and drama in a secondary school whose catchment area included the sons and daughters of the scientists who worked at the Atomic Weapons Research Establishment near Aldermaston. Splitting atoms in the classroom was child's play for such a group! Despite parental pressure, the Head steadfastly refused to sanction O-levels within the school. CSEs were the order of the day, and the whole staff team was encouraged to write and submit Mode 3 versions for approval by the local CSE board.

Those were heady days indeed for a new recruit to the profession! Individual teachers had the power to design a course and its assessment framework, the responsibility for delivering the content in whatever way they chose, and the opportunity to sharpen judgement about standards through discussion with other teachers at the regional moderation of candidates' work. Professional autonomy had a real ring to it then. Although research into Mode 3 CSEs has indicated that they were often *perceived* as of less worth than the more traditional O-levels, (Whitty 1983), there were some remarkable whole school responses to this opportunity which transformed the educational experience and sense of achievement of many students.

At conferences about the ASDAN Award Scheme I often refer back to these days, reminding the audience that professional control of the curriculum is an experience within living memory of many present. I watch those of my own generation smile at the recollection, whilst younger teachers blink in surprise at the accounts of what went on within the context of CSE Mode 3. For the latter group, talk of teachers having total control of what to teach and how to teach is an alien concept; as is talk of a time when individual teachers devised the assessment framework (which included large elements of coursework), set and marked the final examination, and then moderated their overall assessments in discussion with teachers from other schools. Today it seems strange to contemplate a scenario from another era where employers and further and higher education trusted professional judgements about a course whose upper grading possessed the same currency as O-levels. Yet this was the world many teachers inhabited in comprehensive schools twenty years ago.

What happened to change it all? How did the locus of control shift so dramatically from the schools and teachers to government quangos. And why? And what have been the consequences for teacher-led curriculum development?

Ten years on from the Schools Council's inception, the oil crisis of 1974 and the upward spiral of youth unemployment generated pressures for a more centralised control of curriculum development. James Callaghan's Ruskin College speech, in which he challenged the relevance to the world of work of much of what was being taught in secondary schools, heralded the dawn of a new relationship between the government and the profession (Callaghan 1976; 1987). Bernard Donoughue, senior policy adviser to the Prime Minister at that time, in reflecting on the background to what became known as 'The Great Debate' wrote:

'We positively relished an opportunity to breach what we regarded as the negative hold which the teacher organisations had maintained over the determination of educational objectives and practice' (Donoughue 1987). This represented a significant shift in ministerial attitude to curriculum control. No longer was the profession to be entrusted with the sort of privileged influence it had enjoyed since the emergence of the Schools Council. The days when a Secretary of State for Education could declare, as George Tomlinson did in 1947, that 'the Minister knows nowt about the curriculum' were over (Kirk 1985). Shirley Williams's criticism that schools were paying insufficient attention to respect for industry and wealth creation was echoed by others:

> It has in recent years become a 'truth universally acknowledged' that education should be more closely linked to the world of work and with the country's economic performance, and there has been increasing pressure on schools to assess the relevance of their curriculum to their pupils' future working lives.' (HMI 1982, p. 1)

The emphasis was on 'Economic Utility' (Bailey 1984), and it led directly to a number of work-related curriculum initiatives, such as TVEI, Mini Enterprise and Young Enterprise and, ultimately, a national framework for the accreditation of work-related competences – with the National Council for Vocational Qualifications (NCVQ) as the quality controller. One outcome of this was that other vested interests (such as employers) began to exert some influence over curriculum matters, with consequences for the professional autonomy of teachers.

At the same time as elevating the significance of the 'enterprise culture' the Conservative administration legislated for more control from the centre. Inevitably these centrally directed curriculum developments have had a bearing on the position of teachers. Although the 'autonomous professional' is a cherished concept (enshrined in the 1944 Education Act's notion of 'partnership' between LEAs, central government and teachers), it has taken a battering in recent years – compounded by the imposition of contractual duties through the Teachers' Pay and Conditions Act of 1987.

> Degradation of teachers began long ago. Kenneth Baker didn't exactly help when he imagined he would make the system more effective by measuring it. From then on, teachers were not to be trusted to organise their own time. 1265 hours were to be demanded. There were doubtless fruitful spin-offs from this but for many staff that was the

end of Saturday morning supervision of sports and other voluntary activities; they thought, 'stuff it, if we're not going to be valued'. I think that marked a sea change in attitudes and levels of commitment. I believe that it is not simply coincidental that many complain of the deterioration in the levels of state school sports (Jim Harnes, in Crombie White 1997, p. 113).

Jenny Ozga's analysis of the way in which the profession has become 'proletarianized' charts the process of attrition by which autonomy has been chipped away.

In terms of the strategy of overall control of the teaching force, the insistence on the contract signals the final abandonment of indirect rule as a strategy of control. Other policy initiatives had earlier signalled such a departure, especially those that threatened teachers' licensed autonomy in the classroom: for example the reform of the exam system, the contract compliance insisted on by MSC [the Manpower Services Commission], teacher appraisal schemes and parental choice/control. These initiatives alone, in the context of declining support for the service, made the idea of the autonomous professional difficult to sustain. The pay dispute and contract made it impossible. (Ozga 1989, p. 36).

By 1988 the reassertion of central control and direction of the curriculum, and the rout of the profession, was nearing completion. Despite massive opposition to its consultative document the government majority was such that it was able to legislate for a prescriptive curriculum which clearly delineated areas of knowledge and assessment frameworks. The changes represented by the 1988 Act and subsequent legislation in the 1992 and 1993 Education Acts gave the Secretary of State unprecedented powers to decide what should be in the curriculum, how it should be assessed, and how the results of this assessment should be reported. The latter development was particularly significant in the context of parental choice and open enrolment, because the annual media production of 'league tables' supported the application of the marketplace ideology to schools and colleges. The result was predictable.

25,000 individual cost centres now compete with each other for customers. Education has become a commodity to be bought and sold; schools and colleges have become the providers of a service to consumers; teachers have become the deliverers of a curriculum to the specification of the government; delivery is evaluated against performance indicators created by the market regulators (who are not the professionals) and institutions are audited to check on their mechanisms of quality control. (Crombie White *et al.* 1995, p. 14)

As the 1980s came to a close, teachers who had struggled to implement the GCSE in time were now being required to address programmes of study and attainment targets. Records of Achievement were in the ascendancy and local management of schools (LMS) was focusing minds wonderfully on squeezing quarts from pint pots. Teachers were screaming against initiative overload.

And yet, despite all this surrounding turmoil, the germination phase of the Youth Award Scheme had been completed.

THE EMERGENCE OF THE AWARD SCHEME

Following publication of *In and Out of School* (White and Brockington 1978), the Schools Council agreed to fund a dissemination programme to promote the 'social and community education' ideas espoused in the book. Between 1980 and 1982 a series of regional conferences were staged around the UK. One of these, in Exeter in 1981, led to the setting up of a 14–18 curriculum working party chaired by Richard Pring at Exeter University. The principal aim of the group was to share and spread 'good practice' amongst the participating schools and colleges in Devon.

Concurrently a local trust was persuaded to make £2,000 available for assisting with the development of selected initiatives. I had the job of sharing out the funds, which meant visiting each of the schools involved. The Deputy Head of one of the Exeter schools, Brian Fletcher, invited me in to discuss an idea for curriculum enrichment. He had constructed his own 'award scheme' to offer accreditation to his fourth year group for a whole range of achievements that were not recognised within the traditional examination framework. 'It's not a question of passing or failing; it's about rewarding success,' explained Brian. 'I want to encourage a variety of activities and I need a base where the students can do things'. The emphasis was on the word 'do'. Brian Fletcher needed equipment for the 'base', and the Schools Council project was able to offer £700.

That was 1981. TVEI was launched two years later. Exeter was one of the first wave of 14 consortia of schools to be funded in the 'pilot', and

Brian's school took advantage of the funding to extend the Award Scheme within the framework of the personal and social education curriculum. The TVEI resources were used to promote the scheme as a curriculum opportunity for all fourth and fifth year pupils in the school. In 1985 Brian Fletcher became Head of Coombeshead School in Newton Abbot and, under the leadership of an energetic Head of Year, Rita Rose, the school became the driving force for developing the scheme within a regional consortium of local secondary schools. Television South West offered some sponsorship and the Award Scheme gained credibility with local employers. 'I only wish I could have done it when I was at school', said one father, echoing the views of many parents. In October of 1987 the BBC featured the Scheme on the 'Education Programme', and the interest generated led to the setting-up of two other regional consortia in Avon and Berkshire.

These three consortia of teachers worked together as a loose-knit federation for two years to revise and re-write the materials for national dissemination. In the spring and summer of 1990 a series of regional conferences was staged in Taunton, York, Edinburgh, Liverpool, Birmingham, Cambridge, Bristol, Keele and London to offer the scheme to interested teachers in other LEAs. By September 3,000 young people were enrolled on the scheme. A year later this figure had grown to 5,000. By 1993 it was 30,000 and, in 1995, the number of student enrolments pushed past the 100,000 mark.

ENABLING PROFESSIONAL PRACTICE

In seeking explanations for the rapid growth in popularity of the Award Scheme it is difficult to disentangle observations about the quality of the product from those which relate to the wider social, educational, economic and political context within which this development has taken place.

Teachers often express unease about the 'market-place' ideology that forces schools into becoming competing cost centres, where excellence is adjudged on a range of performance indicators that are increasingly being reduced to the lowest common denominator of numbers of pupils gaining 5 A–C grades at GCSE, irrespective of the nature of the intake to the school.

'My impression is that my professional judgement counts for very little. School performance is determined by a narrow band of statistical indicators (5 A–Cs), with little recognition given to the starting point of pupils. I work in a very demanding school and have never worked harder in my life. It galls me that no matter what I do these efforts and those of the vast majority of pupils that I teach will remain unrecognised under the present system of measuring school performance. (Geoffrey Osborn in Crombie White 1997, p. 106)

Little notice is taken of the school's record of success on a whole set of other indicators like creative or sporting achievements, or moral atmosphere. Perhaps this jars with a body of people who have a deep-seated commitment to the importance of the *affective* as well as the *cognitive* domain. Indeed, new recruits to the profession, including escapees from industry and commerce, are often attracted to teaching precisely because it is about working *with* people.

Increasingly, these new recruits and many of those attending further professional development courses are encouraged to adopt the concept of the 'reflective practitioner' (Schon 1983; Pollard and Tann 1993), where the individual teacher is encouraged to see himself or herself at the centre of a dynamic process in the classroom. Kolb's cycle of experience, reflection and reformulation (Kolb 1984) is at the heart of this process at all levels of the education system, and there are plenty of signs that this affects practice enormously – a practice which is influenced by personal beliefs and constructs.

Teachers have a strong sense of values. They teach because they believe in something, and they want to see it conveyed. They have a conception of the 'good life' and the 'good citizen'. They know what kind of society they would like, what kind of personal and social values they wish to encourage, what knowledge they wish to convey, and how. All these things are interconnected. Teaching is, at heart, a moral craft. (Woods 1995, p. 30)

The issue here is to do with values – the belief systems that underpin policy and practice. At the heart of most disagreements about education are various conflicting beliefs about the purposes that it should serve and the values that it should embody. Examples of conflicting values are not hard to find, although very often they are submerged within a sea of political rhetoric.

For instance, do teachers as a whole share Margaret Thatcher's view that 'there is no such thing as society', or John Major's assertion in 1992 in response to media reportage of delinquent behaviour amongst young people that 'society must condemn a little more and understand a little less'? Such statements reveal a lot about the value system that under-pinned the Conservative administration. It was one that excluded whole groups of people. In educational terms it was a value system that sup-ported selection and restricted access, that marginalised school refusers and disruptive pupils, that celebrated individual as opposed to com-munity advancement; that resulted in an expansion of private schooling at the expense of the public sector; that acknowledged and even cele-brated the concept of a 'sink school', because the 'market-place' would operate to resolve the problem. It is a value system that has con-sequences for the kind of society our children will inherit. And it is a value system that may well be in conflict with the value system of a body of people committed to notions of a fairer society and equality of opportunity.

As someone who made a career out of research and now teaching, I value the importance of learning immensely. It is clear to me however that we are in danger of excluding pupils from this process by reward-ing those who achieve only the highest attainment levels. For the majority of pupils in our school this is simply not a realistic target. If we are to educate all pupils we need to widen the routes into education and not place insurmountable barriers in their way. Learning is a lifelong process and we should be aware of our responsibilities ensur-ing this continues. Over-reliance on one academic route is bound to create 'casualties' and this under-class is much in evidence in our schools. (Geoffrey Osborn in Crombie White 1997, p. 102)

There is also a reaction amongst teachers to the prescriptive structure of the National Curriculum and of the NCVQ framework, both of which seem to rely upon the idea that students will progress in neat, linear steps towards clearly stated outcomes or objectives. Here the assumption seems to be that knowledge gained or skills acquired can be measured precisely, and provide the yardstick for describing (and funding) success-ful students and effective establishments. Critics of this 'outcomes related' approach point to the narrowing consequences of such a focus (Jonathan 1983; Hodkinson 1992; Hyland 1994). This was part of Alan Smithers' concern when he described GNVQs as 'a disaster of epic pro-portions' (Smithers 1993). This approach also ignores the movement that had been gathering pace in the 1970s to recognise the significance of the learner's engagement with the *process* as well as the *content* of the curriculum. It is as if Bruner has been rendered irrelevant (Bruner 1960; 1990).

In discussions about ways forward in relation to the 14–19 curriculum, it is often asserted that 'the devil is in the detail'. It seems to me that one of the problems we are confronting is that the focus has been on the detail of the map at the expense of the territory itself – examining the daubs and dashes of the picture instead of studying the framework of the canvas. Although the recommendations of the Dearing review were informed by the issues and implications raised in the excellent report *Learning for the Future* (Richardson *et al.* 1995), it failed to grasp some of the concerns expressed.

We have a divided and divisive system in the UK. One-third of our young people 'succeed' in acquiring sufficient 'points' to merit entrance to university, one-third achieve some limited success, often regarded as second best because of its vocational orientation, and one-third drop out at the earliest opportunity. The system only serves a minority of people very well indeed, and we need to ask some searching questions about why this is.

In addition, most debate about curriculum issues focuses on course design and content for the statutory sector, allowing the independent sector to select its response. Yet any debate about the ends (and means) of education can only make sense in the context of a consideration of the *whole* range of provision in the UK and the purposes that each part serves. It comes back to values of course.

What are we trying to achieve through our system of formal education? What do we want from the many billions of pounds that are spent on the public sector and the lesser billions spent on the private sector? What qualities do we want to develop and celebrate in young people? What knowledge, skills and competencies are going to be most useful for them and for the country in the next century?

Nearly twenty years ago, in describing a curriculum framework under 'areas of experience', HMI had struck a chord with many teachers who believed that traditional 'subjects' ought not to be held up as the sole focus of schooling (DES 1977). This view has been recently reinforced by those such as Howard Gardner in his writing about 'multiple intelligence' (Gardner 1993), or Richard Pring in his eloquent appraisal of the 'liberal ideal' (Pring 1995). There is growing acceptance of the need to recognise and celebrate a broader perception of ability and intelligence.

'It seems to me there are three basic elements to teaching which are

parts of what I call the 'golden cracker'. The first involves getting to
know the child, the second involves the child practising skills, doing
exercises, being occupied in consolidation of learning and the third is
what I have called the alchemist's stone – the teacher's skill in inter-
vening to stretch the pupil's learning. . . . To mark the learner's mind
we need to know its intricacies, its preferred learning styles, its different sorts of intelligence – motor, linguistic, spatial, musical, logical,
scientific, personal. We need to know that the pupil's mind stands
ready to do a deal with the other end – the teacher's extraordinary
skill as an alchemist to the mind in transforming mental slavery to
freedom. At this end lies the golden cusp of the teacher's skill: his or
her ability to open the mind. (Brighouse 1994, pp. 29–30)

It is fertile ground for implanting a curriculum model which addresses
the concerns of teachers mentioned above, and which supports the
notion of the enabling and creative professional. The Award Scheme's
capacity to meet the needs both of individual students and teachers
whilst addressing institutional concerns and priorities is clearly very
significant.

CONSUMERS' VIEWS OF THE AWARD SCHEME

Through the various sets of student workbooks, targeted at different
levels, the Award Scheme offers an 'off the shelf' curriculum enrichment
package, which can embrace or extend what classroom teachers are
doing already. Work experience, health education, personal and social
education (PSE) the expressive arts, sporting activities, and such like,
are all included. The remodelling of the scheme over the years in
response to identified need has taken place whilst preserving the
essential ingredients of success. New programmes to cater for 'special
needs' such as 'Towards Independence' and 'Workright', have been
developed alongside the introduction of a 'Universities Award' which
has been welcomed by UCAS in relation to student applications to
university.

The Platinum Award really does complement the studies of sixth form
students. What we particularly notice here is that it increases the confidence of the students, greatly improves their self image, and gives
credit for activities that are beyond the ordinary curriculum
and which play an important part in their personal and social

development (Sister Brigid Halligan, Head of St Mary's RC High School, Liverpool).

This is as true for Key Stage 4 as it is for the post-16 phase. Areas of experience that have been squeezed or marginalised because of National Curriculum requirements can be nurtured and enhanced by the accreditation offered by ASDAN. And the accreditation itself is now worth something in the marketplace. The acknowledgement of its value by higher education providers and employers' organisations, in response to the mention of the Gold and Platinum levels in the UCAS guide for applicants has enhanced its image for those aspiring to university entrance (UCAS 1995). Students recognise that admission tutors are looking for a more extensive profile of achievement than that provided simply by A-level or GNVQ points.

The Platinum award is very good for UCAS applications. It shows that you can be committed to other things, that you can take responsibility, and that you've got a lot more going for you. I feel I've gained a lot of time management skills and a lot of confidence. I'm more able to communicate. I'll give anything a go. (Ann Withall, aged 18, Ilfracombe)

The emphasis on 'core skills' (and now 'key skills', following the 1996 Dearing review) means that those programmes that offer a template for both demonstrating and accrediting these are becoming increasingly attractive. The allocation of a points tariff for 'key/core skills' by UCAS will enhance the value of ASDAN's higher-level awards yet further. Indeed the Dearing review drew attention to the potential of the ASDAN award scheme for recognising a wider range of achievement, including 'those with exceptional ability' (DfEE 1996). This facility to 'kitemark' its awards with the NCVQ logo, for specific core-skill accreditation at Levels 1–3, made a big difference for ASDAN. Students engaged on A-level or GNVQ courses can look to the ASDAN Universities Award for a means to demonstrate their competence in the personal skill area.

I'm doing four A levels – History, French and English, and I'll be starting General Studies next year. I'm hoping to go on to university to study Law and eventually to be a family law solicitor. I don't think there's anything else apart from the Award Scheme that helps us to work with people, to communicate and stuff like that. (Emma Harris, aged 17, Bromsgrove)

My plans for the future are to go into medicine, especially surgery. There's a lot of competition out there for medicine, so having something like the Platinum award gives you that little bit extra. It shows that you can do a lot more than just pass examinations (Samah Aliman, aged 17, Liverpool).

The ASDAN Award Scheme also provides an opportunity to demonstrate application of knowledge in pursuit of activities that are seen as inherently worthwhile (and enjoyable) by the majority of students – so that the accreditation of 'core skills' is part of a much broader process for students and staff. The 'enjoyment' aspect is clearly important too.

I definitely recommend the Scheme. It's good fun. I'm learning a new computer language, doing special effects stage lighting for the school play, and work experience for a theatre company called Stage Electrics. It allows you to do what you want to do and at the end it gives you a qualification which can be useful in later life, especially when you're trying to get into university. (Chris Tomlinson, aged 16, Bristol)

Students find the challenges accessible and relevant. Very often they discover that they can obtain accreditation for things they have wanted to do anyway – passing their driving test, travelling on an 'inter-rail' ticket across Europe, running a fundraising charity event, organising a period of work experience, improving their information technology skills, and so on. Motivation is enhanced at all levels. For teachers the scheme offers the opportunity to be involved once again in curriculum design and implementation, and in the follow-through process of accreditation. The Mode 3 style consortium and moderation approach touches a chord about 'professional judgement' with older teachers, and stimulates the enthusiasm of younger staff.

ASDAN scheme gives teachers greater professional control to enrich the opportunities students have to work and learn. The accreditation framework enables students to take a more active role in their own education and make some investment in the learning process. (Julia Holingworth in Crombie White 1997)

It may be this dimension that is actually the most important. It harks back to the significance of the affective domain mentioned earlier:

most of us acquire knowledge and skills in a manner that is more influenced by the context in which we learn or by our feelings at the time . . . learning is a matter of challenges to and reformulation of personal theories and personal constructs, and that the role of the teacher is to lubricate these processes. (Crombie White *et al.* 1995, p. 27)

Not only does the Youth Award Scheme provide a curriculum enrichment programme for teachers that embraces much of what is cherished under the heading of PSE, but it offers a way of accrediting it as well. It makes sense of the emerging emphasis on 'core skills' by helping students and teachers gather evidence of attainment through settings that provide contextualisation for the knowledge gained and skills developed. In rewarding students' success through its stepped programme of challenges, it demonstrably increases motivation. It achieves all the aspirations expressed by HMI ten years ago in *Better Schools* for a curriculum to be 'broad, balanced, relevant and differentiated' (HMSO 1985). The evidence is clear, as teachers coming to the scheme for the first time listen to fellow professionals describing the sixth form 'enrichment' experience it offers for applicants to higher education, as well as the benefits for those with special educational needs.

As I take part in the regional moderation of young people's work that characterises the accreditation structure of this particular Award Scheme I am reminded of those heady days in the early 1970s at the school near Aldermaston, where CSE Mode 3s were the common experience. I observe teachers exercising professional judgement in a way that both highlights their creative imagination and demonstrates what this imagination can actually achieve. For ten years I have witnessed the remarkable expansion of the scheme, and marvelled at the way in which teachers have developed the original ideas, whilst sustaining and retaining the underpinning principle of rewarding achievement.

The Youth Award Scheme is a child of its time – the offspring of teachers who had been touched by the Schools Council or the early days of TVEI. However, unlike many other initiatives which rose and fell during the 1970s and 80s, it has been able to ride the two horses of economic utility and liberal education. It addresses the concerns of employers and university admission tutors with its accreditation of practical skills and personal qualities, whilst offering a curriculum that fuels the imagination of teachers and students. It has squared a very remarkable circle and is a living testimony to the potential for innovation within the profession.

NOTE

1 The Youth Award Scheme is one of a number of curriculum programmes managed by the Award Scheme Development and Accreditation Network (ASDAN) – a not-for-profit organisation, representing the consortia of participating establishments, which is based in the offices of an educational charity in Clifton, Bristol. The curriculum development aspect of the Youth Award Scheme is run from within the University of West England (UWE) Faculty of Education at Redland, Bristol. For further information about the Award Scheme and other ASDAN programmes, telephone 0117 923 9843.

REFERENCES

ASDAN (1996) *The Universities Award* This video film about the Platinum/FE Level 3 Award of the ASDAN Award Scheme offers comments from students and teachers involved with the scheme.

Bailey, C. (1984) 'The challenge of economic utility' in C. Bailey, *Beyond the Present and the Particular.* London: Routledge and Kegan Paul.

Brighouse, T. (1994) 'The magicians of the inner city' pp. 29–30 of the *Times Educational Supplement*, 22 April 1994.

Bruner, J. (1960) *The Process of Education.* Cambridge, MA: Harvard University Press.

Bruner, J. (1990) *Acts of Meaning.* Cambridge, MA: Harvard University Press.

Callaghan, J. (1976) 'Towards a national debate', speech at Ruskin College, October 1976, reported in *Education*, 22 October 1976.

Callaghan, J. (1987) *Time and Chance.* Glasgow: Collins.

Crombie White, R. (1997) *Curriculum Innovation: A Celebration of Classroom Practice.* Milton Keynes: Open University Press.

Crombie White, R. Pring, R. and Brockington, D. (1995) *14–19 Education and Training: Implementing a Unified System of Learning.* London: Royal Society of Arts.

Dale, R. *et al.* (1990) *The TVEI Story: Policy, Practice and Preparation for the Workforce.* Milton Keynes: Open University Press.

Dalton, T. (1988) *The Challenge of Curriculum Innovation: A Study of Ideology and Practice.* Lewes: Falmer.

DES (1982) *Teacher Training and Preparation for Working Life.* London: HMSO.

DES (1988) *The National Curriculum 5–16.* London: HMSO.

DES/HMI (1985) *Better Schools.* London: HMSO.

DES/HMI (1977) *Curriculum 11 to 16.* London: HMSO.

DFE (1992) *Choice and Diversity.* London: HMSO.

DfEE (1996) *Report on the Review of Qualifications for 16–19 Year Olds* (known as the Dearing post-16 review) London: HMSO.

Donoughue, B. (1987) *Prime Minister: The Conduct of Policy under Harold Wilson and James Callaghan.* London: Jonathan Cape.

Fowler, W. (1988) *Towards the National Curriculum: Discussion and Control in the English Educational System 1965–1988.* London: Kogan Page.

Gardner, H. (1993) *Multiple Intelligence: The Theory in Practice.* New York: Basic Books.

Harlen, W. (1973) *Science 5–13 Project.* London: Schools Council.

HMSO, (1985) *Better Schools,* cmnd. 9469. London: HMSO.

Hodkinson, P. (1992) 'Alternative models of competence in vocational education and training' *Journal of Further and Higher Education,* 16 (2) pp. 30–9.

Hyland, T. (1994) *Competence, Education and NVQs.* London: Cassell.

Jonathan, R. (1983) 'The Manpower Services model of education' in *Cambridge Journal of Education.* 13 (2), p. 9.

Kirk, G. (1985) 'The growth of central influence on the curriculum', in G. Kirk, *The Core Curriculum.* London: Hodder and Stoughton.

Kolb, D. (1984) *Experiential Learning: Experience as the Source of Learning.* London: Prentice Hall.

Labour Party (1995) *Excellence for Everyone.* London: Labour Party.

Lawton, D. (1984) *The Tightening Grip: Central Control of the School Curriculum,* Bedford Way Papers no. 21. London: University of London Institute of Education.

Morrell, D. (1966) *Education and Change: the Annual Joseph Payne Memorial Lectures 1965–66.* London: College of Preceptors.

NUT (1995) 'Teachers' Views of 14–19 Education' *A Pilot Project* Goldsmiths College and London Institute of Education, available from NUT, Hamilton House, London.

Ozga, J. (1989) *Teachers as a Workforce,* Open University E208 Course Unit 19. Milton Keynes: Open University Press.

Pollard, A. and Tann, S. (1993) *Reflective Teaching in the Primary School,* London: Cassell.

Pring, R. (1989) 'The curriculum and the new vocationalism', *British Journal of Education and Work,* 1 (3) pp. 133–48.

Pring, R. (1995) *Closing the Gap: Liberal Education and Vocational Preparation.* London: Hodder and Stoughton.

Richardson, W., Spours, K., Woolhouse, J. and Young, M. (1995) *Learning for the Future: Initial Report.* London University Institute of Education Post 16 Centre/Warwick University Centre for Education and Industry.

Schon, D. (1983) *The Reflective Teacher.* London: Temple Smith.

Secondary Heads Association (1994) *Pathways to Achievement.* London: SHA.

Seifert, R. (1987) *Teacher Militancy: A History of Teachers' Strikes 1896–1987.* Lewes: Falmer.

Skilbeck, M. (1984) 'Curriculum evaluation at the national level', in M. Skilbeck (ed.) *Evaluating the Curriculum in the Eighties.* London: Hodder and Stoughton.

Smithers, A. (1993) *All our Futures: Britain's Education Revolution* (a *Dispatches* report on Education) Channel Four Television with the Centre for Education and Employment Research, University of Manchester.

Stenhouse, L. (1967) *Culture and Education.* London: Nelson.

Task Group on Assessment and Testing (TGAT) (1988) *National Curriculum: A Report.* London: Department of Education and Science.

Tomlinson, H. (ed.) (1992) *14–18 Education and Training.* London: Longman.

UCAS (Universities and Colleges Admissions Service) (1995) *Guidance Notes to Candidates Applying for HE Entry in 1996.* London: UCAS.

Walker, J. (1979) *Changing the Curriculum: The GYSL Experience.* Sheffield City Polytechnic.

White, R. and Brockington, D. (1978) *In and Out of School.* London: Routledge and Kegan Paul.

Whitty, G. (1983) 'State policy and school examinations' in J. Ahier and M. Flude (eds) *Contemporary Education Policy.* London: Croom Helm.

Whitty, G. (1985) *Sociology and School Knowledge* . London: Methuen.

Woods, P. (1995) *Teaching,* Open University EU 208 course, 'Exploring educational issues', Unit 2. Milton Keynes: Open University.

Index